Moon City Review
2014

Moon City Review is a publication of Moon City Press at Missouri State University and is distributed by the University of Arkansas Press. Exchange subscriptions with literary magazines are encouraged. The editors of *Moon City Review* contract First North American Serial Rights, with all rights reverting to the writers upon publication. The views expressed by authors in *Moon City Review* do not necessarily reflect the opinions of its editors, Moon City Press, or Missouri State University.

Correspondence should be sent to the appropriate editor, at the following address:

Moon City Review
Department of English
Missouri State University
901 South National Avenue
Springfield MO 65897

Submissions are considered at http://mooncitypress.com/mcr/. For more information, please consult www.mooncitypress.com.

ISBN: 978-0-913785-46-1

moon city press
springfield missouri

Tao—the Road by Jacek Frączak
Pencil and color-crayon on paper, 25" x 19". 1995.

Table of Contents

Fiction

Jim Ray Daniels *Survivor's Guilt* — 1
Vanessa Blakeslee *Stand By to Disembark* — 17
Jon Chaiim McConnell *Salvage* — 34
Conor Robin Madigan *Reasons for Loving* — 58
Megan Giddings *Roy Orbison Saved From Heart Failure* — 61
Danilo Thomas *The Steeling* — 64
George Looney *A Very Old Music* — 72
Zeke Jarvis *Crying Class* — 87
Amanda Marbais *Bottle Rockets* — 128
Amber Sparks Two Stories — 155
Bryan Merck *Fiery Chariot* — 158
Matthew Fogarty Two Stories — 160
KV Wilt *The Dump: Bermuda, 1960* — 162
Alex Mattingly *Alfred, Lord Pennyduck* — 170
Matthew Vollmer *Academy Girls* — 184
Khanh Ha *The River of White Water Lilies* — 210
J.T. Robertson *The Dodo, the Balance, and the Bee* — 223
Phong Nguyen *The Story of Ill-Begotten* — 233

Poetry

Amorak Huey Two Poems — 10
Pat Daneman *Polly's Mother Sang Opera* — 14
Phoebe Reeves *Fernald, Ohio* — 16
Laura Dimmit NBC Nightly News, *Live From Joplin* — 29
Gary Wilkens *Surfing Near Pali Gap* — 30
Tim Craven Two Poems — 31
Jenna Rindo *What Is Salvaged From My Son's First Buck* — 41

Melissa Boston *Soutine, Your* Carcass   42

Lisa J. Cihlar Two Poems   44

Brandon Rushton *Maintaining the House of a Deceased Loved
    One Is a Paraphrasing of the Cinematic Inheritance of Grief*   52

Ricardo Pau-Llosa Two Poems   54

Jeff Hardin *My Life According to Little Proofs Assembled*   56

Luci Brown *Of Another Nature I Did Not Know*   57

Albert Abonado Four Poems   66

George Looney Three Poems   81

Darren C. Demaree *"What the Fuck Are You Telling Me?"*   94

Christopher Locke Two Poems   95

Roy Bentley *Vengeance*   98

Brian Simoneau *Each Pleasure*   113

Angie Macri *Spoon Flat, Ash Flat, Big Flat*   115

Gary Leising Two Poems   116

Kellie Wardman *This Yin and Yang Is Good for Something*   135

Emily May Anderson *Daughter*   136

Noel Sloboda *Hollywood Cemetery (Richmond VA)*   137

Kirsten Hemmy *On Considering Whether to Live in America:
    A Love Poem*   138

Richard Newman *Gift Shop at the Gates of Hell*   151

Nancy Carol Moody Two Poems   152

Gabriel Welsch *Faith*   154

Brittney Scott *The Weight Aurora Carries*   163

Timothy Geiger *The Labor*   164

Keegan Lester *Numinous*   165

Eve Strillacci Two Poems   166

Meg Eden *The Excavation*   179

Cynthia Marie Hoffman *[I sing the alphabet]*   180

Hali Fuailelagi Sofala Two Poems   181

C.D. Albin Two Poems   204

Doug Paul Case *The Old Queen Has the Gym*   207

Dan Lambert Two Poems   208

Ken Haas *God's Widow*   243

Alan Michael Parker *Letter to the Buddha, Including
    an X-Ray of My Foot*   244

Naomi Shihab Nye Four Poems   254

Nonfiction

Amaris Feland Ketcham *Afterthoughts of the Bloom* 46
Geoff Watkinson *Fathers, Guns, and LSD* 110
Allison Doyle *Who You Are* 140
Jody Reale *There's No Telling* 191
Katy Resch *Loss* 230

The Missouri State University Literary Competitions

Samuel Nichols *Hermanos de Sangre* 100
Christopher Crabtree *Learning Chess* 109

Art

Bobby Ross *Stories* 119

Translations

Santiago Vizcaíno *The Storm*
   Translated from the Spanish by Alexis Levitin 220
Benny Andersen *To a trap*
   Translated from the Danish by Michael Goldman 221
Salgado Maranhão *Sea Drift IV*
   Translated from the Portuguese by Alexis Levitin 222

Interview

Julia Greene *A Telephone Conversation With Naomi Shihab Nye* 246

Reviews 258

Contributors' Notes 274

Staff

Editor
Michael Czyzniejewski

Poetry Editor
Sara Burge

Nonfiction Editor
John Turner

Fiction Editor
Michael Czyzniejewski

Reviews Editor
Michael Czyzniejewski

Assistant Editors

Kelly Baker
Terry Belew
Jessica Boykin
Anthony Isaac Bradley
Natalie Byers
Patrick Chism
Joel Coltharp
Amanda Conner
Heather Cook
Derek Cowsert

Christopher Crabtree
Renée Dunn
Matt Kimberlin
Lora Knight
Dane Lale
Antony LePage
Timothy Leyrson
Joseph Lucido
Madison McFarland
Bailey Gaylin Moore
Kate Murr

Andy Myers
Allys Page
Rob Pickering
Angela Rose
Kathryn Schlimpert
Sierra Sitzes
Caleb Stokes
Taylor Supplee
Jeff Van Booven
Satarah Wheeler

Advisory Editors
James Baumlin
W.D. Blackmon
Lanette Cadle
Marcus Cafagña
Jane Hoogestraat
Jennifer Murvin
Richard Neumann

Special Thanks
Karen Craigo

Jim Ray Daniels

Survivor's Guilt

Mr. Wojo, the scout leader, shuffled and dealt the cards to the other fathers at the picnic table across the large common room from where Al sat. He could hear the suction of their mouths off beer bottles and the click of flipped cards. Through the thin wall of the bunk room behind him, the other scouts breathed the deep uncomplicated breaths of the young and tired.

"Alvin, why don't you get some sleep," Mr. Masch sighed. "We'll wake you if your parents make it." He paused. "I mean, they will make it. Just maybe not till morning."

"Yeah, get some sleep, Al," Mr. Wojo said. At least he knew better than to call him Alvin. "Snow's really coming down out there." He nodded to the window across from him. Al looked, but from where he sat, it was just a dark square. No moon, no stars. No streetlights, no cars. His parents had promised to drive out and take him home for his championship basketball game tomorrow.

Stony Creek, the scout camp, was an hour north of Detroit. Al's first campout with the troop, and he hadn't wanted to miss it or his game. That previous summer, he had f from a rare illness that had forced him to miss a third of the school year, and his parents were still cutting him slack for surviving. He was trying not to be the sick kid anymore. Fall had been a failure as he struggled to catch up in school. They'd decided not to make him repeat fifth grade so he could stay with his friends, but his friends back on Rome treated him as if he still had something they still might catch. Three months equaled three years in kid time, and his parents and teachers simply did not understand.

"I'm OK," Al said, so softly that it wasn't clear anyone had heard him. A wispy cloud of cigarette smoke hung above the men's table.

☾

He had a fever that wouldn't quit. The doctors couldn't figure out what was wrong, eventually settling on viremia—viruses cruising through his bloodstream, stopping wherever they felt like it. He didn't want to eat or move or think. Sometimes Al thought he was willing himself to be sick, holding the thermometer too tightly. What was it about the world that had made him sick, even with spring erupting outside the tiny window of his bedroom, trying to intrude, impose its green medicine? He lay sprawled in a daze while the world spun curveballs around him. His mother brought him meals on an old wooden tray that had been in the family forever.

"This tray makes me happy and sad," his mother said. "I don't expect you to understand that." Al's grandparents on his mother's side were both dead. His grandfather had died from cancer—a long, grim illness that wore Al's grandmother out so badly that she died shortly after. At the end, they both had eaten off that tray.

His parents had no way of contacting the camp. No phones nearby that someone might answer late on a Saturday night. And if his parents were dead … Al forced himself to stop. His father was a good driver when he wasn't drinking, and he wouldn't be drinking. Al could remember little of the drive up on Friday night—the skies already dark, snow piled up to the roadside reflectors, even before the storm hit.

Al had fired a .22 that afternoon at the rifle range. His foggy glasses had clicked against the side of the rifle, which recoiled into his shoulder and tilted them askew. A stray dog had bounded through the snow behind the targets, and they all stopped shooting while it passed. The closest house was miles away. He wanted to call out to the dog, but it was already disappearing into distant snow.

He retrieved his paper target and examined it closely. All twenty of his shots had missed.

"Not quite ready for your marksman merit badge, Snyder," his patrol leader, Wozniak, said, looking down over his shoulder. "Hell, I could hit that damn target with my eyes closed. With my back to the range, I could still at least hit the fucking thing."

Swearing was something scouts did, Al noticed. And spitting. He'd have to work on spitting. If he was going to stick it out. Earn some patches to sew on his uniform, or on a red vest like the older scouts wore.

Aside from Mr. Wojo, the men on the campout seemed to act as if their wives had tricked them into volunteering with some fairy tale about bonding with their sons. They mostly stood around smoking cigarettes while the boys completed a series of outdoor activities focused on survival skills. How to build a fire in the snow. How to cook in the snow. How to stay warm in the snow. How to pee in the snow—that seemed to be a favorite, though no lessons were necessary. Everybody had their scout knife and their scout flashlight and their scout backpack. Al wished that his gear wasn't so new. He tried to scuff his backpack with snow.

The older boys snuck cigarettes. Boy Scouts was a Little Man's Club. The fathers had come of age and spent their military years fighting the Korean War. Al's father had spent his military service in Detroit—his friend's father knew a colonel who had adjusted his orders so he could stay home with his new bride. He'd survived by taking the easy way out. His father had not volunteered for the campout.

"I don't want to be in scouts," Al had told his father. "None of my friends joined," he said, unsure who currently counted as a friend.

"You've got to be a leader, not a follower." One of his father's basic tenets, and it had led him to start his own business wholesaling nonperishable grocery items to most of the small Mom and Pop stores in the Detroit area. Which led him to work sixty-hour weeks and avoid smoking cigarettes and drinking beer in the great outdoors with the other fathers.

"Give it a try," his father said. He had been a scout once, and his old scout handbook was among the few items he salvaged from the fire that burned down his childhood home. It still carried smoke in its pages. Al was giving it a try. His father, after a discussion with his mother, had agreed to drive up after work Saturday to bring him home for his game. Al had moved up to starter halfway through the season. If they won the championship, he wanted to be in the team photo—some proof that he was back.

He'd counted six photos he should have been in while paging through last year's yearbook.

Al heard the creaking of a bunk behind him, and the heavy clunk of someone landing on the floor from the "Willies" side of the cabin.

One side was called Jakes and the other side Willies. They'd had a big pillow fight until Mr. Wojo let out a piercing whistle, then they all retreated to their separate sides to sleep. Jakes and Willies—Al wondered who'd thought of that. None of them were named Jake or Willie. Al, sitting in the corner of the common room, was stationed in Boy Scout limbo. He'd have to ask his father about this Jake and Willie thing. If he showed up. If he was still alive. If the world was still round, and the sun hadn't given up on them.

Many of his father's customer's were Arab store owners from the inner city of Detroit. They loaded up station wagons or pickup trucks with cases of noodles and spam and candy bars and cigarettes and whatever else was on their lists as they pushed the large open carts through the wide aisles of the warehouse. Al often helped his father on Saturdays before things like scouts and basketball came along. He missed those afternoons in the dark, scuffed-up warehouse, his father, relaxed, joking, buying him lunch at a Greek place down the block, letting him order one of their sweet, flaky pastries for dessert. When they returned home after work, Al often felt a strange, cold pang of not understanding something about his parents.

Chubby little Ralph Morton emerged from the Willies' open doorway and slipped outside in his long johns to pee, then hurried back in and stood in the doorway, rubbing snow off his bare feet. The men glanced up, then returned to their cards. The other boys called him Moron. They joked that the T was silent. Ralph spotted Al in the dark corner and slipped in next to him on the rough bench.

"You in trouble, Alvin? Did you pee your pants? You want your mommy?"

Al was afraid to speak for fear of breaking into tears and earning his own cruel nickname, but he was able to hiss out "Moron," and Ralph, after rubbing away fake tears, trudged back to his bunk.

Was he going to be Alvin to the whole troop? The only Alvin everyone knew was from "Alvin and the Chipmunks," and they mimicked the famous shout of their manager Dave: "AAAAAAAAAAlvin!!!!!!!!!!!" He'd heard it the first couple of years at school, but it died out after the other kids got to know him. Here at scout camp, it was back again.

"There were no chipmunks when we named you, Alvin," his mother had explained. "There was just your grandfather, Alvin."

His mother. He couldn't think of her being gone, hurt, or even just stranded in the storm in their dark car. He did want his mother. He loved her above all else. She who had nursed him through his illness with patience and tenderness and boundless love.

The men were clearing off the picnic table and stowing their empties. "Al, it's time, buddy," Mr. Wojo said. standing above him, hammy fist on Al's shoulder. "In the morning, they'll be here, I promise. Now, go to bed."

"They should make a rule ... look at that kid. Scouting ain't about that," Al heard Mr. Masch mutter. Al had the top bunk in the far corner, one that had not been taken in the mad rush of friends grabbing bunks for each other Friday night. Beneath him slept Lenny Kowalski. Lenny the fatherless. Lenny the large. Lenny the cruel, who no one wanted to share a bunk with. If his own father was gone, would Al end up like Lenny, full of a sickness that would never go away? Lenny's muscled arm draped itself down onto the floor, and Al was careful not to step on it. The troop had a pecking order of coolness, but Lenny, a constant hissing fuse of anger, seemed to be on an entirely different list, a list of one. If scouting was such a social thing, what was a misfit like Lenny doing there? Maybe someone made him join, too.

Al carefully climbed up, then began his wait for morning, unimaginable morning. He remained motionless, believing that nothing could happen as long as he lay still and breathed softly. But each breath seemed to stutter its way out straight from his heart. How could Mr. Wojo promise him anything? His brain buzzed. He stung himself with doubt.

During his long night on the top bunk, Al twisted and wrung out the idea of his parents being dead like a cloth that would never dry. He was suddenly at their funeral standing between two coffins while all around him people applauded. He wasn't sure what he'd said to elicit the applause, but it seemed to go on as long as he wanted it to. He'd live with his grandparents. His teachers would hold him up as an example of quiet courage. The girls, oh, the cute girls would all walk home with him. The bullies wouldn't dare touch him. He'd be a superhero with the power to convince people to be nice to each other.

His fantasy was like a big stage—when he stepped out of the bright lights and behind the curtains, a shadow dropped down, darker than even a night without moon or stars. The cold shadow of grief. For a moment. For a moment, had he wished them dead?

For hours, the electric surge of panic hammered relentlessly against sleep until sleep softened and began to absorb the blows like a thick sponge. Sleep told him he would be safe in its moist cave, in the warm depths of his sleeping bag. Sleep took him.

In November of the previous year, before he got sick, Al's dog Trixie died. One day he came home from school and took off his wet boots and set them on the steps to the basement, like usual. He walked into the silent kitchen, where his mother sat, smoking, her eyes red, mouth slack.

"Sit down, Al," she said.

She had baked homemade bread, a rare treat. The smell of her delicious misshapen loaves mingled with cigarette smoke in an odd mix of comfort and strain. Al put his hand on a loaf: still warm.

"Can I have a piece?"

"I have to tell you something first."

Al stayed slumped in his chair. His book bag dropped to the floor. He struggled with wanting the bread before it cooled, and with his mother's grim expression. "I had Trixie put to sleep today."

Al looked around the kitchen, stunned. She had removed the bowls, the dog food, the leash. Had she even picked up his last crap in the back yard?

"He was OK yesterday. He—he—I didn't get to say good-bye. How could you do it? How?" He ran out of the kitchen and into his room. He lay on the rug where Trixie had slept just last night. His mother had vacuumed, but the rug still smelled of dog. Al pushed his forehead against it. He grabbed handfuls and held on.

Later, his mother came in and sat on his bed. "He was in so much pain. It didn't seem fair to keep feeding him pills. I wanted to tell you first, but I had to do it before I lost my nerve."

"You should've let me say good-bye. He was my dog."

"Al, we usually don't get the choice to say good-bye." His mother tilted her head back and ran her hands through her hair. "You're stuck with the last stupid things you said to people, you're stuck wishing you had another chance. Wishing you knew it was the last time."

"But you had a choice."

"I said good-bye for you."

☾

Al woke to the cabin stirring. Exaggerated groans and cursing. From below, Lenny kicked the bottom of his bunk. Al's whole body lifted slightly, and he landed rigid with fear. Life was going on for the other boys, but his was stopped. His was turning blue. Lenny would be sorry. Lenny would seek forgiveness.

He thought of Trixie again as the scouts ate cereal and drank cartons of orange drink at the picnic tables, and the men swilled coffee and started back in on the cigarettes. Trixie was gone, and he had already forgotten too much—he closed his eyes and tried to picture her, but on the jostling bench, it was impossible. His parents had not arrived at first light like he had imagined. The other fathers said nothing to him.

After breakfast, they bundled up and headed out to learn more survival skills. If his parents were dead, none of those skills would help him. He wanted to wait at the cabin for news, but Mr. Wojo gave him a tired smile and insisted that he join them. "It'll be good for you," he said.

They were learning how to make a snow shelter. The important thing was not to panic, the young instructor stressed. Keep moving. Stay warm. Focus on the work.

Most of them were using their entrenching tools to dig snow caves on the side of Mount Baldy, the high hill in the center of the camp. They spread out, looking for promising nooks and wind-curled drifts from last night's blizzard. The sun reflected harsh off the snow, and Al couldn't look anywhere without squinting. His heart jolted and throbbed against his ribs.

A group of older scouts worked together on an igloo. Laughing and boisterous, their deepening voices echoed over the hillside. Al moved to the far end of the spread-out troop until he was nearly alone. Lenny was next to him, digging frantically like a starving dog or squirrel retrieving a remembered bone or nut. Lenny's caves kept collapsing, but he didn't seem to care—he just moved to a different spot and began again.

Al slowly tunneled into a beautiful drift sculpted by wind into a frozen wave until he could squeeze inside—dark, moist, his warm breath steaming against the snow. What had he last said to his parents, besides "good-bye"? His mother had washed his basketball uniform. Had he thanked her? His father had scolded him for leaving the bathroom a mess. His mother was wrong—he couldn't even remember the last things. His silent tears disappeared in the snow. He could hear the instructor talking to Lenny. He'd give a prize—a blue ribbon—for best cave.

Al made his opening smaller, packing snow around the edges. "What, are you burying yourself, Alvin?" he heard Wozniak's muffled voice through the thick, dense wall of his cave.

They were learning winter first-aid when Alvin heard the faint whine of his father's station wagon rise up the hillside.

He jerked his head around and squinted to where the road curled in the distance. He spotted the car fishtailing, gaining traction, losing it, gaining it again. He turned and ran, tumbling through waist-high snow, tasting it cold in his mouth, against his face.

"Snyder!" he heard Mr. Wojo shout behind him, but Al was gone. He angled down to meet the car outside the cluster of cabins. He waved to his mother, and she waved back.

When the car stopped, his father pressed his forehead against the steering wheel.

Al pulled at his mother's door with his thick gloves till it opened and she emerged and hugged him to her chest. He was gasping for breath. He didn't care if the whole troop was watching. He squeezed her hard.

"We're so sorry, Al," she said. "Your father tried that hill half a dozen times before we turned around last night. Nobody was getting through."

His father came around the other side and clapped Al's heaving shoulders. "Hey," he said. "What's all this fuss about?" He looked up the hill and waved to the other scouts and their fathers. "Geez, Al, grow up a little." He gave him a light shove toward the cabin. "Hurry now, get your gear."

Al tried to pull himself together. He felt a bit like Dorothy at the end of *The Wizard of Oz* all wicked witches dead, the family together again, but it was like all the Munchkins had returned with him and were staring, the two worlds at odds with each other forever, no balloon in the sky, just the threat of flying monkeys.

He gathered up his backpack and sleeping bag, and his parents took him away. All along the road, people were digging out their cars. Snowplows and salt trucks rattled their chained tires against the pavement like sleighs.

The car was warm from both sunlight streaming in and heat churning out the vents. Almost stifling. They all quickly lapsed into silence. Al knew his parents would not always be coming to the rescue. His father breathed out a loud sigh. Al felt poison guilt rising dry in his throat. He wanted to tell them that he'd never been sick. He wanted to tell them that for a moment he'd wished them dead. To ask them if they had wished him dead during the long months when he lay at the end of the couch like an unstuffed pillow and he watched dull daytime TV. Did you wish? Did you wonder? He leaned over from the back seat and put his head between theirs. "Did you ever build a snow cave?" he asked. "Did you ever learn how to survive?"

Amorak Huey

The Letter X & the Magic Act

Cut your girlfriend in half, she holds it against you for weeks.
Every time you kiss, you taste disappointment
like stale tobacco, raspberry wine coolers,
tattoo ink—all that passes for possibility. Pick a card,

any card—the man with the ax is wild

maybe because you're eighteen in a dark corner
of a dark parking lot, telling scary stories

while the dashboard light drains the battery
in your Firebird because you read somewhere
fear shares brain electrons with the urge to get romantic.

To smash the wristwatch is the easy part—
unless you return it restored
you have done nothing worthwhile.
Technique matters but the show matters more,

no such thing as cheap applause.
Stopping time's just another sleight of hand flimflam,
it's easier to creep yourself out than you'd expect,

and the various lives that stretch ahead

are more complicated and less important
than this moment
when your skin is an electric fence,

when what you want will never be this obvious again,
when you've revealed your secrets,

made your best case—

in that darkness, there might be danger.
To touch each other while we can is the only response.

Amorak Huey

In Praise of Charlotte Giattina's 1988 Monte Carlo SS

With a first line from Robert Lowell

Each season we scrap new cars & wars & women,
we sense early the value of fast & untouchable.
Heat lightning fills our horizons, that searing
impossible kind of love our favorite songs know all about.

We learn early to brag about fast girls, untouchable cars:
Trans Am, Camaro, Mustang, Firebird, we have wings
& nothing is impossible, not even love, though we know nothing,
we start over each night as flat as prom photos, airbrushed tattoos

& Trans Am T-shirts, all horsepower & eagle wings,
so much swagger & shimmy & skinny hips, we are peacocks
in airbrushed yearbook photos, we tattoo each other's names
on unseen skin. The lines we draw kick up dust

as we swagger & shimmy down skinny backroads, peacocks
& rooster tails, working up the nerve to hold hands,
fingertips touching unseen skin, color outside the lines, dust
to lust, ashes to crashes—unrequited violence,

iridescent rooster-crow confidence we hold in our hands.
All these girls, their lips & graduation gifts: MR2s, Fieros, Preludes:
our lust grows up fast & crashes with gleeful violence
into the revved-up bric-a-brac of being eighteen—

these girls, their fire-breathing: no way to know what's prelude,
what's final act when each season brings new cars & wars & women.
We are consumed by acceleration, the flotsam of being young—
we are blinded by this heat lightning. This searing.

Pat Daneman

Polly's Mother Sang Opera

We heard her, never saw her—
voice like liquid in a glass, ice
crackling, cold condensing
on its curves as it slipped
through our fingers. We imagined
what we did not see—
black curls, lace dress, her face
a sad older version of Polly's.

Though what did older mean to us?
When you are sixteen there is no other age,
no other way to look than tempting,
from the pink on your lips to the space
that opens when you spread your legs,
tan all the way into your underpants.

As for the real woman, who could say
if she was ugly or more beautiful
than her daughter, or if there was a bottle
on the bedside table? No one was allowed
in Polly's house, even best friends
got no farther than the front porch—
Polly leaning out, lifting her heavy hair,

from above, the flood
of music, dark forest
of words we did not understand.
At home our own mothers

ironing, sleeping, smoking,
while we stood at Polly's door
not knowing what we were
waiting for.

Phoebe Reeves

Fernald, Ohio

For three years they drank from the well, after
it was contaminated, after men in suits
with bottom lines and military secrets knew
of uranium dust swept into groundwater.

At night, dirty from their play, the boys would come in
and she would run them baths, soap up their heads
and rinse, as they crinkled their eyes shut,
suds and water swirling down the drain.

She toweled them off, tucked them into bed,
and smelled the soft fall of their clean hair.

Vanessa Blakeslee

Stand By to Disembark

The day after a few of the ship's factory workers pulled a joke on him, Crazy Paul flipped out and beat up a table with a gaff. Rumor was that the Army had found Paul mentally unstable after too many tours in the Middle East and let him go—how many tours was too many, Quentin wanted to know, but didn't ask. Dang, their crew leader, sent Paul up on deck for a time-out. At lunch break Crazy Paul told them that he'd been wandering around to clear his head when he happened to pause outside the wheelhouse. "We're not going to off-load in Dutch Harbor," Paul said. "I heard the Captain talking."

A ripple tore through Quentin's gut like an eel. Everyone within earshot leaned toward Paul, barraging him with questions, except for Quentin's bunkmate, Jason, who sorted fish and worked the cutter beside Quentin most days. Jason's gaze fixed on Paul as he shoveled stew from his bowl with chopsticks, eating like the Asians on board. They loved Jason for that reason.

"You can't just go around saying that," Quentin told Paul. "Besides, we've got to off-load."

"Will you listen?" Paul replied, blinking and stuttering. He clenched his fork and adjusted his hardhat. He'd scrawled U.S. ARMY on the back in slanted block letters, despite his discharge. "The company's planning to off-load at sea. That means we're going to have to fish another trip before Cascade lets anyone off. Another three months."

"Bullshit," Quentin exclaimed. "That's breach of contract."

"How else you gonna get off this ship if they don't?" Paul retorted.

Marcel, the most overeager worker on board, chimed in. "Yeah, Cascade Fishing gonna fly in a helicopter just for you?" He was always needling.

Quentin ignored this. "They don't want to risk a lawsuit," he said to Paul. "There's at least a dozen other guys who have contracts up, same day as mine."

Paul wagged his head. "It's an old trick, I'm telling you. Companies do this all the time."

"And nobody does anything about it?" Quentin asked.

"Nope," Paul said.

Back down below, Quentin spied the gaff that Crazy Paul had used to beat the table and fought the urge to grab it and do the same thing. But instead Quentin took a deep breath and started sorting fish. He and Jason faced a giant mound from the nets dropped in earlier—a few big halibut, weighing about a hundred pounds each, had wedged like boulders among the catch, mostly Atka mackerel. The men threw out the halibut because by law they couldn't take them. Quentin used to try and save as many as he could, sprint up on deck and heave them overboard. Not anymore. "Let Cascade Fishing breach contract," he said. He was chucking fish onto the cutter table so hard that every so often one skidded off. "When I get back, I'll be outside the company office in Seattle first thing, with the meanest lawyer I can find."

"What're you going to do?" Jason asked with a scoff. "Run to the captain?"

"Watch me," Quentin replied.

He said this in spite, but then decided that the civilized approach might be better for his weary brain. At shift change, he climbed to the wheelhouse and rapped on the door. Not until a solid minute had passed did he realize how loud he was banging, and quit. The captain swung open the door, bellowed, "Jesus, what?" They'd met rough seas and the door bounced against the wheelhouse.

"What's this I hear about you not letting us off?" Quentin demanded.

"Well, what you gonna do if I don't?"

Quentin launched into his tirade about the lawyer, so wracked with fatigue that the argument sounded like a drunk's speech, even though he couldn't recall the last time he'd had a drink. None of the men who wanted off seemed to have the balls to raise hell like he did. Unless this lack of restraint was another sign of his unraveling—his brain snapping and crackling like aluminum foil in a microwave, his sanity dangling closer to the gangplank. He focused his remaining energy on his words, stopping just short of threats. He said, "You've got to get me off this ship. I won't make this easy for you."

"Don't worry, you've made that clear," the captain replied. Then he slammed and latched the door.

At dinner, Quentin piled his serving into a bowl, brought it to his bunk, and collapsed. Soon after, Jason entered and asked about his talk with the captain. Quentin didn't reply.

Before Jason left his bunk in the morning and when he turned in for the four hours and fifteen minutes of sleep they were allotted every night, he prayed under his breath. Quentin could never make out the words, and he felt guilty when he caught himself straining to hear, but couldn't help it. Jason was a couple of years younger than Quentin, a Mormon kid who'd screwed up his mission trip. Someone found out he'd slept with a girl and reported him. Two months ago, he signed with Cascade as a sort of spiritual quest—or punishment, depending on how you looked at it. Otherwise, Quentin couldn't tell Jason was Mormon. He didn't put on any kind of special underwear when they dressed, not that Quentin made a habit of looking.

Maybe Quentin had signed up for something similar, although he hadn't realized it at the time. Maybe the job wasn't about making twenty grand in one shot like his friend Oakley had bragged about back home. Maybe Quentin was seeking to prove something, now that he was head of the house, albeit temporarily absent. Since his mother had begged him not to enlist in the military—not to return in pieces, like his father. His war had been the everyday kind, the battle to earn his keep and his family's, too. But whatever Quentin's motivation when he stepped off that Alaska Airlines plane in Dutch Harbor— quest, punishment, or greed, pure and simple, hardly mattered now.

That night when Jason whispered his prayers, Quentin mouthed a few lines of his own. He wanted to be sure no one heard, even though the ship never slept but emitted a constant boom. Silence. Boom. But exhausted as he was, he couldn't sleep. The thoughts never stopped. How could you be such an idiot, to listen to Oakley? What kind of moron signs up for a job as dangerous as a tour in Afghanistan—at least there you might have risked your life with your friends. How naive could you be? You deserve to lose your fucking mind. He swung his legs over the bunk and pulled on his clothes.

Above deck, the tail end of summer had ushered in darkness. He lurched for the railing and caught his breath; he couldn't remember the last time the Alaskan sky hadn't been bright with sunlight for all but a few hours. How cold it was out there in the wind, the sun gone. The ship bucked and pitched, its lights cast over the side, but he hung on, inched forward. He ought to be on a safety line. Walls of waves, dark gray, arose like moving hillsides that disappeared to black. A terrifying abyss. If a man jumped, he'd never be found. He felt a hypnotic pull from those giant waves and kept staring into them, even when he knew he shouldn't. The ship rolled upward then; he stumbled and retreated. Once again below, soreness and sleep overcame him.

Nights, Quentin dreamed of sorting fish. They piled up high as the decks. He was stomping around in ten inches of freezing saltwater. His frosty breath spewed clouds as he sorted and tossed the catch. Jason called him over, showed him a silver salmon, eerie among the green-black mackerel. "I don't know what he's doing this far out," Jason said. "Must have gotten lost in a current." Then Jason chucked the salmon to Crazy Paul, who sliced off its head at the cutter. The silver salmon, headless, slid onto the packing table where the Vietnamese with cigarettes hanging from their mouths packed the fish into the metal freezer trays.

"Stand by to haul back," the ship's loudspeakers droned.

Quentin awakened to aching wrists and cramped fingers. Marcel stuck his head in the cabin doorway, bellowing good-morning profanities. Quentin's feet hit the rocking floor. He gripped his bunk's edge, legs adjusting automatically as if they'd grown springs in place of bones, but moving his sore limbs felt like trying to bend lead. He grumbled for Marcel to clean up his mouth; why did he think he was such a big shot? But the punk ignored him and barked another string of gibberish. How Quentin wished he could pound that chiseled ex-linebacker's jaw. He struck his pillow hard, panicked, and caught himself. Back home he'd been the one to break up fights.

All six in the cabin tugged on their sweats in the shadows, then their Grundens suits and wool-lined rubber boots.

That morning Quentin told Dang he couldn't work below in the factory anymore, something Dang didn't like to hear from his fastest sorter. When he asked why, Quentin just mumbled please and something about needing a break, inwardly shoving aside flashbacks of the unsettling nightmare.

But deck work was as grueling and dangerous as the factory. When the nets were hauled back and stored along the ship's sides, the loose fish fell out; trapped between the nets and deck walls, they rotted. Above deck hung gutted fish which the Japanese deckhands strung up on lines to dry in the salty, open air and sunlight, an old practice. The Japanese ripped off chunks of the shredded fish as they hurried underneath. Once in a while, one of them offered Quentin some of the jerky and he did his best to respectfully decline. Inhaling fish stench as he jumped nets, ran winches, and wielded his gaff was enough to nearly make him vomit, never mind the sight of the men feasting on those nasty dried strips of fish.

For now, though, the deck saved him from talking in circles with Jason, Crazy Paul, and the rest over the captain's decision to off-load or not. The talking in circles was the kind of behavior his father had begun to display, his first symptoms of dementia and short-term memory loss. His father had worked for over twenty years as an air traffic controller, and Quentin was convinced the intensity of the job did him in. When Quentin was in tenth grade, his father's behavior changed drastically—his mother discovered missed payments, which didn't make sense since his father always prided himself on keeping their finances in top shape. His father had been only forty-eight when diagnosed with early Alzheimer's. Now he was in a home.

It was a gorgeous day on ship. Quentin's head felt lighter, probably because he was no longer bent over an endless pile of fish. At shift-break he headed down to the galley with Mike, one of the few others above deck who spoke English. Mike was a recovering crystal meth addict. Quentin had never seen him take a shower or change clothes in the six months they'd been aboard. The cold made detecting all but the most putrid smells difficult—most of the time Quentin was thankful for that. Still, he cringed at the dirty layers of fish scales decorating Mike's neck and wrists, the fuzzy brown of his rotted teeth. He was like something they might dredge up in the nets—a barnacled, malformed half-man, half-creature of the deep. His presence made Quentin miss the clean company of his friends. They'd all played baseball together on his high school team. Those who'd gone to college close to home would be getting together this time of year for weekend games in the park.

"Did anybody come up and ask if you wanted to get off yet?" Quentin asked.

"Nope," Mike said. He frowned and scratched his elbow. "But there's supposed to be a list. You gotta sign your name if you wanna get off."

In the galley, seven factory workers claimed they'd signed, but no one recalled who was going around collecting names. Quentin choked down his skirt steak and potatoes, furious. Was this a joke? It was like the whole goddamn boat was playing a trick on him.

Before second shift he stormed up to Sasaki, the crew leader on deck. But Sasaki started shaking his head before Quentin finished. "No list," Sasaki said, arms folded. "We unload at sea. You stay."

"Sorry, not staying," Quentin answered. "If there's a list, my name better be on it. I'm getting off this ship when my contract's through."

Sasaki jabbed his finger into Quentin's chest, then his own. "Good workers stay."

His father had been a good air traffic controller, Quentin thought. Exceptional, his coworkers had said. Quentin's family had thrown the retirement party, rented out a reception hall. His father's condition was partly genetic, the onset triggered by lifestyle stress. Quentin had dismissed this in signing the dotted line with Cascade. He was young and fit; what did he have to worry about? Not until he'd spent a few weeks in the factory and witnessed Crazy Paul's PTSD, plus the stories of crewmen lost overboard in rough seas, the gruesome tales of severed fingers and gauged eyes, did he swallow his gullibility. These men were scarred, pushed to the brink for so long some of them had forgotten anything different—as if Cascade had fed them through the cutter. He told Mike to flag him down if Mike spotted the officer with the list.

"Relax," Mike said. "Cascade loves to pull this shit. It's not like they won't let you off, eventually."

The loudspeaker cracked to life: "Stand by to haul back."

I should have stayed below in the factory, Quentin thought too late. Now he was stuck above deck, without a single friend, about to lose his mind.

And more nets were coming in.

He glanced around for the first mate with a clipboard, taking names. But he didn't see anyone but the crew. Lately, in the factory, he had caught himself forgetting what he was doing, and he'd stand there momentarily confused. Then the terror would set in, as he fought to stay alert around the humming cutter while the ship pitched and rolled. If he ended up losing a hand or puncturing an artery, what then? He might as well have gone to Afghanistan. He couldn't recall ever seeing an officer with a list go around and take names of those who didn't want to renew their contracts; the very conversations of the previous forty-eight hours blurred into mirage. Was it possible he was dreaming up this list, that his mind was so far gone? Or maybe the officer had come around, but dazed by fatigue, Quentin had missed him.

"Stand by to haul back," the loudspeaker boomed.

The enormous nets dragged up from the sea, full of squirming catch. He flashed to the days ahead—more sorting, packing, and then freezer break, when they took out the trays of packed fish from the hydraulic freezers, removed and hauled the frozen blocks to store at ship's bottom. Usually the ship was rolling, and the blocks slammed into the men's chests as they caught them.

He and Jason had been assigned freezer break after Jason had just come aboard. They became friends quickly—Jason pulled him aside when one of those fifty-pound blocks of fish flew out of an unlatched freezer and might have killed Quentin right there. They were getting no rest, and Jason developed a raging fever. Quentin didn't think the kid would last a week.

"Stand by to haul back," the loudspeaker droned again.

Quentin clung to a mast and closed his eyes. The only other sounds were the mechanical groans of the ship, the sea and wind. Bursts of Japanese. He needed to give up his obsession over the list because it was driving him crazy, but then he would have nothing solid to keep him going. The list had to exist, as sure as those black walls of icy water—now churning and white-capped as far as the eye could see.

The nets pulled in and dropped, and something was wrong. The Japanese waved their arms and shouted to one another. Embedded amongst the enormous stack of flapping mackerel, tusks, ribs, and skulls protruded. A few of the Japanese crew scavenged for smaller bones to hide in their boot flaps and underneath Grundens suits. Some held up skulls and passed tusks back and forth. Sasaki shooed his men away from the catch, but they ignored him.

Word spread quickly. Soon everyone from the factory emerged from below and surrounded the odd treasure. Quentin crowded next to Crazy Paul and Jason. Mike dug through the pile with the Japanese.

"What is this?" Quentin asked Crazy Paul.

"The Walrus Graveyard," he replied.

Quentin shot Jason a quizzical look. "I've never heard of a walrus graveyard."

"Me neither," Jason said.

"It's where the walrus go to die," Paul said. "They know by instinct."

Quentin asked why the Japanese were so excited, and he and Jason craned their necks to hear Crazy Paul explain how the Japanese took the tusks and bones back to Japan to grind up for potions. Walrus tusk potion was worth a lot of money in Asia. The scene was like his dream about the silver salmon, and Quentin began to wonder if this was another Arctic mirage. Like the land he thought he saw the other day, which prompted his nighttime stroll, just a trick of the horizon after too many hours of sunlight.

Mike held up a tusk like a trophy and picked his way out of the wriggling catch. "Better hurry up if you want anything," he said. "Captain's on his way, and we're supposed to dump all of it back." He shouldered the tusk, made tracks for below.

"You want anything?" Quentin asked Jason.

"Nah," he replied. "But hey, someone came around the factory asking who wanted to get off."

"Who? Where'd he go?"

"Some officer handed out the list, said to pass it around below. I didn't sign it, so I don't know."

Quentin picked up a broken walrus skull and hurled it overboard. The swirling, washing machine-madness swallowed it in an instant. Back to rest in its watery tomb with the others, he hoped. The walrus graveyard gave him some comfort: He envisioned his body floating through the depths, joining theirs. Then fear shot through him so hard, he lost his balance. Grab hold of your mind, he told himself. The mind is more powerful than the body, more resilient. You're an Olympic athlete, or on desert patrol. You're an elite fisherman of the Cascade fucking fleet.

He asked Dang if he could return to the factory, and Dang agreed but switched him out with Crazy Paul, who was working cutter. Paul hated authority and resented taking orders from the Vietnamese in particular, despite Dang being the most mild-mannered supervisor aboard. In Vietnam, Dang had been an accountant, but his degree didn't count for much in the U.S. Quentin had talked to Dang about his family. Dang and his father were probably the same age.

Jason smirked, tossing the good fish onto the table where Quentin now commanded the cutter, slicing off heads. Crazy Paul kept his back to them as he sorted fish. Jason held up two wet-rubber-gloved fingers at Quentin, making a rabbit-ears sign. Their running joke about Crazy Paul was that he had a little rabbit inside his head that talked to him.

Quentin flipped Jason the bird for finding his situation so funny—getting paired with someone widely deemed the voyage idiot. But once Jason glanced away, Quentin's smile fell. How long until his only friend would realize that he was as deranged as Crazy Paul, and make fun of him? Just how crazy was Paul, after all those missions outside Kabul? How disturbed might Quentin become, if forced to fish another three months in the Bering Sea?

Quentin decided to test Paul. He fed the cutter slowly, and the sorted fish backed up on the other end. Paul eyed them piling up; Quentin had thrown off his rhythm. Paul muttered to himself as he hurled the fish toward the cutter, and the little chattering rabbit flashed through Quentin's mind. He laughed, the first reprieve he'd felt in days. God, it felt good. Great, even. If only he could laugh more, he might cling to sanity.

But Paul flew into a fit. Seizing a gaff, he banged away at a post. Jason and Yasek, the biggest worker on board, were laughing so hard that their breath billowed out white and quick around them, as if from the steamy nostrils of sea monsters.

Dang swung over to their cutter, gestured to Paul. Through the holes in his knit face mask, Dang's eyes narrowed. He raised his chin, asked sharply, "What's going on?"

Quentin nodded toward Paul and made the rabbit ears sign, still grinning. Dang guided Paul to the side and told him to take a break. Then Dang dragged Marcel over from the packing table so they wouldn't fall behind, and the ray of hope vanished in Quentin's chest. Now he would have to deal with Marcel—a kiss-ass whiner with a mediocre work ethic besides. Right away Marcel grabbed a fish wrong. The fin stabbed him through his rubber glove, and he yelped.

Quentin yelled, "How long you been on this ship? Seven months? Or were you always this much of a dope?" He should have held back, but Marcel opened up a ruthless anger in him.

Marcel sorted even more slowly now, wringing his hand, rubbing his fingers through the pierced rubber glove. He wanted to be an actor when he finished with Cascade, get on a reality TV show—maybe part of the reason he drummed up drama, although Quentin couldn't care less. He should leave the cutter, go back to sorting, not only for his sanity but his paycheck. Their bag wage depended on how many fish they processed, which was why he sorted fast. If he was going to lose his mind or a limb working a commercial fishing vessel, he was sure as hell going to make the most money he could.

"Come on, you piece of shit," Quentin said to Marcel. "Get to work."

"You can't order me around," Marcel replied. A smug smile broke over his face, and he puffed out his chest. "I've got the list."

Quentin flicked the switch; his cutter ground to a halt. The ship swooped up and down in the charging seas, and he waited a moment. Then he used gravity to his advantage and lunged at Marcel, who swatted a fish in his face. Stunned, Quentin grappled for his stocky opponent but his hands slid all over because of the wet gloves. Quentin was shouting that he was going to kill him for hitting him in the face with a fish, and to give him the goddamn list.

Yasek and Jason broke them up. Yasek pressed to Quentin's ear. In his Polish accent and in between excited huffs of breath, he said, "I know you are thinking of home. Settle down."

Quentin gulped air, nodded. He was too close to leaving with his twenty thousand in the bank, the hardest money he'd likely ever earn in his life, money he needed to get on his feet when he got back, to pay his mother rent so they wouldn't lose the house. Dang bawled out Marcel—never were they to abuse the catch for such a stupid disagreement. Quentin seized his chance. "Give me the list," he ordered Marcel. "Now."

Dang nodded, and Marcel whimpered in his throat, fumbled underneath his gear. Quentin held the pen in his freezing fist and scribbled his signature in big letters that looped over the names above. Marcel returned the paper and pen to the plastic baggie for safekeeping, then slithered back to the packing table. Quentin picked his way through the fish, back to the cutter. The metal whirred to life, and he wondered how his father was doing, if he'd remember his name or if he'd be too far gone. The day his father had lost his temper in the control tower, rattling his coworkers and jeopardizing dozens of airplanes, had been what forced his early retirement. All those hours in that control room had amounted to what, exactly? Quentin wasn't sure, and he didn't have any clearer sense of how he wanted to spend his life. Only that whatever he did, run a restaurant or coach baseball—hell, even if he joined a monastery, prayed and made cheese every day, he'd better make it count. To live without enjoyment made no sense.

Crazy Paul slipped back to his place and resumed sorting without a word. Quentin focused on the cutter but was glad to see him return. He felt sorry for the trick he'd played on Paul and told him so at shift's end, although didn't admit this to Jason.

The next morning, word sailed through the galley that the vessel would off-load at Dutch Harbor and remain in shipyard for two weeks. Those who didn't want to sign a three-month extension could leave. Quentin's jaw slackened with relief. Soon he'd be on the couch, watching the World Series. If he wanted to he could take a nap during the game. He'd be able to sleep through the night: eight, nine, ten hours if he wanted. He could even invite a girl over.

In the shower, he cried.

The Aleutians made a beautiful sight on either side as they sailed up to the mainland, even though the islands appeared little more than big, treeless green rocks. Quentin and Jason pointed out interesting sights to one another. They could see for miles. Off the side of the ship, a pod of orcas trained their young to hunt by toying with a seal. The bigger, older whales positioned themselves farther out and watched the young from a distance. Some of the pod racing alongside the ship propped their heads out of the water and spun around.

But the way the whales played with the seal bothered Quentin. "They've been tormenting that poor seal for miles," he said. "How much more can it take?"

"If the whales don't train the younger ones to hunt, they'll all die," Jason replied. "It's smart. It's survival."

"Well, I don't like it."

"Every creature needs to eat. Which means killing. At least the fish don't have much for brains, and it's pretty painless."

"And our brains, and bodies?" Quentin asked. "What about those? The no sleep, the frozen blocks almost decapitating us?"

Jason shrugged. "Brutality has its limits. I guess that's why you're on the list."

They spotted Dutch Harbor in the distance as Quentin's final shift ended. Those whose contracts were finished ate, showered, and stood by to disembark. In the cabin, Quentin donated his sweats and gear to the men who were staying. He handed Jason his rubber gloves and gaff.

Marcel stuck his head in the door. "So when you coming back?" he sneered.

"There are a million ways to make money besides doing this," Quentin said, zipping his duffel bag. "I'm going back to college, first semester I can enroll."

He bounded onto the deck wearing his street clothes for the first time in months, waved good-bye to Sasaki, and shook Dang's hand. He guessed those men would stay on that ship for years, and hoped that didn't happen to Jason. He was the last one Quentin bade good-bye to.

"Don't dream of fish," Quentin said, thumping him on the back.

"I won't," Jason replied, grinning. "Only women."

Quentin was halfway down the gangway when he realized Jason was calling after him. How strange to take in the ship from that angle. He teetered with his heavy duffel back up the gangway, suddenly unsure which direction felt more like prison—the days spent onboard or the unfathomable ones ahead. He wondered if during his time at sea, he'd passed the point of no return. If when he got back, it would be too late for his mother to save the house. If his father wouldn't recognize him. As soon as he asked the question, he was certain of the answer.

At the deck rail, Jason waved his arms wildly. The sweatshirt Quentin had given him fit too snugly on his broad frame. Jason cupped his hands around his mouth and shouted down at him: "Don't worry about the seals."

"What?" Quentin yelled back, squinting.

"The seals," Jason called, "when the whales play, they always let the seals go."

Overhead, the Arctic sun gleamed. Quentin stepped onto solid ground and into Jason's enormous, fluttering shadow.

Laura Dimmit

NBC Nightly News, Live From Joplin

Two nights after the storm, my mother and I sit
on the couch, watching as Brian Williams reads
the evening news. He is broadcasting live, just
five miles from here, a dripping blue tent mostly
obscuring the battered shell of St. John's hospital.
Weeks from now, we will learn that the tornado shifted
the entire hospital on its foundation, twisted it
by three degrees—on paper, such a delicate measurement—
but Brian Williams doesn't know that tonight, and neither
do we. When the segment ends, after a specialist from
the Weather Channel has repeated that this damage is
the worst I've ever seen, I wonder about ratings, how
the whole country can watch us grapple with shock,
as we wait for the death toll to stop rising, for the rain
to stop long enough to start clearing roads, salvaging.
It feels like a city-wide out-of-body experience,
seeing our landmarks suspended from inside the lens
of each major news network, watching our neighbors
be interviewed, waiting to see our stories pulled
from the debris right in front of our eyes.

Gary Wilkens

Surfing Near Pali Gap

Splitting bottle-green mountains,
charging the rhino of the toothy foam,
my heels kicked to heaven, my face turned
to the cold hells, the ocean a cat in heat

—*Oh fuck, I'm drowning*—

then crimson fire in the sand,
Ha ha there is no more Jonah,
the whale has shit him out,

into the stars behind the night,
where a boy holds a seashell
to his ear, hearing only his heart.

Tim Craven

Neuroanatomy Practical

Smaller than you thought.
More like your idea of a dog's.
You cup it, softly. Your thumb fidgets
over the fissure of a temporal lobe.
You lift it up to the side of your head
and imagine your own, sitting in there,
firing, immortal.
On falling to the ground
would it crumble or shatter
or liquefy or combust or bounce
back up into your hands, intact?
When she (sixty-six, Caucasian, lymphoma)
donated it to science, was this the promised
research? You consider biting into it
as you would a peach, and, were it not
for the toxic preservation agent, you might.
In ten years' time you will think,
what a privilege it was to hold that brain,
brim-filled with tomato soup recipes and original sin,
and smells of late-summer and oboe lessons,
and self-taught Italian and the night sky:
the Plough, the Bear, the Big Dipper.

Tim Craven

Research

It's one in the afternoon and the stench
of my whiskey breath bounces back at me
off the nape of your neck and
I tell myself that this is research.
You've called in sick to stay in bed
so we donate these hours to each other
because outside is minus something
and littered with dirty snow
and full of strangers working in factories
and where the only boy you ever loved,
the one you thought you'd marry,
slammed his father's car into a telegraph pole
going ninety up Bluebell Wood Road
and you'll never know whether he meant it.
You ask me to tell you something real so
I show you the scar on my chest where a
girl once pushed a cigarette straight
though the base of a styrofoam coffee
cup acting as a makeshift ashtray on an
afternoon like this.
Molten plastic fusing with skin
is as real as it gets. I'm the king
of nothing and I can spend all day
teasing out that quiver in your breathing
I heard last night.
Have you heard of reverse paranoia,
where the world is making every effort
to make us happy, despite our best attempts?

When I stop holding you and find my shoes
I'll never see you again but I'll remember
your boyfriend who died at twenty-two,
because he is real like my breath
on your neck.

Jon Chaiim McConnell

Salvage

Out far on the ice where the sawing is toughest there are, scattered beneath, all of the lost things of the city. Things that have been swept out within the year and then frozen deep into the lake.

I ask July again if this is true.

He says that of course it is, where do I think he got his lamp from? And then he stakes that lamp high on the ice and lights it by the fumes. The earliest morning domes in around us.

Unfurling his blanket of oily tools, Emory sits close in the lamp glow and assigns me a saw. He tells me to make note of its number, since assignments are strictly regulated. You watch after it, he says, and start believing what we tell you.

What have you found in the ice, then? I ask him.

This coat, he says, for one. A display of platinum watches from the mall. A dog that he buried at home.

I ask why he couldn't have left him buried here.

And July says that he was missing. Not abandoned. He tells me to remember the difference.

Emory tells me to hold my worry until I need it. He points into the dark after a moment. And then I walk.

The sky is gray and the lake ice is gray and I can hear my steps crackling and just make out the globe of the lamp in the distance like a tremoring eye. The men I came here with have told me that this feeling low in my gut is simply the pull of the relics below. My metal tongs sting through both layers of gloves and I wonder whether any place is better to dig than another. Even shortly into winter this ice has been building for months and, in some places, is forty feet thick.

I begin to saw into the lake by digging shallow, tiring squares. One deeper in from the next.

A curling staircase down, like Emory showed me, that seems to take hours.

By ten feet I've sawn past a table leg. It is suspended with the jointed side facing and there is no stress and no damage that I can see, as if carefully taken apart one day and then lost on the next.

By twenty feet I've sawn past a jewelry box with the name etching corroded, turned over mid-freeze, spilling necklaces that tendril away like golden thread.

And by thirty feet I've found what looks like a set of toy cars arranged in a whorl. Almost meticulous. Worth taking. As I struggle to set my small lantern on the step above my head the flicker of it begins to catch in the lake all around. Very slowly, it illuminates. The light gently spreads. And in the ice beyond there is a silhouette of a bicycle. A still bubble of trapped fish. A constellation of boots, half -bottles of beer, and what I think is a totaled minivan.

In my exhaustion it seems like my chiseling echoes for days.

It is easy to drag my prizes back, still smoothly encased together and fastened to my tongs by the length of rope I thought I might otherwise need. By the fogged watch that Emory gave me it has been only an hour and twenty minutes. He is there at the camp site hugging a colorless messenger bag to his exposed chest to warm some life back into the leather. July has a pile of ivory spoons. There is a wire of pain from my hand to right temple that I need to stop walking to shake off and suddenly I am colder than I've been all night. There is something to worry about: the idea of my body failing before the thaw. I've lost all of the feeling on my skin.

July brings me a sip from his water and he asks if I've found what I'm looking for, found something of mine, on only my first outing with them.

And I say, No, but I think that I've found something new.

The ice block blackens on the drag home. When I won't tell my wife where I got it or what's inside or why I've developed a gentle limp to my right leg, she leans her head all the way back and asks me to the ceiling that I keep it away from our daughter. It is Sunday and I'd promised to make breakfast. Our daughter's name is Ballantyne and she is three years old, and after she places a single hand onto the cold face of the block she immediately begins to wail as it sheaves an entire layer of dirtied ice to the living room floor. I leave the breakfast to simmer and prop my girl against my leg. I yell to my wife that nothing's the matter and if we had any real friends around I suspect they would say we're too old to be raising a child. That's how I imagine them to be. I suspect that they would say that all the time.

My second night out on the lake I'm able to get within a hundred feet of returning to camp before my back seizes up entirely and I lurch forward, kept from falling only by the weight of the heavy new finds that I've carved out and lashed to myself. I'm left considering the frozen murk. On this dig I've salvaged a coil of garden hose, an eyeless rocking horse, and a set of board games that may need to be put in the oven to dry. I'll need to find space for it all at the house. From deep beneath me there's a noise of the low pressing shift of the lake and in the surface's scored reflection I can see that the moon has now risen behind me.

Emory asks if I've died in midstep.

And when I look up he's there, keeping his distance, crouched with his thermos of milk.

I tell him I've begun having doubts about myself.

He tells me that hundreds of years ago the Iroquois used to tunnel into the frozen lake to spend out their winters with only the possessions they could carry. Then they made do or they died of starvation. Strange, isn't it? Considering.

He asks me to look at what he's found. He pulls a small porcelain goose out from a zippered side pocket in his coat and turns it slowly in his hand and then shuffles forward, closer beneath my dangling face, so that I can get a clear view. He says it's terribly made. Look at the way the eye paint has missed and the beak bleeds a little to the chin. There's an odd bend in the legs.

Why does everything need to be perfect, though? The pain against my spine has grown so intense that it's begun to numb itself away. And I say that the thing doesn't look so bad to me.

July says that, from a distance, it looked like I had died in mid-step.

And Emory pauses and smiles and says that he thought exactly the same thing, then pats him on the shoulder.

The both of them are leaning above me, shifting their stances in the lamplight in order to see the knots that they're tying around my arms and my waist. I'm prone on a thick gurney of ice. My finds from the night are tied to me. It will take four, maybe five hours for them to drag me the entire way home.

Emory cradles my head and shares some of his milk. He wants me to know that, out here, we take care of each other.

When I ask the two of them how many others there have been, they consult for a moment and then tell me there have been a few dozen. Over the years. Men more than women. Though, before me, nobody had really thought to keep count.

I can't entirely tell when the lake sliding beneath me turns to sand or to the asphalt of the peninsula park's running path, but soon there are trees above me. And then power lines. My finds are clinking together behind us. Emory and July aren't speaking often and when they are it's low and to themselves and they laugh together, pleased. When I ask what street we're near or what buildings are around they only say that we've made it to land.

The first time they showed me their entire collection it was lined along the girder sills beneath the Thirty-Eighth Street bridge, surrounding a moldered twin mattress, fastened with twine. And I don't know if the look now on their faces is worry, or disappointment, or simply the long pull of the cold, but it's the same look they had then, showing me their home, waiting for me to ask if I could participate, too.

I ask if anyone has ever died on the lake before. With them. That they know of. July says that I would be the first. I'm turned sideways and I come to a stop and then Emory leans down and begins to unfasten my straps. He says that he thought he told me not to worry about it.

That I should never worry about it. That I should think of who lived instead. Isn't that us, right now? I'm left alone on an ice block in front of my house.

I wouldn't say I dream through it, exactly. It's more that when my wife's face appears over me I can't help but to picture her stilled in an ice floe. Found in the spring. Lost months before when the tide pulled her from the driveway after she had foolishly raked leaves with her back to the harbor.

☾

When my wife speaks to me she speaks from the buttons on her shirt and she whispers so softly that I need to ask her to repeat herself several times. I find her hand already wrapped around mine and I tighten our fingers. She tells me the original block of ice in the living room has shed another layer onto the floor. She put the others with it. I'll need to be the one who cleans everything up, is all she was trying to say. She makes herself laugh and I can hear the dog thumping his tail outside in the hall. I am in our bed. It seems as if all of the towels in the house have been draped across my chest and my legs, even the ones that we never use because they either shed their fibers or maintain their smells or have been discolored by young nephews visiting with acne medicine. There's a knock on the door and then Bally enters without waiting for a response, holding a pale green towel against her chest. That one we don't use because the dog has chewed holes along the edges. She quietly crosses the room to lay the towel over my feet, turns, and then leaves.

I realize there's so much more in the lake but I ask to sit the next weekend out at the camp in the name of recuperation, and they seem to understand. July says that he's glad—they'll have more to find for themselves now. When they trudge into the distance beyond the radius of the lamp I stretch my legs out in front of me until they pop and wait for the splintering pain to subside. There's a feeling like strings plucking against my lower back. I wouldn't have made it very far by myself on the lake in the first place. They practically had to carry me here.

There isn't much to the camp besides the crates that we sit on. Beneath the tarp that covers Emory's tools is his usual selection of blackened handsaws and medium-gauge chain and a length of cloth twisted and tied through the straps of twelve headlamps, none of which have batteries. There are assorted pipes and pliers and cleats. Long-weathered picks with their ends in old sheaths. All of us inert. I suddenly worry about the blood pooling in the spots above my legs and I begin to knead and I think that I can hear the creak of the trees lining the peninsula, where the sand meets the lake. Far, far behind me.

☾

I'd fallen asleep for what I think was the second time when July presses the cold neck of a wine bottle against the side of my face.

I say that he's salvaged more quickly than usual.

And he says that what he's salvaged is dessert wine. Three-quarters full. He snaps the corked mouth off with a pick.

The two of us drink from our gloved hands and it's sweet in a way that I've never had before and speckled through with needles of ice. July says to breathe on them a few times to make sure that they melt, that it's not glass. And when I ask if we should save some for Emory, July waves his hand and I can hear the thunk of an axe in the distance. July says that Emory doesn't drink. That he wants to get to know me some more. That I came back when he thinks that not many would have, and he's curious why.

The walks back to shore are regimented and single file, Emory leading, all of us holding a rope. As dawn warms the snow it will get loose enough that a single low gust of wind will cloud our vision for a half hour. And, even though we're never more than a mile onto the lake, it doesn't take that far to get turned around. They made sure I understood these things, first day.

So as the wind shifts from behind us and begins to billow I can hear Emory singing low and off key. Without words. Simply a noise to focus to. Soon, July joins him. And, when the snow begins to hang to where I can no longer find where the ice on the strip of land before us meets the sky and the rope in my hand seems to extend out into nothing, I close my eyes. They pull me along in a gentle way. As though I'm a child. They've seen how I need that sometimes. There's a practice to the way that their voices join together.

It's morning when the first block of ice finally splits apart in the living room. I'm ready with a handful of paper towels and the small trash can from near the front door that we never use. My wife takes her hands away from Bally's ears—as the fissures widened and the trapped air escaped the whistle it made filled the entire room, sharply, and loud. Bally comes to kneel beside the toy cars and flip them onto their wheels, taking the paper towels from my hand to dry them. She asks who they belong to. I look to my wife, who says nothing and then kneels down beside us. I tell Bally that they belong to her and, as I try to think of how to explain further, she arranges them into a long line on the floor and begins to roll them as well as she can to the opposite wall. Some of them make it and then softly crash. Some of them don't. There's one that gives her trouble and so I crawl forward to show how for these cars that click you need to pull backwards first and then let them go. And, before the aged mechanism fails from years of neglect and the tinny engine recording almost immediately begins to bleat static, it does work, beautifully. For just a brief moment. For more than we could have hoped.

Jenna Rindo

What Is Salvaged
From My Son's First Buck

I stand in his room remembering his birth
face, gray and wrinkled, suddenly
visible after I push him from my womb,
the cord gristle twisted tightly around his neck,
his mouth open for calories lost to the kinks in our connection.

Now his bedroom door is closed.
Spent shotgun shells fill containers
on his four drawer dresser. His trash can over-
flows with Mountain Dew bottles and the brown
paper wrappers of high protein power bars.

When he's away up north hunting I come into his room
looking for clues in his backpack's zippered compartments.
I find a slip of paper, extra credit from last year's bio teacher.
He had carried his buck's heart to school in a cooler to be
dissected. It looked not just mammalian but oddly human.

I can barely remember my son latching onto me
and how I let down every defense.
I finger the smooth points of his first rack,
dated, mounted, centered over his single bed.
The wide-spread antler was once velvet covered.
The skin that nourished it shed piece by piece.

Melissa Boston

Soutine, Your *Carcass*

The butchering
is out of order.
Hung by its hock

on the six hook,
its softness
is still visible,

its skin yet to be
removed as you
would turn

down a sock;
the entrails
and ribs are doffed,

but from anus
to sternum
its cavity remains

pulsed in red.
Your eyes
follow this slit

to its head,
and look!
Its own little eyes

stare away,
and it reveals
its perfect

little teeth.

Lisa J. Cihlar

An Insignificant Life

Her life will not be defined by sorrow. The sparrow that hits the window and dies in the jaws of the feral barn cat is one of thousands. Therefore insignificant. Everything eats. Her father never names the beef cattle or the feeder pigs no matter how cute and nuzzly they are. She calls them by name in her head only. All the cows are Bossy, all the pigs are Bristle. The chickens are too many and peck feathers from each other's heads. The unnamed cocks fly at her with spurs extended. She has had blood running down her legs.

Lisa J. Cihlar

Liar

Peonies make me angry,
flaccid after rain
as a loose woman
after a terrifying orgasm.
I have seen a new yellow
varietal in January
seed catalogs. They look
less wanton than the reds,
whites, and pinks.
I would plant them
in my plot if they were not
so dearly priced.
Foxgloves give me a headache.
I think if I blend them
into my pesto
I might kill someone.
Joe asks me,
Who thinks things like that?
Even though I secretly
know I do not have a novel in me,
it becomes my excuse.
Poems don't usually kill people.
Peonies are usually
beautiful in poems.

Amaris Feland Ketcham

Afterthoughts of the Bloom

"Does Amaris need a flower remedy that starts with an 'A'?" Aurora asked as the pendulum circled in a slow clockwise spin. She held the pendulum—a small crystal affixed to a pewter chain—so that the crystal swung a half-inch from the central plain of my left palm, where the device could read my chakra's energy. Aurora watched the rotation as she cycled through the alphabet—"Does Amaris need a remedy that starts with a 'B'?"—and moved only to the next letter if the crystal continued clockwise. The pendulum changed direction, zipping around counterclockwise with the letter H. We made a note and then continued through Z.

Aurora changed her voice when she inquired of the pendulum— she made herself sound sweeter, as if trying to impress the small crystal. Maybe she used the higher pitch to try to control the ideomotor effect, where she might subconsciously and reflexively control the diagnosis. The involuntary movement of a diviner's muscles has been used to explain mystical energies involved in dowsing for water, moving the planchette across the Ouija board, or rattling the tabletop during a séance. Which is to say, I had doubts about the mystical achievements made possible by flower remedies, but I was willing to sit with Aurora as she divined my problem.

The two of us sat in folding camping chairs on my front porch. The summer sun had already started to bake the dirt yard and the adobe house. Even though it was morning still, we could feel the heat collecting, radiating off my home. I used my right hand, the one free of the ceremony, as a shield from the sun so I could make eye contact with Aurora when she looked up from my left palm's business. She had short, fluffy red hair, wore a bright yellow tank top and some old jeans with intentional daubs of acrylic paint on the thighs.

Aurora was one of the first people I'd met after moving to Albuquerque, one of my first friends in my desert life. She'd dropped out of college our sophomore year to study massage therapy and natural therapeutics. She worked in the school's homeopathic store still, selling detox teas, Asian-themed dietary supplements, sagebrush creams, lavender oils, and of course, flower remedies.

When we finished going through the alphabet, Aurora opened her *Bach Flower Remedy Guide to "H."* "Does Amaris need a Holly remedy? Does Amaris need a Hornbeam remedy?" The crystal continued clockwise above my palm, but I thought of the ideomotor effect and flinched.

"Amaris, I know you're skeptical, but can you at least pay attention?" Aurora asked. My eyes must have glazed over while I thought of how silly the term "flower power" was and how much Aurora would hate it if I called this divination by that name. I mumbled an apology.

Aurora knew that I had little faith in many healing practices. When I'd been living in Kentucky, my mother would take us to the doctor, a man who often recommended prayer to heal everything from depression to brown recluse spider bites. If we pressed him, though, he'd eventually find some antibiotic samples to give us. Once, I had a stubborn wart that no supply of duct tape would kill, and when I finally convinced the doctor to break out his stash of liquid nitrogen, he spilled the whole cup on my foot. I limped away from Western medicine, but I never ceded myself completely to its alternatives.

Also when I was a child, my mother trained with a Reiki master, practiced radiating healing energies through her palms. I had some wrist problems that the town doctor had diagnosed as either tendonitis, broken bones, carpal tunnel syndrome, or inverted carpals. He suggested I had sustained the injury from falling down while playing basketball. My mother hoped to heal me with her palm's heat. I could feel warmth from her hands, sure, but my carpals remained inverted and continued to pinch nerves, and my tendons still swelled and what was wrong stayed wrong. I doubted alternative medicine as much as I doubted Western medicine.

"I'm trying to take this seriously," I said, "but in my own way."

"I just don't want this to be like that thing with the priestess," Aurora said.

A few years before, I had divination with an Ifa priestess from Puerto Rico. Every aspect of the process had fascinated me—a lot of shells and earthenware sprinkled with gin, the only liquor blessed by African gods. The priestess assigned me to collect two hundred pebbles from river shores, clean them, and then wash them in gin every day. The religious charge would help fortify my bond with a particular river goddess, one of great valor, who would help me say "no" to people.

"No, it's not like the priestess," I told Aurora. Years had passed, and I was still collecting the pebbles and putting them in an emptied gin bottle. Aurora had understood my incomplete ritual as a sign that I wasn't committed to my well-being and that I didn't take alternative healing seriously.

"OK, good, because I think that this will help," Aurora said, straightening her hold on the pendulum's chain. A flower remedy is more powerful and predictable than Western medicine, she said, particularly new pharmaceuticals, which had fewer trials than the flowers. The flower remedies had been around for almost a century.

Edward Bach had created the first mother tinctures of flower remedies in the 1930s. An English homeopath and physician, Bach had intuited the cures through a sort of psychic connection with plants—when he felt a negative emotion, he would seek certain flowers' energies to heal himself. His methods were distinct from the ethnobotanical explosion of the previous century, when, say, Alexander von Humbolt collected information on the aboriginal uses of different plants, how the locals cultivated their plants for medicine, food, clothing, dye, cosmetics, rituals, and other uses. For example, for centuries people in New Mexico had been using yucca leaves to cure sunburns and scratches, mixing the leaves and roots in shampoos, rubbing the coarse trunk fibers together to make fire, kneading the ash with dough to make a bread blue and paper thin, sewing with the sharp spines on the leaves, and dying wool with the seeds. But Bach didn't conduct interviews—his was a more sensitive, perceptive approach.

Bach found that if he collected sunlit dewdrops from the flower's petals, he could preserve the energetic essence with brandy and have access to the healing tincture year-round. He listed thirty-eight remedies, ranging from agrimony to impatiens to willow and curing everything from self-hatred to inattentiveness to my personal favorite, vague fears.

She recomposed herself before asking, "Does Amaris need a honeysuckle remedy?"

The crystal raced counterclockwise. According to the backward spin, I was in a "negative honeysuckle state" and needed to supplement my diet with the remedy. My diagnostic criteria included wistfulness, nostalgia, and an inability to form a connection between my past and my present. While I didn't know that I was ill to begin with, and I had little faith in the clockwise-counterclockwise chakra test thatdelivered a diagnosis without a proper set of complaints, I agreed with the inclusion of nostalgia as one of my discerning symptoms. I could view myself as in the process of knowing the pain a woman feels when she fears she'll never return home—homesickness, repining.

Along with the remedy, the book recommended that I should repeat certain positive statements as mantras. I could not see myself staring in the mirror and repeating the affirmation, "Every day is new and exciting." Nor could I possibly envision myself closing my eyes on the bus with a sigh and saying, "Remember, life is happening now."

This mirror-talk was the dopiest recommendation that I could think of: It would better serve a late-night comedy skit than my life. Aurora pointed to the potential transformation after taking the remedy—the patient would be able to form a living relationship with the past, to carry what was once beautiful from a collection of yesterdays into the present. "Just try it," she said. "I'll make you some honeysuckle and maybe it will help. You don't have to say the mantras out loud."

I agreed.

I didn't know where Aurora found the honeysuckle flowers in peak potency. The remedy recipe calls for the flowers to be within two days of full bloom, and while honeysuckle can bloom throughout the summer, I'd never seen the bush growing in Albuquerque. Since Bach had lived in England, his remedies included different indigenous flora than what grew in our high desert home—oak instead of juniper, holy instead of cane cholla cactus. Dew is also hard to come by in the desert, and I would have liked to see someone testing a prickly pear's energy field by rubbing their hands around the cactus' flower. But that desire was only my cynicism coming out. The desert has plenty of its own cures: rub aloe on your skin for sunburn, chew fresh chamomile flowers to quit smoking, stick a garlic clove in the ear for an infection. Not all are so ordinary, either: There are cures for the evil eye, excess rage, a soul that wanders too far while the body is dreaming. Maybe British flora and rituals could be transplanted to the American West just as easily as an Anglo might learn the Eagle Dance. Maybe it was a matter of perception, acceptance, and soul-searching.

I didn't help Aurora bottle the flowers in the brandy, but she instructed me on the recipe for future reference. After you pluck the blooms, place them in the brandy, cap the jar, and put it in a window for one day. The sun, Bach says, has power to infuse the energy of the flower into the brandy. Allow the bloom and brandy to warm in the sun, then let it sit out one whole night. The next morning, cut the contents with fresh spring water. Fifty-fifty. Place the jar and all contents in a dark cupboard. Wait until the blooms begin to blanch and then remove them. Voila, mother tincture.

Aurora stopped by the next day with a glass dropper bottle labeled in her handwriting: honeysuckle. I knew that the process should take at least a week, and asked whether she'd had some on hand at the natural therapeutics store where she worked.

"Yes, and this is a potentized batch," she said. Homeopaths always seem to make up words that shouldn't exist. I must have arched an eyebrow, because she said, "It's been diluted to the fourth potency."

I asked how the remedy could be stornger if it's been diluted. Potetentization releases the honeysuckle's energy from its physical matrix through serial dilutions—one tenth the mother tincture, then one tenth the second tincture, and so on, until in this case, the fourth round. Shake or "strike" the remedy between each dilution, because "succussion" increases the effect of the treatment.

I pulled some of the liquid into the eyedropper and squirted four drops under my tongue for quick absorption. The remedy swished around my taste buds, but didn't burn when I swallowed.

"It's sweeter than I imagined," I told Aurora.

"Take it four times a day until it's done and you'll feel better. You really have to stick to the regimen, and finish the bottle. You have to believe in it," Aurora said. She really harped on the belief part. Belief, interior reflection, psychosomatic results—these are the necessary components of placebos.

I'd never been good at following prescribed orders. I couldn't even self-medicate reliably, although on Friday nights, I drink a little unpotentized bourbon. I didn't want to bring the tincture to work and take two dropper doses there. While Aurora carried with her a purse-load of vials—essential oils and flower remedies and massage gels and Mason jars of detoxifying teas and mint sniffers—her work at the natural therapeutics store had normalized these items. My work expected me to be normal, to play within the rules, to keep my elbows off the table when I ate, to speak when spoken to, to coordinate my blouses and slacks and heels. But I decided to comply with her prescription.

During my lunch hour, I started roaming around downtown. I walked to Civic Plaza and stood on the concrete stage. Watching the people below cross the plaza, enter cafes and unwrap burritos, and sit in swooshing purple dresses to chat on the phone, I tried to remember when the built world had been a sort of parkour playground, where each piece of the urban environment was something to interact with, to climb, touch, or hop over. The downtown professionals did not jaywalk—these people all crossed the street when the white, LED man promised a safe passage. I remembered how, into our twenties, we rolled skateboards up and down wheelchair ramps, investigated the inside chambers of landscaped juniper bushes, waited on the islands between lanes for traffic to ebb before racing across busy thoroughfares. We used to steal late-summer roses, ripened apricots, and fresh rosemary from the city. The people downtown passed awesome lavender bushes without stopping to crush the buds between their fingers. I tried to release my impulses toward mischief and mystery. I said from the stage: "Every day is new and exciting."

Brandon Rushton

Maintaining the House of a Deceased Loved One Is a Paraphrasing of the Cinematic Inheritance of Grief

Snow is not so much snow as it is reason
to turn off the porch light—

grief stacks up with the woodpile, split

blindness by burning both ends of the fog:

All winter the attic asks for its ghost back.

This ice-braided stairwell. Frozen fern.
Geese flocking southward carrying
something that looks like chromosomes.

After he died, I tried to grow a new father.

I pulled the hair from his razor
and planted it in the yard.

Specter changes its name to dictator. Leaving

things that are trying to live
between couch cushions. Ink pen. Pocketknife.

I scrape together

a dollar in different kinds of coins.

Please, excuse this low-budget film of memory.

Blood tends to taste like doorknobs—these days
I hold them longer as your hands.

In the kitchen I let a glass scatter itself
over the linoleum.

I, this janitor of couldn't-quite-sneak-my-way-through.

It is all along time.

Bone friction in the treetops. The cold crawling in

under the shingles.

Bees dying in the window jamb,s
me, scooping them out with a spoon.

Ricardo Pau-Llosa

Friends

Every now and then, you have to count on them,
but let's hope it's only now and then.

It's better to be on your own, to move this sand
over here and that coconut over there—by yourself.

That way the world is always a mirror,
a file, a record, a standard.

When you have to ask for help, the image
that should shine forth gets muddled.

And, of course, when the storm comes,
you never see lobster, never the palm

when the sun scorches, never a chicken
when the cook is walking about.

Never the hatchling tortoises frantic
for moon water when the gulls are staring.

Ricardo Pau-Llosa

Didn't Last Long

Sooner or later, I was bound to trade my shadow
for a sweet female crab. How delightful it is to change

something yours, entirely yours, for something
you are going to lose. Of course, it all depends

on how you look at things. When the delectable female came,
I didn't even glance anymore at my things.

There they were. I felt their presence. Like the wind
in the branch, the heat with which the summer

lines its suit of sand. Laughter and hearing,
chewing and flavor. They are never lost,

only stray from sight a little because something
new comes in which doesn't forgive glances.

Who said that the new makes demands
and the old has to allow itself to be sought?

Oh, my sweet love, take a good look at me, and at yourself.
Goodbye is the shadow of Welcome.

Jeff Hardin

My Life According to Little Proofs Assembled

What if the prologue
                steals its best ideas from the epilogue?
I won't deny I am an empty shell washed up, stripped clean.
A truth?—
        or simply one more thing I'm likely to believe?

*

Unsurpassably, I've waded in,
             gone under long enough to let the water heal.
Those people who trail off midsentence are maybe gathering deeper breath.
Some words undulate;
        others pull the curtains closed.

*

What more proof
       than how the snake slides in to scan the henhouse.
We're mostly flat rocks on uneven ground.
The airy lightness of mimosa blooms,
             their repercussive shock across
           the yard ....

*

Always, to get to what's beyond,
          I cross, first, a bridge of a single breath.

Luci Brown

Of Another Nature I Did Not Know

Somewhere in my house there is another house. With three kids and a torn marriage. A mother with eyes like coconuts and a smile not even half that. She bakes cobblers at midnight. Waking me to wonder why our bedroom smells like fresh apples. Why children laugh and I clutch my abdomen. There is nothing there to hold. And Joshua passes her in the hall each morning as she says, *It's okay to feel the weight of solitude thickening the air.* He glances back at me, goes to brush his teeth. On Friday, I felt the man in the back yard. He couldn't get the flower bed to form into a marriage. I told him it smelled like April from this angle.

Conor Robin Madigan

Reasons for Loving

After it happened, she was unsure that it had and she lay in the sun room and didn't know what to do. Her brother had always hated trains and wouldn't travel. He was convinced people died on trains all the time. This had become an obsession for him. He went pale when cars pulled up with troops from the war, the covered caskets, the heads bobbing about inside for no one to see. He was ten and his mother held him close. The railroad was no place to take a child, Joseph and Mary, she said. Son after son, up to see their daddy's work. Young boys to see their dead brothers home. Daughters and nieces who wrapped their arms around their own little torsos when caskets rolled free onto the landing, wishing to nuts they held their bothers, cousins, and fathers. Men coughing and spitting down patches of darkness. Teetering cars crushed men in a snap. Old sun-dried blood, and bloated tar bubbles. Carrion birds and lice and hollow hobos raided rotted shipments boiling in the sun. Bodies from the whorehouse, bodies from the mines, bodies. And those long shimmering lines, hot and endless.

She lay on a couch and hammered her heels into the armrest. Soon they'd all be home and responding to their families with monosyllables. She puttered around the row house, the image of the mashed up man remarking itself to her with every fifth or eighth heartbeat of forgetting. The dryer in the basement ran down the clock of an hour. Beau would be racing. He'd roll down to York in neutral. The only sounds in the Falcon, the wind, passing cars, silence between siblings. Beau told her how to do it. It was a matter of gravity and fluid dynamics. Disgusting. The wheels turned.

Marty had taken her to the zoo when they visited his rich father. Bears watched her, a tall thin meal. Starving wolves fill up on stream mud and go until they pull down a burdened beast to eat and together purge out their insides of stagnant gut rot. A daughter of monosyllables. Barks in the den. At the battlefield the plaques told her the men ate only cherries, the heat of summer killing droves before battle, diarrhea pulling them down into the earth with all their fluids. Men have such drained bodies. Women can soak up so much, can be filled, a cup wanting. A woman smashed would-be potential, dashed against the steel and tragic, but the man—the man's body—once moving and alive, just died, leaving his place of work. The dry, withered face stopped its droll and labored animation. The cup was never there. Some men. Not her brother. That and weddings; they'd been to a zoo, the battlefields and weddings without mother. She didn't travel. Marty had grown up the day Janey was born.

Daughters can do that. Sons can be born dead to fathers. Tight eyes and a mouth open and silent save for great breaths of shaking terror, like some sea creature brought from its dank selfish hole. Not daughters. Bears watched her. They had to get rid of a plug. Birth after hibernation. To grow the cold of a glacier inside her. Purging, unplugging—the animal delights of birth. An ice released. The mine kept its unborn, like a deranged plugged-up miscarriage. The bodies lined up on the football field where sons battled to win a chance to enter coffins lined in pink satin.

"Why can't a goddamn woman just do it herself?"

"Maybe they will," Beau said.

"It'd be a lot cheaper, I'd bet."

"In the future, when we're on the moon driving around up there, I bet there's gonna be a way." She liked him best like this: working on his car, letting her dreams become his considerations. "Imagine having one in space."

"It's impossible."

"What, why?"

"Birth needs gravity, I'm pretty sure."

"Phooey."

"They can't just plunge it out of you like a clogged toilet."

Railroad picnics maybe changed all that. An unused part of the rail, back near a pond, got shined up and ready for the guests. Families trickled over a hill down to a long stretch of solitary rail where a caboose held lunch and liquor and a party. Janey wore her blouse. Beau brought his girl. A loudspeaker thinned out Speedy West and Jimmy

Bryant, and young adults danced like the kids. The grunters laughed and sat under the shade in folding chairs. Chocolate pudding came in waves. For one day a year, there was a reason to wear a suit, bring your hat, shine your belt and shoes, offer condolences, hug your old pal, hold your own torso waiting for your dead brother to trickle over that hill down to a long stretch of solitary rail.

Megan Giddings

Roy Orbison Saved From Heart Failure

Jenny writes a letter to Roy Orbison asking for his hand in marriage. She promises him love, fidelity, pancakes waiting for him in the morning, foot rubs, admiration, even those pancakes with bacon crumbled into the batter, kindness. She finishes the letter: "I don't care if you're older than me, I don't care if you're already dead, I know you're the one for me."

Roy Orbison was the inspiration for Doctor Octopus of Spider-Man fame. His signature oversized sunglasses gave the villain an element of cool menace that horn rims, goggles, or a spiked helmet couldn't capture.

When Orbison's house burnt down, he sold the property to Johnny Cash. Cash turned it into a beautiful orchard.

Whenever Jenny needs someone to talk to, she writes to Orbison. She sits on bar stools dashing off postcards, her journal filled with missives, and when she sits in physics class, Jenny re-explains the theories in her notebooks in simple language that even a musician from the past could understand.

From "On Why Orbison Matters": "You could feel his pain in every note he sings. Every note was an elegy to his dead wife, his burned sons, his failing eyes."

When Jenny's parents died, she spent the weeks after slumped in different positions listening to *Crying* on repeat.

All those white and pink flowering trees in the Tennessee sunshine, the trees reaching out under the bright blue sky.

Roy Orbison with six metal arms flings Spider-Man up and away from him. He opens his mouth and sings the chorus to "(They Call You) Gigolette" as Spider-Man soars across the New York City skyline.

An antique shop on Detroit Street has a table made from an Orbison-Cash tree. Jenny likes to visit it on Saturday mornings, resting her hands on the soft wood. She does this and says a silent prayer for the lost children, the parents, herself.

"To hear Orbison's voice for the first time is to realize all the possibilities of the human voice. His incredible range (three and a half octaves!), his silken delivery like a caress to the ear, reminds the listener that the divine is truly attainable."

Eight p.m. and Michigan December dark, Jenny sat in a green Ford Taurus, caught in a ditch. Her parents stood outside, snow dusting their eyelashes and hair as they argued about the best way to free the car. She discusses this moment over and over in therapy, unsure of why it sticks with her twenty-four years later.

With great power comes great responsibility.

Jenny draws a pie graph of life as she knows it: sleeping, time-machine building, eating, correspondence, watching episodes of *Doctor Who*, music-listening, mourning, walks.

The Teen Kings wore button-down shirts in gingham beneath tight suits. Orbison on lead guitar, alternating between geology training, alternating between teacher training, alternating between rhythms, alternating between singing, alternating between fantasies of crowds screaming as the band comes out on stage.

"Pretty Paper" was on the radio. Jenny leaned her head against the cool window, holding a blue-wrapped present on her seven-year-old lap. Jenny didn't know most of the words, so she crooned a wordless melody while thinking about lit-up trees and brand new books wrapped in shiny silver and gold.

By the time Spider-Man returns, Orbison has fled the scene. He could be in the lab conducting experiments. He could be meeting with the Sinister Six. He could be playing a show at Madison Square Garden, playing three different guitars simultaneously to the crowd's delight.

His voice painted her heart indigo.

Frank Booth in a bolo tie. He mouths the words as Ben performs "Crying." Emotions like an earthquake fissure his face. Jenny is uncomfortable with how much she relates to him in these moments.

"It's a shame that Orbison has faded from the nation's imagination. No other musician has the spirit of the West so exemplified in his voice."

Jenny hides her blueprints behind a large, framed black-and-white poster of Orbison. She has told no one what she is actually doing. Her friends and colleagues assume she is secretly writing fan fiction or falling into video game after video game.

The orchard's apples have been rumored to be able to help people sing better for an hour after eating. One man claimed baking them into a pie made his wife fall in love with him. A girl claimed two bites cleared up her grandma's glaucoma.

On October 27, 2042, Jenny perfects her time machine. Her hair streaked white, her demeanor calm. She spends a sleepless night weighing the consequences of her planned actions, then travels to Hendersonville, Tennessee, on December 6, 1988, defibrillator in hand.

Danilo Thomas

The Steeling

My brother and I vandalize the cleanness of sky. We drag our bodies through maggots lining tin gutters. We shine in the shadowed streets of this town. Dirtied with snow and plow salt, we creep to the head frame in the mine yard. We creep over the fences, creep over the barbed wire. The fences are silver. The barbed wire is russet and dull. Creeps, also. The gallused lean on broken limbs. Their steel staircases hacked twenty feet shy of the arsenic ground. The lattice of the head frames rot. They chip onto the ground and the ground soaks in lead and mineral blight. This gallus shows us what we've done. My brother and I drag our besotted bodies along these beams to reach the staircase, and the crows: and not the stars that never dangle ropes for us, will not meet us halfway. My brother's shoes are slick. Grease and dirt wadded in the groove of flange, rats in rat-clusters. My brother's shoes have weathered soles. My brother's grip is lax on the rails. He clenches his teeth when he falls. My brother's coat blackens in descent and shadow, and pigeons. He twists. He twists like the twisted, soldered steps. He stretches his arms to brace. The rush of him into concrete. The ground does not give, does not give him away. Where the steel is black each rivet-head holds steel panel to steel panel. Each rivet-head chipped and rusted, the crow's nest has wounds: scabs of paint, scars from boot heel. The crows have flown to the sky, the sky that is crows forever. The stars are lights left between their flying bodies, are minnows the crows starved looking for. The minnows between their black bodies. There on their wings. The minnows' bellies are silver. We vandalize. The spray of red blossoms from the finger. The mist of paint falls on my brother's broken body, the blood in my brother's hair. His hair, his crushed face in the tallow waste. The paint coats. The blood spreads. I take the bottle from my pocket. I look at the stars. The sky stalks them. In our town of orphaned metal, I am under the moon's solitary glare, Earth-gazing. Brighter lights dwell alone in those distances. Below me, the wheelhouse settles in rust. The wheelhouse, corrugated tin, disappears around its own thin nails. The tin rattles. The tin slaps. The echo of it sings in the wind. The wheelhouse sheds ice to pile scree, defeated, and does not put the sheave into motion. The cable has gone. The sheave does not twine the moon in wire to hoist the dead from this earth. The buried platform will never bring my brother to me. Those cords have rotted. Those cords are midnight entrances painted in red at cold heights. Those cords, won at the top of gallus frames, make us dirty, make us harder, and choke until we vomit. I place my palms on the rail of the crow's nest. I tilt the bottle. A last drop. Shattered inches from my brother's face. Splash of glass. Wet concrete. The moon's reflection. The moon is interred. The moon is waning gibbous. The moon is my brother's tombstone, the epitaph etched with meteors, and speaks of holes in the flesh of an abused chippy that walks heeled through this town. She dances for a starved wolf that slams ivory tones from the piano in some dirt-floored saloon. She cringes while she waits for the next drunkard to throw the next bottle to chip the next hole from her cheek. That hole is a sky. The stars are chips of marble fallen to the stonemason's floor that engraved the moon. And the moon is so white. White as my brother's bones. His slick skull. His skull is cold, a stone in a river. The moon is that stone. The black river the sky made of crows. The sky is not clean. The stars are minnows. They are belly-up. Their bellies are silver.

Albert Abonado

The Last Pearl

I'm not sure when I learned about the robbery
that became the reason my parents sold their little grocery store.
I was just happy I would no longer be pried out of bed early
on Saturday mornings, only to find myself in Chinatown
in the back of a van crammed full of merchandise:
cans of jackfruit, bags of rice whose elephant logos belonged
in my dreams or mud-colored crabs whose mouths bubbled
when I lifted them from their crate. The crabs must have wanted
directions to the nearest source of salt or a good spot to lay
their eggs since they knew my family loved
their roe. I would have said the Atlantic, but the language
of crabs doesn't generally mix with oxygen, I suppose.
Most of the time, I slept. I should have kept
a journal of all the dreams I had while waiting
so that I could look back on a day like this and say
The building full of gardens was the day we purchased a windup bird.
The dream with miniature saints hovering over my bed was the day
a tire burst in the middle of the expressway.
I just remember the officers who frequently tapped
on the window of the van wanting to know where
my father was and why he was double-parked
or the steamy meatballs that came in little
paper boats or the time no one let me use
their bathroom when I had to pee so badly,
when I pinched back what was a certain flood.
My father yelled at every store owner who denied
me, informed them that was illegal,
how they were not allowed to deny us

access because bathrooms were a constitutional right,
and everyone in this country is guaranteed a bathroom.
I don't remember the details of how it all ended.
I assume I probably did end up peeing
in a bathroom, but the possibility my urine wound up
in a bottle or jar emptied out in a hurry doesn't seem
so unrealistic since my bladder was rather small
back then. The only thing I know is true
is the Chinatown where I saw Asians
with whom my friends liked to say
I shared an intimate relationship, a claim based
on a document they say anthropologists once discovered
on Ellis Island, detailing the mysterious bond
that allows Asians to exchange information across
vast distances without speaking to one another
directly. Sometimes, I told my friends, Asians don't hear
voices. We hear a series of whistles and clicks
that we decipher like Morse code or whale songs
so when I told them about the robbery,
they were surprised when I said
it was another group of Asians who held
my father at knifepoint, who told him to lie
on his belly like a slug, who warned him
that if he contacted the police, they would cut
off his balls and the balls of his children.
My friends didn't believe it was possible
for Asians to commit violent acts against
other Asians because that would violate
a moral code written in kanji on our spines,
that really my father must have seen men wearing
very convincing Asian masks, and with people
out there with disguises that believable,
it's a good thing my family got out
of the business when they did.

Albert Abonado

Diagram of a Man With Very Tiny Wings

after Rachel McKibbens

In the language of children, I don't have the word for tragedy.
I can only insist on the importance of being witness
to terrible, unfortunate events. On a piece of construction
paper, I attempt to explain the idea to my niece
with the following: I draw a man without arms falling
from an invisible building. *This is sadness.*
I intend to explain to her that the man can no longer look
behind him. He has already forgotten the reason for falling.
He can only look towards the ground expanding
as he approaches, except I'm unable to say any of this.
I say, instead, that here, a man mastered the art of flight.
This is a miracle: limbs that move so rapidly they became transparent.
And what about this picture I drew of a building collapsing?
No, someone started to carve a monument of flowers from stone.
Those are not graves on the page, but the names I gave
to my footprints, names that belong to my godparents who sleep
in another country. Let me start again: This cloud is disaster.
You cannot see all the fish made of lightning that swim
inside its belly. This is where the man falls from, where the buildings hang
upside down, why it rains cinder blocks and furniture
in some parts of the world and every window is a rung
on a ladder that doesn't end, but disappears. This cloud is responsible
for every dark corner of our home, the figures you don't see
that I can't talk about, stalking our hallways, who don't need
eyes or teeth to be weapons. They are the ones who gathered
the dust we left behind and made it into a calendar.
We wake up every morning to shake the days from our spines.

Albert Abonado

Cave Song

Whatever is the name of the empty space between the eye and brain is
    where
I assemble the cancer scars on her body, that region she points
to but remains hidden beneath her plaid shirt, the marks she says extend

from hip up her ribs and into her armpit. In a remote part of myself
that does not recognize light as a substance, a gap she may only touch
with sweetness, I see a column of bats rising out of her.

What am I to do with the one who arrives with an armful of bananas,
    but is also
a pillar of unending dark out of which all these animals ascend
    screeching towards
the exit? I fold both over in my mind, from wet stone to blood song

to starshine. For every day she returns to us again out of the storm
of our aisles, I remind myself that she is more than shroud or gingerroot.
I unlearn the face I stitched together with leather and wire. I pry open

the jaw and empty it of morning. If all repetition is holy, then praise
her hands, the psalms dusted with her sugar, the nails that dig
and peel what still requires ripening. Praise

the ones who reach out, mouth first, for a little taste of what's left.

Albert Abonado

The Man Root

"They say I'm not human," the thirty-nine-year-old says softly. "Whatever they want to say, that's fine. I guess I am a Tree Man."
— *"Indonesian 'Tree Man' trapped in his mutating body"* The Los Angeles Times, *July 16, 2010*

In a period of documents,
even I am fascinated

by the kind of fruit I will bear
after the rainy season,

the color and odor I blossom
around my wife, if I will wake

from a dream about falling
because of the small melons

that drop softly from my elbow
in my sleep. I know about

the people who follow me, curious
if I thrive on just water and light.

They want to ask if I can bury my feet
deep enough to nourish myself

on their dead, if I am related
to the orchid or the banana tree.

What animal nests in my limbs?
I sometimes forget the difference

between children and lizards. Perhaps
I will one day find myself

pulverized and pressed into a sheet
on which they write their contracts, sign

their names into my blood. Let them say
the saplings I cultivate in my garden came

from my teeth, that I graft my face
to other trees so one day

I can watch myself walk
in a field of myself, that my speech

is nothing more than dirt. Let them take
metal to the ground around me

to see why nothing grows in my soil
or how far down my roots must go

to find the kind of dark I swallow
when they are not looking

George Looney

A Very Old Music

First time I saw Karl he was on his riding mower, and at first I thought he must have his daughter on his lap. Folks round here often do that. Keeps the little imps entertained, or at least distracted, for a spell. If I hadn't had the time to get a better look, that's what I'd have gone away thinking. Just a father keeping his daughter from getting cranky before dinner. But I was walking slowly that day—weighted down with burdens no one looking might readily see any sign of—so I was close enough long enough to see, as the sun angled just so through the trees lining the lawn, the truth of it. That here was a man out mowing his lawn who had a second head on his shoulders. A woman's head at that. And though I could see she was saying something in his left ear, it would be awhile before I heard her speak and learn she only spoke Greek. And not modern Greek, but the Greek of Homer, of the Old Testament, a Greek of mystery and faith and everything that goes unwitnessed in this fallen old world.

A Greek few folks can understand even in Greece itself. Karl had no idea at all what she was saying, but she was almost always saying something in that sore left ear of his. No wonder the man seemed to have a permanent lean to the right.

God sure does like to keep things entertaining. I mean, after all I've witnessed in this world just a walk down an unassuming street can bring me face to face with another enigma, more proof that the miraculous and the tragic are as much a part of this desperate world as the mundane. If a man with a woman's head on his shoulder talking Greek in his left ear isn't sign of God's hand in all this, I don't know what is.

☾

It wasn't Karl's feminine tormentor that brought me to this little town in the middle of nowhere, but the pine woods that make up parts of the Chattahoochee National Park. Pine woods being the best places to find scarlet snakes. Leastways, that's what my reading up on them told me. And Subligna—what folks here call this ramshackle version of a town—sounded like Latin to me, like it was the name of something holy and mysterious. Like faith had to be strong in a place with a name like Subligna.

Faith has always been strong in me but, like a scarlet snake, it has burrowed down into the sandy loam that must be all that remains of my soul, and it only comes out some nights to remind itself of the world it burrowed down to get away from, to convince itself that to stay hidden is best.

My preaching days are over. Can't get up in front of folks and convince them to love God with your own faith burrowed deep within you and fearful of showing itself in the light.

Sometimes, having a whiskey in Marlow's, I stare at Gloria in her waitress getup looking so much, in the dim light of that tavern, like Rachel it damn near has me ready to go deep into the Chattahoochee Park to hunt for a gator to feed myself to. But no gator can swallow me enough to cleanse me of my sins, or consume the ghost of the woman who haunts me with her body and her music and that perfect face I held in my hands and kissed one last time in the midst of a gator's guts and the shouting and cries from the congregation. Only the snakes hold out hope for me. If I can hunt down the scarlet snake whose markings spell out the depths of my sins, I can cut off its head and carve it and cook it up with some onions and peppers, and once I've eaten that snake maybe then I'll be able to forgive myself. I'll know that snake when I find it. I'll be able to read my sins in the bands that cross its legless body. This I believe.

It takes a lot of faith to keep going in this world, Karl can attest to that.

We drink together, Karl and me. The woman's head growing from his left shoulder only drinks ouzo. I've seen her knock back over a dozen shots of the licorice-tasting stuff at a sitting. One night not long ago, after the seventh or eighth shot of ouzo, she started singing what must have been some ancient sea chantey. It could have been what that fellow Odysseus heard the sirens sing, him bound to the mast and calling out to his crew to let him go. Their ears stopped up with wax, they couldn't hear him, or the sirens. His own plan. That must have been the worst of his torment—that he had willingly participated in what would deny him his chance to have such incredible longing fulfilled. His body become nothing but desire lashed to the mast; it must have seemed absolute cruelty how his crew ignored his transformation in their midst from a creature of skin and blood and the passing of time to pure emptiness crying out to be filled.

The voice in which the woman's head sang the untranslatable song was so lovely everyone in Marlow's stopped what they were doing to listen. Not one of us had any idea what words she was singing, but we all knew how it made us feel. Me, all I could do was think of Rachel playing the organ, how those hands of hers could turn the notes of any hymn into a promise of consolation and repair, of the mystical healing only possible with touch. That woman's head was busy seducing every man and woman within earshot.

I don't know what kept me from grabbing Karl and kissing the lips through which that singing poured. After all, I've already kissed the bodiless head of a woman spilled out of a gator's opened gut, so kissing that singing woman's head on Karl's left shoulder wouldn't have felt so strange at all. Guess the mixing of the music and the whiskey just made it so I couldn't move. Mesmerized is the word for it. Most of us in Marlow's were mesmerized.

That such music stirs up rawer passions don't surprise me none, either. One man that night in Marlow's got up on the bar and took out his member and tried to put it in the mouth that music was coming from. Thank the Lord for Russell, the bouncer, who knocked the drunk off the bar and dragged him to the door and out into the street. Russ left him there crumpled in a heap of bawling flesh. 'Course, it's not like some of the rest of us hadn't had the same thought. That music made those lips a promise of such pleasure it was remarkable more of us weren't thrown out that night.

Other nights—and tonight's one of those—the ouzo makes the Greek-speaking woman's head go quiet. Karl gets this smile on his face when this happens and has been known to buy a round for everyone in the place. Not tonight, though. Tonight he just smiles and sips his whiskey and sneaks looks at that quiet face. He's told me on nights when the ouzo quiets her he can turn and gaze at her alcohol-becalmed face and almost feel a kind of love for her. He's told me once or twice, when she's gone quiet after enough ouzo, he's almost kissed her.

After Karl told me that I started having dreams of being back on that stage wallowing in the filth that spilled out of the sliced-open gator with Rachel's perfect face in my hands, and then I'm sewing her head onto my left shoulder—or in some versions having someone else sew her head on my shoulder—and she is with me and I'm kissing her and the things her tongue does in my mouth are a miracle. Sometimes, though, when I dream of taking on the head of Rachel, it's not a good dream. Rachel's head, beside mine, just turns away from me, refuses me, and the pain of my longing for her, and her refusal of me, twists my body into a grotesque grimace of the human form, and all I can do is a sad and stumbling two-step in some bar where the sawdust on the floor rises with my every graceless step into clouds that could be the edges of storm fronts moving in to lay everything to waste. Dreams can leave us in places as bad as any the world can ever take us to.

Gloria's looking particularly fine, and the way that waitress getup announces every curve of her ample body's almost enough to send me out to hunt snakes in the woods. But it's too dark already to have any real shot of finding the snake with my sins on it. Dark enough who knows what I might find. The other evening, when it was still much lighter than this, I stumbled over an exposed root and my hand reached out and clutched the trunk of a fir to break my fall and I felt what turned out to be words in Spanish carved into the tree. Though shallow now, when they were first carved into the tree they must have been carved deep. Only part of the sentence remained, and I only recognized a few of the Spanish words, but I had heard of the man who had long ago carved his signature under that almost-gone sentence. Hernando de Soto was the name scrawled under the sentence that I believe spoke of his longing for gold and his despair over how it eluded him. Too often what we ask of the world goes unanswered, though maybe the odds get better when what we desire of the world is help in repenting. Maybe the longings of the spirit are what the Earth most wants to satisfy. Like to think that could be so, that in time the Earth will send up the scarlet snake with my sins etched on its skin so I can be saved and made whole again. So that the ghost of a woman's perfect face will cease to haunt me.

Some nights I stay in the woods 'til dawn. On clear nights the stars reflect in the calm water of Lake Conasauga with such accuracy it's almost as if there's another world in this one. A better world maybe, I think on such nights. A world where a gator doesn't swallow up a woman and carry her face inside as if it were holy. Where a sister doesn't have to hunker on a stage pressing the severed hips and legs of her brother to her chest. And where a preacher doesn't have to hold in his hands, filthy with the innards of a gator, the bodiless head of a woman he loved in sin. On such nights sin almost falls away from me, and off in the distant, dimly lit dark I imagine a naked woman humming hymns she'd played the hell out of on church organs. I picture Rachel headed in my direction, and as she gets closer the music she hums changes, grows more fervent, almost as though the music she makes with her lips and her tongue and the depths of her throat is a kind of Geiger counter, ticking more and more rapidly as she nears the man who loves her beyond all faith. It's my body she's seeking those nights, and sin has no hold on any man or woman alive in a garden with two identical skies.

One night lying beside Conasauga, listening to the muskellunge now and then leap from the lake's calm surface and fall back to the black water sending ripples through the second sky so that its moon seemed to shiver with some forbidden passion, I thought of Karl and his Greek-speaking second head and wondered which head Rachel would have kissed more if she'd ever made love to Karl. Almost asleep, I pictured Rachel moving atop Karl the way she had moved over me so many times, and then Rachel was kissing the woman's head, and the woman's head whispered something into Rachel's mouth. Asleep and dreaming, what the woman's head on Karl's left shoulder was saying was louder and more insistent and it wasn't Greek at all, ancient or modern. "Rachel," she whispered. "Love me, Rachel," she said and gently bit Rachel's lower lip. And Rachel's body and Karl's body blurred and became one body and it was Rachel's head on Karl's shoulder and the two heads were kissing and Karl's body stopped below the ribs, ending in a jigsaw-puzzle jaggedness of flesh and bone and someone was whimpering off in the darkness of some rotted-out stage and it was me.

Though it was hard to make him understand about the snakes, how I'd come to believe our sins are written in colors and patterns along their bodies, Karl gets how difficult it is to find the one snake with my sins inscribed on its skin. "Think of all the sinning that goes on every night and every day in this fallen world," I've told him. "If all sin is recorded on the skins of scarlet snakes, imagine the odds of coming across the one snake in all the world with your sins written across its legless body." How unlikely salvation is, Karl gets more than most.

"Faith takes each of us on a different journey," he has said to me before.

"And gives each of us different burdens," I added. Both Karl's heads nodded at that. Tonight Gloria's whole body seems to lean towards the Earth, and her smile is a sort of pained thing that doesn't fit her face. Makes me think that if I were to slip her uniform off I'd find bruises on her body, and the bruises would form arcane symbols on her flesh, runes that, if chanted correctly into the night air beside a lake high enough up a mountain that the moon in the sky and the moon in the lake could converse, would be both a prayer for strength and a blessing of tenderness. What I don't want to think I'd find beneath that waitress getup is scales instead of skin, scales whose colors spell out my sins with such clarity they could never be forgiven.

Karl's Greek-speaking woman's head, quiet most of the evening, is all of a sudden ranting. "Someone must've watered down the ouzo," Karl says. As his tormentor spews what sounds like a barrage of curses in ancient Greek, Karl tells me when she's like this he gets to where he believes he could kill her. "Right now," Karl says, "I'd like to take a knife and shove it in her mouth and push it up till it pokes out the top of her skull. I'd like to skewer her," Karl says.

What stops him is what always stops him. It's Karl not being sure what killing her would mean for him. "If all it would mean," he's told me, "is that I'd have to lug a dead woman's head around with me the rest of my life, I'd do it in a minute. Hell, maybe they could even cut her off me once she's dead."

"Would they throw me in jail? Would it be murder," Karl has asked me more than once, "or would they charge me with attempted suicide?" What scares Karl the most is that killing the woman's head that drunkenly rants in Greek most nights into his left ear might be the death of him, too. "Just how much a part of me is she?" Karl has said. She's gone quiet again, and he glances at her without turning his head.

Gloria brings Karl and me another round, and another ouzo, too. Karl's drinking Stroh's and I wonder what kind of hangover he might have in the morning. Folks say mixing different types of alcohol is a prescription for a major hangover, and, since Karl and the ouzo-drinking woman's head share one body, it seems a bad idea for Karl to be downing beers.

"Karl, maybe you should drink whiskey, or vodka." Something more akin to ouzo, is my point.

"I'll be damned if I'm going to let her determine what I drink." The way he says this, it's clear how much she's already taken from him.

Sent away, is the more accurate term for it, Karl has said. "My wife and son, my siblings, almost all my friends," he said, giving me a little smile. Seems that, though he's had this woman's head on his shoulder all his life, it wasn't 'til she started speaking that he started losing everything that mattered to him. Karl's told me she'd been mute most of his life. "Then," Karl said, "when we were baptizing our son, right there in church she started in to speaking what turned out, according to the priest, to be ancient Greek. He said he recognized a word here and there. No one could ignore her after that."

She was quiet the night he told me this, just a little muttering under her ouzo sweet-stinking breath. Occasionally what I'd call a whimper. "Can't even work no more," Karl said. Said his boss told him that since she started talking, having him around made everyone else in the shop nervous. "Disability pay's what I live on now. Only one hooker will even deign to service me," Karl said, "and she makes me pay double." I laughed at that but stopped when I saw the look on Karl's face. Hell, even his tormentor's face gave me a look that told me how offended she was. She muttered something in that arcane Greek of hers and swallowed more ouzo.

"Miracles do happen, Karl." I mean to offer him some semblance of hope that he might one day be free of his foreign tormentor, but Karl takes what I say differently.

"You might call this a miracle," he says with a nod to the left of his head, "but she ain't no miracle. This here's a damnation, is what she is. Some sort of demon," Karl says. "Not even hell wanted her so I got stuck with her. I gave up long ago trying to figure out what sin I'd committed," Karl says, "to justify this. Must have been so awful

I've blocked it out. Repressed the memory of whatever I did to earn this vexation is what I've done," Karl says. "If you come across a snake out in the woods having trouble crawling for the weight of the sins inscribed in its scales," he says, "that's the one with my sins on it."

Karl not only knows of my searching; he knows I used to be a preacher and that I worked with faith healers back in the day. "Too bad that gator ate that boy healer," he said once. "Sounds like maybe he could have freed me of her. Maybe he could have spoken to her in what used to be called tongues and convinced her to go back to hell. Don't know if that Phineas could have helped me none, though," Karl said. "Hell, I'd be afraid what might happen if she were to swallow one of his worms." I didn't bother to remind him it was Phineas who swallowed the worms, not those in need of healing.

Phineas and the boy and all the rest are gone now, so it's not like it mattered that he was confused as to what they did. None of them are doing anything no more. And all I'm doing is trying to find a snake with my sins on it to cut up and fry with some onions and peppers so I can eat it and be set free from the ghost of a woman's face that haunts me every bit as much as Karl's second head haunts him, that head humming something that sounds very old and very sad in Karl's left ear.

Humming don't seem to work for me like it worked for Jebediah. Every afternoon I head out into one of the pine forests. Some I can hike to and others I have to drive to, they're so far off. The Chattahoochee National Park covers some ground. I make sure the sun is almost ready to drop down out of sight before I start in to humming, and the tune I hum is the closest I can recall to what Jebediah used to hum when he was out gathering snakes. Jebediah's music brought snakes out of the Earth every time. Must be I have the tune wrong. My ear for music was never all that exact, though when Rachel played a church organ I'd swear every note echoed in my body for days.

Gloria's humming as she brings Karl and his tormentor and me another round. It's no hymn she's humming.

"What's that tune?" Karl says. His tormentor has started whistling what Gloria's humming.

"What? Was I humming?" Gloria says and smiles, and goes back to her humming with a look on her face like she's listening to herself to try to name that tune. Not one of us can say what tune it is but it's catchy, that's for sure. Not only is Karl's tormentor whistling it in his left ear, Karl and I start in to humming it, too. Pretty soon all four of us are going at it like it's some symphony we're performing, each of us taking a different pitch.

Several of the other Marlow's regulars join in and soon just about everyone drinking in this dive's humming this tune not one of us can name. Jimmy over at the bar is using his unwashed beer glasses as percussion, and Gloria is dancing with the music we're all making, this music she started without knowing she was humming. Seems everyone in this bar was waiting for something to call them out of themselves, to get them to celebrate just being here and having had enough to drink to make a song no one recognizes infectious enough to pull us all into it. Karl is kissing his tormentor and it's something to see.

I want to remember this tune and take it with me into the woods. Maybe this is the music that will bring out my snake and let me kiss the ghost of Rachel's face a last time before letting it go. Gloria's looking at me with her arms out. In the uncertain light of this place, she looks enough like forgiveness to get me up and moving in front of all these humming fools in this place of faith they call Subligna. Could be I've still got some dancing left in me.

George Looney

What Can't Be Said, Ever

How disparate murmuring blends
into the mournful notes sung
by a lady jazz singer long dead.

As if sound itself were in the mood
to chuck it all for love,
or some more obvious despair.

How the best man gestures,
wineglass blooming in his hand,
toward the couple, quoting Eluard

about forgetfulness being necessary
for preserving the individual,
which is not what this ceremony's about.

How pale & exposed shoulders giggle
dim light, the bride & her court
the secular equivalent of a choir of angels

praising what they believe
must be God. How
when Bird slipped his soul into the sax,

God, he'd have said, was
the sound that filtered in
from Avenue B & made his

flophouse an absolution he knew
he didn't deserve. How
despair wasn't what Bird would have

called that sound, nor delight.
How all he'd have said was
it wasn't for the dead. Only

for the living, Bird would've said,
& did, with his sax. How
short our time is. How indescribable.

George Looney

Insomnia as Accomplice

To think the night is
more than darkness
can accommodate

is to set the mind
at odds
with itself. The mind is

no place to hang out, or look to
for comfort.
Insomnia's a bargain

with the body's decay,
one that ignores
the adage time can't

stop itself. From chanting
in a dead tongue
to a missing god

to the worship of things
like blown-glass
Elvises, TV provides

little solace. After three
in the morning, time
is no longer relative.

It breaks into the body,
an intruder
with hose over its face

so its passing resemblance
to something human
comes off as

some sort of joke, maybe,
or an insult. To
take on what passes

for what's left
of the imagination
at such an hour assumes

that to still be awake
is a curse
that can be lifted

if time can be found
& forced
to say the right words. Elvis

can't be found in glass
caricatures. Desire's
not enough. To sleep,

believe the moon isn't
hiding anything
on its other side that can't be

dealt with. That the mall
on the edge of town
goes dark & plays Sinatra

till dawn. That even light
knows when
to give up the ghost,

to pack it in & hunker down
& hum itself
to anything resembling sleep.

George Looney

Distance as Unreliable Narrator

From this moraine miles off, the lake is
the edge of an argument
convincing enough the sky forgives

any intent. History has
never satisfied us. Not
the way stories told in bars do.

Like the one about the blurred photo
taken by a doctor, drunk, fishing for trout.

Something breaks the surface of
what in the photo is
a festering of light. Those

who need to believe believe they see,
clearly, what isn't clear at all.

It's prehistoric, believers say
when it shows up on the late local news.

Nothing's as convincing as local legend.
Distance just makes things unreliable,

& any argument's just an excuse
to accept the relegation of light to one side of

something as pernicious as the moon
with its fever of a face some refuse to see,
though no one claims it's not there.

Like ghosts, & the stories that keep them
from getting out of town.

The lake haunts us all here, the stink of
its terrible & majestic death

giving depth to the most innocuous
anecdote. This watery dying,

though, so huge & so close it seems
a part of us, is too much
for any one of us, alone, to contain.

Sightings are inevitable, slippages
from what's inside us. Out
is what they want, these images

we imbue, because we must, with meaning.
Loss is too easy a way out, though.

It's what we manage to hold in
that ends up doing us in, the ghosts

of every image that escapes us
singing old tunes & toasting
our corpse, that argument no one can be

said to have won. Children laugh
& splash one another in the lake

to cool off. At our best, we give them
floating ducks to hold onto

as they flutter-kick through what,
at our worst, we'd have
broken by the slithery back

of something so ancient we don't have
a name for it anymore. History is

our happening on the world & bringing
to it the sad, irredeemable shape of meaning.

Zeke Jarvis

Crying Class

Lisa always did her homework. The journaling, the rehearsal, the emotional exercises: She never went into crying class unprepared. This week's homework had been to watch YouTube clips of letters to dead pets or grandparents. The goal was to let students see what inauthentic grief looked like so that they would only display authentic grief. Lisa had watched two clips about dead cats (the worse one was titled "Poem for My Dead Cat," and it featured a twelve-year-old who tried comparing her family's old cat to Athena for her wisdom and courage) and one about a grandfather who had fought in the Vietnam War and killed himself. They were all very, very bad. She wrote in her journal that she was embarrassed for all of the people in the clips, and that made her think about how she might have made that one cop feel when he pulled her over for speeding. She hadn't believed that crying actually got women out of speeding tickets, but she'd been progressing thanks to the crying class, so she decided to try it out. The cop had torn up the ticket, but she knew, looking back, that she had been fake in her crying.

Lisa took her usual seat in class, sitting behind Karl, the old man who always brought up the fact that he would probably die alone, and in front of Aubrey, the mess of a college girl who was taking this course as part of some court order. Lisa opened her notebook and took out a pen. The last note that she'd taken read, "Cry, don't pout!" She looked at it for a few seconds and then erased the exclamation point. Their teacher, Mr. Downes, looked at the clock, then went to the front of his desk and sat down. "Crying," he said, "is a practice, not a lack of control." He picked at one of his nails, in the absent-minded way that he usually did when he made one of his more striking points. "Practice is something you do often, it's something you're good at. A lack is something that you do because you can't do any better." Mr. Downes stood. "But that's exactly why you're here: so you can do it better."

Mr. Downes stood while Lisa wrote down "practice = better." When she looked up, Mr. Downes was furrowing his brow and frowning. His face looked so wrinkled, so natural, that Lisa felt ashamed by her own failed attempts to cry in a genuine way. Still, she tried to remember that this practice was measured not just against Mr. Downes, but upon a spectrum, where she was above the bad criers on YouTube but below Mr. Downes. And, unlike the dead-cat kid, Lisa would get better. Mr. Downes let a single, quiet sob out. Behind Lisa, Aubrey blew a gum bubble until it popped. The air slowly wafted out around Lisa's neck. Mr. Downes put his hand over his eyes and let two more sobs out. After a few seconds of silence, he looked up again. "Anyone," he said, "why do we put our hands over our faces when we cry?"

Lisa knew the answer, but she was also trying hard to pace herself so that her attempts to demonstrate her knowledge and discipline didn't make her the butt of more jokes from her classmates. Although this class only met one night a week in the evening, she still felt awkward leaving class, seeing other students joke around while they avoided her or looked at her with a strange type of pity. After a few seconds of quiet from the class, Mr. Downes said, "Oh, guys, you're going to make me cry."

It was a joke that he'd used before, but it still got a few chuckles. Lisa raised her hand. She saw Mr. Downes do a sweep of the class with his eyes, seeing if anyone else would participate. His eyes eventually settled back on Lisa, and he nodded at her. "Go ahead."

Lisa didn't even have to look at her notes. "Most people are afraid of their tears. They don't want to appear weak, so they cover their eyes when they cry."

Mr. Downes gave a quick smile that he then let drop. "Very good, Lisa. And, if people generally hide their tears, then what does it mean when we let them show?"

There was another silence. Lisa knew the answer. It was it shows that we're not afraid, and that will put us in the position of power. But she hated to always be the one to answer, especially after the longer pauses from the rest of the class. Eventually, Aubrey said, "To creep people out."

Mr. Downes laughed. "That's one way of putting it," he said. "It's more about power. You need to remember that. You don't just creep people out; you control the situation, because you play emotional jiujitsu."

Aubrey mumbled something that even Lisa couldn't catch. Lisa couldn't tell if Mr. Downes didn't hear it or if he didn't care. After every class, she wanted to go up to him and ask him why he didn't yell at Aubrey more. Or the class when they didn't participate and then laughed at Lisa for participating. But he was so in control most of the time that it seemed like he must have had his reasons. Karl turned around to look at Lisa, then looked back towards the front right away. His eyes looked red. He put his head in his hands and looked down at his desk. There had been one good student towards the beginning of the course. A young man with long hair that hung over his eyes. He'd dropped partway through. Or, he'd quit coming, anyway. Looking at Karl, Lisa realized that the young man might've killed himself.

Mr. Downes began to pace in front of the class, his arms folded. Mr. Downes had a strange trait. He seemed handsome even though his face didn't look particularly attractive. It wasn't bad, it just wasn't one that you'd say was handsome if you were looking at a picture of it. "The delicate balance," Mr. Downes began, "between communication and manipulation. That is what we must be mindful of." He stopped at the light switch and ran his finger around the plate. "Andrea," he said, "how do we preserve our emotional truth while being effective criers?"

Andrea was a middle-aged woman who would knit during class, who would never volunteer to participate, but who seemed to grasp the core essentials of the class. She also only ever wore jeans and a sweatshirt. She looked up from her knitting. It looked like a sweater, but Lisa couldn't tell how big it would be when it was done. It had red and blue stripes, like Ernie's from *Sesame Street*. "We find the tragedy in any event."

Mr. Downes smiled. He looked a little sad behind his smile, and Lisa wondered if he was getting ready to cry. Maybe he was always getting ready to cry, just in case. "Well put," he said. "Can you think of an example from your clips from this week where you could've outcried the person crying?" Mr. Downes scanned the room. "Anyone, let's let anyone answer this."

This time, Lisa raised her hand without hesitation. Mr. Downes nodded to her right away.

"Lisa."

"One thing that I learned from this week's homework was the importance of timing. I saw one clip where the subject read a poem without weeping or even getting choked up, and then, as soon as he'd finished, he burst into tears. It seemed very disingenuous."

Mr. Downes raised his eyebrows, which pleased Lisa. Mr. Downes' reactions always seemed more genuine when they included his eyebrows. "That's a very good point, Lisa," Mr. Downes said. "How many times have any of us been put off when a crier begins too early or lasts too long in his or her weeping? Any other examples?"

A student two rows over, a slightly older guy who talked a lot about his ex-wife, raised his hand. Mr. Downes pointed at him. "Go ahead."

The man leaned back in his desk and let one are dangle down behind the chair. "As I was searching for clips this week, I came across one that was about going through divorce."

Lisa watched Mr. Downes carefully. It would be easy to be patronizing with this one, but Mr. Downes had a way of correcting without putting you down. After the student had said "divorce," Mr. Downes had put his right index finger to his lips, which he tapped slowly.

The student continued. "Some of it actually seemed like good advice, like trying new things so that you didn't see all these reminders of your ex. But the thing is that this person kept kind of sniveling the whole time, never actually crying. It was really embarrassing."

Mr. Downes nodded. There was a pause; it seemed like Mr. Downes was waiting for more. The student just shook his head. "Pathetic," he said. Mr. Downes pursed his lips. Lisa shifted in her seat and looked around. Karl had started to sketch something in his notebook, though Lisa wasn't sure what it was. "I mean," the divorced guy continued, "I get it, but, it's like, what are you supposed to do, just sit and snivel the rest of your life?"

Mr. Downes went to the board and picked up a piece of chalk. "Exactly," he said. "Crying is about knowing what to give and what to withhold. When you give, you can make people feel more comfortable." Mr. Downes began to draw a circle on the board. "Now,

I know that this might seem like I'm contradicting myself. After all, just a minute ago, I was talking about jiujitsu."

Lisa looked over at the divorced guy. She couldn't tell if he was listening or if he was trying not to cry. Lisa couldn't believe how many times the students in this course didn't let the genuine tears come. She knew that she should be taking notes on what Mr. Downes was saying, but she also wanted to go the guy, to put a hand on his shoulder and tell him that it would be OK.

"And yet," Mr. Downes continued, "aren't there times when you want to make someone comfortable and times that you want to intimidate or disturb them? Think about your boss, lecturing you on why you didn't get a raise." Mr. Downes drew two ovals near the top of the circle. "Or think about your parent telling you that you've disappointed them yet again." He then drew a series of drips coming from the left oval in the circle. "On the other hand, think about the spouse who hears that you've lost a family member. Think about their anticipation as you don't yet tear up, as you're still processing that information. Help them to feel that they're helping you."

Lisa was watching the divorced guy close his eyes and sit when Aubrey blew another bubble. This time, Lisa turned around and looked at her. Aubrey stared back, then shook her head, quickly and in a tight arc. Lisa turned back to Mr. Downes. He was drawing what looked to be long hair hanging down from the circle. "But your crying isn't just about them. It isn't about you, either; it's about successfully navigating the situation. That's what you're here for."

Mr. Downes curved one of the lines that had looked like hair. Lisa was unsure of what it was. It could have been the string for a helium balloon. Suddenly, he stopped mid-curl and turned back to the class. "Mark," he said, pointing at the divorced guy.

The divorced guy opened his eyes. He looked startled. "Yeah?"

Mr. Downes said, "Your ex-wife is not coming back."

The divorced guy, whose name was apparently Mark, looked around. The other students weren't entirely sure what to do. Mark sat up straighter. "What?"

Mr. Downes walked over to the desk and stared down at Mark. "She's not coming back," he said.

The man gave a bit of a laugh, then looked around again. Lisa looked around, too. Karl was frowning hard and Aubrey was covering a smile with one of her hands. The rest of the class was also looking around and shifting in their seats.

"Never," said Mr. Downes. "She's probably fucking some other guy by now, and you need to get over it."

Mark glared at Mr. Downes, then said, "Fuck you," very quietly.

Mr. Downes smiled. "Come on," he said, "just tell me that you can move past your ex fucking some other guy."

Mark shook his head and looked at the board. Maybe he was trying to figure out if there was some clue in the drawing. "Maybe even blowing him," said Mr. Downes. His voice pitched up as if he was trying to be helpful. Mark shook his head again and put his hands over his face. His crying was silent, but clear. Mr. Downes crouched by Mark's desk. "Mark," he said, "show us your tears. It's OK."

Mark shook his head again, but then he took a deep breath, and he stood, lowering his hands. Mark cried for a good five minutes, rotating in a circle as he did. On his third turn, Lisa began taking notes. "Pace your breathing," "posture," and "Tears aren't always what counts." She stopped taking notes every so often just to watch. She realized that it had been a while since she'd cried without being self-conscious. Not just since class began. She wanted Mark to be totally in the moment now. She tried to look at the tears themselves so that, if Mark did shift into performance, she wouldn't be able to tell. But the tears were hard to see. They were like slug trails, only visible from certain angles, and then it was more of a shine than seeing the thing itself. Lisa wanted to ask Mr. Downes about it, but she wasn't sure how to frame her question. She chewed the eraser on her pencil.

After Mark finished, he wiped his eyes and sat. Mr. Downes gave him a high five and the class laughed, including Mark and Mr. Downes. The rest of the class was good, but it was hard for Lisa to focus. She felt tingly. Mark didn't seem like a standout student. She wondered if that's why Mr. Downes picked him. Like the rest of the class, he didn't participate much, but nobody did. Mr. Downes lectured without much by way of exercises. That almost never happened.

At the end of class, Mr. Downes said, "For next time, I want you to think about some of your earliest memories of crying. Think about what triggered it and how you can get back to that." The class all wrote that down, and that didn't always happen, either. After class, Mark talked to Mr. Downes for a bit. They hugged before he left. Lisa packed her things and watched. She and Aubrey were the last two in the room. Lisa left the room but hovered by the door. She heard Aubrey talking. "I've never seen anything like that."

"Class can be intense," Mr. Downes said.

"You know," said Aubrey, "I was thinking maybe I could get a little extra work in. I know I've been behind."

"You'll catch up."

Lisa looked at the tiles on the floor in the hallway. They were beige with little swirls.

"I thought I could give you my number—."

"Aubrey, I have your number on my class roster."

Lisa smiled and started to walk down the hall, as slowly and as quietly as she could. She heard Aubrey say something else, but she couldn't quite hear what. Lisa was almost to the door when Aubrey came out of the room. She was writing in her tear journal as she walked. Lisa ducked out the door as quickly as she could, but she knew that Aubrey must have seen, which was perfect anyway.

Darren C. Demaree

"What the Fuck Are You Telling Me?"

—Ray Mancini, the night after the fight

Roasting guilt, heaped
like coals no one wanted
to carry, they told Mancini
the kid was in pretty bad
shape, they told him the kid
was dying, they told him
his brain was already dead,
they told him about the 14th
round being seconds too
long for the kid. Ray was
alive, pulped, some of him
left in pieces still on the ring
next to the already-fading
opponent he feared more
than any other, because he
knew the kid was going to
come without any end.
"What the fuck are you telling
me?" Ray, I'm telling you
that was no bull you put down,
but the kid was going to keep
at you until the stretcher
had a body to carry. The kid
was a fucking man, intent
on doubling your intent
to win, in the dark if necessary
& even though I keep looking,
I can find no blame for you.

Christopher Locke

Late Return

Harmless really, the dog uncoiled
     its fragile barks, bones arthritic
as shopping carts rivered in icy rust.
I was in my car, behind a door behind
the dog owner, her face all sunflower
     and grandmotherly charm. But her dog
was barking at my daughter Sophie
     running out to see me before I drove off.
So I had to motion, had to say
     Please, your dog, my daughter ….
And then the part I didn't want
     to admit: She was bitten before.
This new dog made Sophie freeze
     tight as December maple, juiceless
and heavy, and the owner smiled, telling
     her, "It's OK, I have seven grandkids
of my own," and took the dog away.
     But in the car, unable to leave, shaking,
repeating to Sophie *I'm sorry*, I remembered
     the first time all those years ago: the way
the dog disheveled her, splashed her
     into the grass, tried to unSophie her,
teeth locking in place like gears oiled
     to their own need, and me too late
to stop it; that stone I still carry.

Christopher Locke

But there are no happy endings, because if
things are happy, they have not ended.
　　　　　　　　　　　　　　—*Donald Hall*

Happy

Portland museum, slight chips of snow
ghosting the windows like ash off
cigarettes; a Maine sky imprisoned
with all the tough angels. We sit in
the building's belly, a café seizured

in beautiful pastries, croissants glazed
like tearful cheeks; popcorn labeled
as non-GMO and therefore, somehow,
healthy. We eat in silence, and I'm thinking
about the Pissarro on the third floor, and

that strange video tower being the only
piece that read "Please Touch," itchy
guards swimming the rooms with hope
you'd drag a finger down a Wyeth
so as to give them a reason. The girls

pipe up, start comparing the best key
lime pies they've ever had, the best
scones: "Nothing spongy," Grace says.
Sophie nods in agreement, mouth full.
My wife offers, "What if we opened

a restaurant and called the kid's meal
a 'Happier Meal,'" and it's my first
genuine laugh of the day. "That's

great," I say. "What would we serve?"
My wife shrugs, noncommittal.

And the nicest exchange we've
shared in days ends as quickly as
as it started, so we turn back
to our daughters, their talk silly,
natural, and yes, almost happy.

Roy Bentley

Vengeance

It's a long time now since Junior Tucker
shot my uncle Ed and then choked to death
on a toothpick from the A&P grocery store.
Ironically, a man whose initials were A and P
had come to my grieving grandmother to ask
if she wanted Junior Tucker dead. Murdered.
She told me that A.P. asked her to say the word
and he'd shoot Junior. Stab him, if she needed
to know that he'd died slowly. My grandmother
said she told A.P. she prayed, for days, and been
shown a verse: *Vengeance is mine, sayeth the Lord,
and I will repay.* I'm paraphrasing, it's been years.
Maybe you've lost someone like that, someone
unrecognized for their gifts. For the great gift of
their presence. To make her grandchildren aware
of the world in which they lived, its seamless dark
and an occasional ray of light in a room, she read
from a book devoted to the notion of vengeance,
the King James Version of the Bible. She read it
to a boy whose name she sang to a failed orchard
when it was dinnertime. When she called, I'd hear
the cries from a branch inaccessible to most adults,
given their weight and inability to climb. If she was
mistaken, letting a murderer live a year or two longer,
praying to be shown how to keep the windows of
the heart open to the likelihood of a caring God
and some form of forgiveness, who am I to say?
It took a while, and a toothpick, but he did die.

The Missouri State University Literary Competitions

Moon City Review is a product of Moon City Press, which is housed in the English Department at Missouri State University. Each year, we'd like to recognize work in our writing programs by publishing a piece of fiction and a poem by members of our student body.

This year, the fiction competition was judged by Ozarks native Daniel Woodrell, author of books such as *Winter's Bone*, *The Maid's Version*, and *Tomato Red*. Woodrell chose Samuel Nichols' story "Hermanos de Sangre" as this year's winnner. Our other finalists in fiction are as follows:

Elizabeth Alphonse
Kelly Baker
Christopher Ray Dean
Kevin Gleich
Ryan Hubble
Anita Lumley
Emily McCormick
Bailey Gaylin Moore
Andy Myers

Kerry James Evans, a Missouri State alum and author of the recently released collection *Bangalore*, served as the judge for poetry, choosing Christopher Crabtree's entry "Learning Chess." The following authors were also finalists in the poetry category:

Elizabeth Alphonse
Terry Belew
Anthony Isaac Bradley
Allys Page
Jacob Monash
Taylor Supplee

We are proud to present the winners' work to you in the forthcoming pages, as we are proud of the work all our students do here at Missouri State.

Samuel Nichols

Hermanos de Sangre

The first time Viejo let me ride with him, I sat up front with the gun. He put it on the passenger-side floor, told me if I saw any fools from Lincoln—"They the ones wearing green, cuz, all over"—to hand it to him, and he'd take care of business. I nodded and looked at the gun at my feet like it was a trophy just within my reach. I was fifteen.

We cruised down 2nd to Balboa, down to Adams and Farillo. He stopped at a gas station—it's a two-hour trip to Mission Porción, where we were to meet up with a priest named Julio Fuentes, who Viejo said was his marijuana supplier. "You tried maría, right?" he asked when we left his apartment. I told him I had, but I'd never smoked before.

Viejo left his pickup running while the gas pumped, and he went inside for beer—"My fuente de vida," he said, laughing. He had me give him the gun before he went inside. It felt smooth and cool, heavy. Viejo tucked it into the back of his pants, under his shirt and coat, before he got out of the truck. He walked into the store, looking left and right like he was crossing the street.

Viejo was taking a while, and the gas pump had already clicked, so I got out, put the pump back, and leaned on the truck. The warm metal side of the bed felt good against my stomach and chest, made it seem like summer. I glared at cars across the street as they passed.

I imagined holding Viejo's gun, pointing it at minivans from Connecticut, Vermont, Oregon. I imagined pulling the trigger, their brakes slamming, cars crunching into each other, the driver at the front frantic. I especially imagined shooting at luxury cars—BMWs, Austin Martins, Bentleys.

I imagined my father's car driving by. Viejo said the last time he saw him he was driving an old Lumina, white paint flaking off like giant fish scales. I imagined him pulling the car into the gas station, stopping right in front of me, asking, "You bang, cuz?"—not even recognizing his own son after frying his brains snorting meth. I imagined pointing the gun at his head, seeing his scabbed tweaker face in the V of the sight, pulling the trigger as I say, "Yes, Papi. I bang."

Viejo came out of the store carrying a six-pack of Dos Equis.

"Esto es todo?" I asked. He usually kept more alcohol than food in his fridge.

"That's the point, little homey," he said as he put the beer behind his seat. "You see the six-pack of cheapy beer. I distracted you, huh? That's what you gotta do sometimes. You'll learn, cuz."

I didn't understand, but after we left the gas station he started pulling thick, expensive-looking bottles out of his coat, ones with real aluminum labels, letters sticking out like Braille. "Dos for Julio. Uno for myself. And maybe I let you keep one. We'll see how you do today, cuz. Ha ha!"

I grinned, looked out the window.

"Oh, almost forgot," he said.

"What?"

"Mi pistola." He kept his eyes on the road, nose almost touching the steering wheel as he pulled the gun out. "Here, take it," he said. I took it and leaned down to put it back at my feet. "Nah," he said. "*Take* it. Manténgalo. In your lap, cuz."

The gun seemed heavier than before. I held it sideways from the barrel, like a boomerang, with my other hand flat under the handle. "Qué haces?" Viejo asked. "Who told you to do it like that? Hold it right."

I put my right hand around the handle, gripped it tight like the end of a baseball bat. It was more comfortable than I expected. My fingers fit into the dips in the handle; the thickness of it was perfect for my palm.

"Ha ha!" he said. "That's mi hermano pequeño." He gripped his hands tighter on the steering wheel. "You like that, cuz? Make you want one?"

"Kind of," I said.

"You Sánchez, all right. Gonna be, cuz."

I didn't really know if I liked it or not, or even if I really wanted to be Sánchez. Viejo had only ever hinted at it, but I knew he'd had to kill people before, for small things, just disrespecting. Holding the gun excited me, but it scared me, too, to like the idea of becoming Sánchez.

I wanted to put the gun down, but I knew it was a big deal for Viejo to let me hold it. I knew he saw it as being a gift, trusting me with the gun, and since he saw me as a future member of Sánchez—maybe a future leader—I was expected to accept and treasure any gift he gave me.

The drive with Viejo was boring, all highway, where nothing happens—like air travel to a gangster. You can pass through enemy turf untouched, and they through yours. It's neutral ground, boring ground. Viejo and I drove up through Palla, Santa Ysabel, Descanso. Miles of curvy roads, Viejo just cruising.

The mission wasn't what I expected. There were no grand villas and lush gardens, only dusty concrete walkways, cracked all over. The bell tower was short, twenty-five feet or so, with a thin white cross on top. The rest of the mission was on a single, long level. The outside was made of crumbling gray stone, with twisted wrought iron grates covering the windows. There were a few tiles missing from the clay roof, and half the chimney bricks had fallen off or out, making it look like a giant Jenga tower. When we got out of the car, the air was acrid, sulfurous; I could smell meth cooking. I thought it was maybe just me, but Viejo took a deep breath and scratched at the front of his neck. He looked like he was home.

One night, when I was little—Viejo was just out of high school and out of the house—I went to the kitchen to get a drink and saw Papi on the couch, watching soccer on TV. He was leaning forward, rubbing his hands on his knees, the rhythmic sound of palms on denim like the swishing of our washing machine. I sat down next to him, leaned against the arm of the couch. He didn't seem to notice, kept rubbing his knees. I studied his face. His nose was short, almost flat; his cheekbones extended far past his sunken eyes. He had three dots tattooed below his right eye, barely visible among the scabs on his cheeks. When I asked him what the scabs were from, he said they were sores from not sleeping. He rubbed his face with open hands and said he needed to sleep soon. I offered to stay up with him until he got tired, offered to talk—"That always helps me, Papi," I said. He didn't want to talk, but he said I could stay on the couch if I wanted. The next morning I woke in my own bed; my water glass was washed and put away. I prayed for my father to rest.

Viejo started walking fast toward the building; I followed. He had given me a little switchblade before we got out of the truck. "You never know, cuz," he said. "Even homies turn sometimes. Always gotta look out." He put a hand on my shoulder, squeezed it. "You got my back, right ese?" I smiled, told him nobody'd get past me. He laughed and slapped me on the back, then told me to give him his gun. I'd forgotten I was holding it. The whole drive I'd gripped it, set it on my lap aimed towards my door. My hand had cramped; it ached as I handed over the gun and took Viejo's switchblade, which seemed more like a toy. I felt like I couldn't squeeze it tight enough, that it would drop from my hand at any moment, that it wasn't really protection, but the illusion of it. But illusion or not, it was another gift, so I took it and thanked him.

Sánchez territory stretched from the train tracks on the East side, to Buena Vista on the north side, 9th on the west side, and Grand on the south side. Twelve square miles, give or take. Our father had built most of it, and Viejo took over once Papi started caring more about lines of meth than territory lines. I was in my bedroom when Viejo walked in the front door of our apartment. He told Papi that Lincoln had come with almost thirty guns on the south side.

Papi had told me to stay in my room for a while, to stay there until he called me out, but I was excited to see Viejo. I hurried to the hallway, peaking around the corner into the living room. Viejo repeated himself, but Papi didn't do anything, just waved him off, then leaned over and put his nose to the coffee table and snorted. Viejo saw me in the hallway, looked at me as if to tell me to go back to my room. I didn't listen.

Viejo repeated himself to Papi, but he ignored him again. "OK, ese," Viejo said. "That's how it's gonna be." He walked up to our father and slammed his face through the glass tabletop, all the way to the ground. He held him there for a few seconds, blood seeping from his cuts, broken glass making new ones. I thought Viejo was going to kill him right there.

"Tú no eres mi padre," Viejo said. "You are Sánchez no more." He told Papi to leave and promised to kill him if he ever came back.

When "Father" Julio Fuentes came out to meet us, he was dressed in khaki pants and a gray flannel button-up. His right hand rested on the side of an AK-47, hanging by his shoulder; he was not a real priest.

Julio looked Viejo up and down, said something in Spanish about him getting thinner. It was the only time I'd ever seen Viejo allow someone to look at him like that. Usually people didn't look straight at him. Some looked at the ground, but most looked around like men on enemy grounds, searching for cops.

Julio didn't seem to fear Viejo. He was relaxed, confident. Too much so. I wanted to say something, tell him to show some respect, but I didn't want to screw up my first time riding with Viejo. Julio didn't say anything to me, and Viejo didn't introduce me, so I figured I should stay cool.

The two started walking toward the building; I followed. We passed under a large archway with dried vines covering stucco. Lavender seemed to be the only thing growing in the flower beds, but it was unkempt, overtaking straining remnants of tulips, lilacs, hollyhocks. Julio opened up the tall front door of the mission and let Viejo walk inside. I tried to follow, but Julio stuck his arm out, stopping me with the back of his hand.

"Lo siento, vato. No niños."

"Viejo!" I called, louder than I'd meant to. "I can come?"

He turned back, looked at me, then at Julio. In the poorly lit entryway of the mission his face looked shorter, his scars larger. I hadn't noticed before, but he was getting thinner. His cheeks looked sunk in, making his cheekbones look like little mountains.

"Ven aca," he said to Julio.

Julio pushed me back a little farther with his hand and went to Viejo. They spoke quietly for a moment. I could see Julio nodding, his mouth closed. He said something to Viejo, all barely more than a whisper.

Viejo called me to him and told me in Spanish that I had to stay in front of Julio at all times while we were in the mission, or Julio would shoot me. I tried not to look scared, but my breath escaped me. I looked up at Julio to see if he was serious. His face was stern; he looked neither pleased nor discomforted by the idea of shooting a fifteen-year-old boy.

The mission was much larger than it looked on the outside, and more impressive. The sanctuary had brown brick flooring, and dark walnut pews with red velvet padding. At the front, two white pillars rose the height of the sanctuary, fifteen feet or so. Between them was a light bronze statue of Jesus Christ, wearing His crown of thorns. Waving robes covered most of His body, with thick-strapped thongs on His feet, teardrop scars on His hands—all brazen, all unmoving, solid. His face was smooth, refined, with a look of genuine compassion, maybe even warning. As we approached the front of the sanctuary, and the statue, I felt Jesus' eyes on me. I wondered if He ever gave my father the rest I prayed for. I found no answer in His face, His eyes blank, His cheeks soft; He had no scabs.

Viejo turned to the right and walked along the front pew and came to a side door labeled "Confesarse."

Everything was darker in the confession room, everything wooden. Three booths with deep purple curtains and padded kneeling ledges lined one wall. The other three walls were blank—no candles, no stand and Bible, no windows. Sitting in the middle of the room, facing the center confession booth, was a chair. A man sat in it, his head drooped down to his chest, his breathing short, haggard.

Viejo walked up to the chair and kicked the back of it with almost enough force to knock both the chair and the man to the floor. It made me jump. I'd never seen Viejo's violence firsthand. He took the gun out and hit the man in the side of the head with the barrel, cutting his ear badly.

"You know who this is, cuz?" Viejo asked me. "Look at his face, homey. Look at it! Tell me who it is!"

Even though I could tell Viejo was raising his voice to scare the man, not me, it made my jaw quiver. He looked ready to kill.

He motioned with his gun for me to go around to the front of the man, to look at his face. Viejo grabbed the man's short black hair and yanked it back, stretching out his thin neck.

The man's cheeks were sucked in like he was puckering, but his mouth was open, exposing teeth like crushed rocks, piss-colored. His shirt was half-torn, and the smell coming from him was noxious. Webs of tiny blood vessels covered the whites of his eyes; the irises were a foggy brown, like a blind man's.

I studied him for a moment, tried to place where I'd seen the face, but couldn't. I wasn't even sure I had ever seen him before. "Who is it?" I asked Viejo.

"Who is it?" Julio asked, raising his voice. "Who is it? Don't play stupid, cuz. Don't play with me, homey. Not here."

Julio stood near the door, hand resting comfortably near the trigger of his gun. His face was too dark to see, but I could see the glint of his eyes, watching Viejo. He still hadn't looked at me since we had gotten there.

"I don't know, Viejo," I said. "It could be anybody. A bum? I don't know. Who is it?"

Viejo's face twisted, nostrils flared, top lip pulled back into a snarl. "What you sayin', homey?"

"I don't know who it is, OK? What do you want, Viejo?"

"It doesn't matter what I want, cuz. It matters what is."

"Well, what is?"

"You still don't know? Come on, cuz. This your Papi. He been screwin' up, being estúpido!"

Viejo smacked the man's ear with his gun again, splattering blood all over his own face, making it speckled. I brought my hand to my mouth to hold back a gag. The man groaned.

"He been throwin' Sánchez all over El Cajon," Viejo said. "Pretending like he still one of us. You know what that means, cuz. You were there. I told him to leave Sánchez. Told him he was out, homey. Sánchez no more. No more!"

I looked back at the man who was supposedly my father and saw what I hadn't noticed before—the three dots below his right eye. They had faded into a light gray, hidden among a galaxy of scabs, but they were still there. I'd seen men like this sleeping beside shopping carts in the woods near train tracks, seen them stand on street corners, Walmart parking lots. But they were men nobody knew, men you might pray for or give a bottle of water, but not men who had families and reputation, men who had sons.

This, though. This was my father, and his body tied to a chair two hours away from Sánchez turf could only mean one thing: He was brought here to die.

"What are you doing, Viejo?" I asked, breaking down.

"Qué pasa, homey? What's the matter? You forget the deal? You forget who you are, little Sánchez? You ain't just a little hermano, homey, mi hermano de sangre. You Sánchez."

"What are you talking about, Viejo? I'm not Sánchez yet. You said it yourself—you said I'd be Sánchez."

"Ha! Cuz, that's right now. You gonna be Sánchez right now."

I didn't know what Viejo was saying, but he made it clear, tossing his gun to me. I caught it clumsily, shaking already.

"This is comienzo," he said. "Initiation, cuz. This is the real deal. Right now. Right now!"

Viejo was fierce, dripping with desire to see his own father killed. I was disgusted, felt like I could puke. I knew he didn't like Papi—neither did I—but I didn't really want him dead. Daydreams and reality were two very different things. At least to me, they were.

Julio still stood in the corner, finger on the trigger of his rifle, pointed at me. Viejo told him to put it down. "He ain't pointing anywhere at you, homey. Put it down. He's got this." Julio lowered the rifle, looking annoyed.

My hands trembled, holding the gun. Viejo stood Papi up from the chair, held him like a hostage. I didn't know why he held him so close, their faces next to each other, blending in the dark. I didn't know why he wanted me to kill Papi, why he couldn't do it himself. And looking at them, my eyes hazy with tears, I couldn't see two men; they'd blurred into one—blood-stained, scab-covered, hellish. I gripped the gun, unsure of who to aim at, unsure if it made any difference. The only thing I was sure of was that there was no turning back, no apologies, no way to say that I didn't want to be Sánchez anymore.

Viejo wasn't simply asking me to kill; he was giving me a kill, handing me a life like a sentiment, a wide-open door into the family I'd thought I wanted my whole life. I wanted to tell Viejo no, to refuse his gift, but I'd be the one dead if I did, and he would still kill Papi anyway.

Viejo took a step back, his face coming into view, shaded. He pushed Papi toward the chair, said if I didn't shoot him he would. He kicked the back of one of Papi's knees and shoved the back of his head; he collapsed face down on the floor.

I watched with the gun still pointed at Papi's head, waiting at any moment for Viejo to jump in and tell me he was tired of waiting and would have to do it himself. But that moment wasn't going to come, and in the end I did shoot—because I had no choice, because Papi had deserved it, because like it or not, Viejo was right; I was Sánchez—was born Sánchez, was raised Sánchez, would die Sánchez.

Christopher Crabtree

Learning Chess

for my grandfather

His hand picks up the black knight to move
in Ls—a cavalry's flanking maneuver
around the checkered board. "This do this,"
he says in his best English. A green tattoo
between thumb and index, smeared by time,
marks him for a guerrilla revolutionary.
He walks to the restroom again—
frequent breaks, bullet hole scars
like extra belly buttons, a bayonet stab
for defeating Japan in the Philippine jungles.
As the black and white armies engage,
he shows me the importance of the middle,
how to open attacking lanes, set up defense.
His fingertip touches the queen, then pawn,
"This eat this." I laugh, say, "Not eat,
take." He laughs. "Oh, sorry. Take—take."
And as I learn my moves, he points out
the hidden traps, teaching me to pick battles.

Geoff Watkinson

Fathers, Guns, and LSD

Before I did LSD for the first time, Foachman, one of my five housemates, made the drug sound like a religious experience. "Dude," he said, "it's so pure. You'll never be the same." Foachman called everything "pure"—it was his favorite word—so I laughed and told him that was ridiculous.

It was an uncharacteristically warm Saturday for late September in New York's mid-Hudson Valley. I was a senior in college and since I didn't believe in God, I needed to find spirituality elsewhere. LSD sounded like just the place.

Foachman was, as far as I knew, the most prominent drug dealer in the area. Throughout college, he'd been picking up pounds of marijuana from Boston or New York City and distributing the goods locally. He ran the business out of our house, the Green Briar, which stole its name from the apartment complex that shared part of our gravel driveway and bordered the back yard. When Foachman wanted to make a lot of money—to go on a "baller vacation," for example— he'd up the ante and pick up a couple of pounds of cocaine.

Foachman had acquired a special supply of acid for all of us to try on that September day. It came from a friend of his in the small New Hampshire town where he'd grown up. Wearing a backwards DC Skate hat, he placed ten acid-saturated sugar cubes in a pitcher, which he mixed with Jack Daniels and Coca-Cola. We rationed the mix between the six of us, drinking it slowly, sitting in beach chairs on our crumbling brick porch, looking out on the three acres that separated us from the local highway.

When the acid started to hit, we tossed a Frisbee between the oaks that rose up towards the sky like stoic warriors. When the Frisbee came towards me, I saw the vibrations of its tail linger behind like a boat's wake. A sparrow sang, sounding like the "Bridal Chorus" I'd heard at the couple of weddings I'd been to. I could taste the leaves that fell from the trees, as if I was sucking on cardboard. My hands didn't seem to belong to my body and it felt incredible to scoop the flying saucer coming towards me out of the air. It was as if I was experiencing the world for the first time.

A few hours later, as the sun began to set, Luke, who lived in the bedroom across the hall from me, came into my room and we listened to Neil Young's *Live at Massey Hall 1971* on vinyl. Young's voice made the walls tremble. Posters of the Doors and the Beatles came to life. Like me, Luke was a scrawny twenty-one year old. Typically, he was sarcastic or passionate. Those who didn't know him had a hard time telling which. He was from Carolina, but prided himself on what he called his non-regional dialect.

As we sat there in the dark, smoking a joint, Luke told me a story. A couple of summers earlier, Luke's father—a renowned doctor who was also an addict—had held a gun to his head for half an hour. They were at his family's lake house, drinking beers on the deck overlooking the lake, the only two home. The doctor went inside to relieve himself. When he came back, the moon shined down on the murky lake and the silver .32-caliber pistol that he pointed at Luke.

"I didn't know it until he came back with the gun," Luke said. "He was off his rocker on coke. Every time he'd been going inside to take a leak, he'd also been blowing a couple of lines. He was so damn good at masking it that one minute he'd seem fine and then—bam—all of a sudden he wouldn't be making any sense and he'd get aggressive."

We lit cigarettes. The smoke curled up to the ceiling, around the lights, and then out the window. It reminded me of the fake gunpowder from the *Pirates of the Caribbean* ride in Disney World I'd been on when I was small.

Luke rolled up his sleeves, exposing a couple of burns on his arms from where his father had put out cigarettes when Luke was growing up, and rubbed his eyes. I didn't want to interrupt him. Even if I had, I wouldn't have known what to say.

"So he sat next to me, with the gun a couple of feet from my head, and started telling me how it was my fault that his marriage was falling apart. The girls' fault—you know, my sisters. I was thankful they weren't home. He made me say it. That it was my fault. Finally, after he rambled on about his childhood and the nature of love and psychology and some other bullshit, he started crying and put down the gun. You know what the sickest part was?" I shook my head. "He hugged me at the end. The motherfucker hugged me."

I couldn't relate to that. My father and I, like many of my friends and their fathers, had a strained relationship, but he was good to me and good to my family. I didn't see him much growing up—he worked long hours as an attorney in northern New Jersey.

I remember my little league baseball games, when I was so nervous to swing the bat that I either struck out or took a walk. I was so scared I'd swing and miss and everyone would laugh. Mom was almost always in the stands, but I can't remember Dad ever being there. I'm sure he was there, sometimes, but when I see myself on the field—the sweat underneath my cap, the brown sandy dirt on my left knee, and me looking to the stands from second base after sliding in safely—I don't see him. When he was there—where he stood or sat— is as mysterious to me as one of the first games when I did swing the bat when I was twelve, the ball ringing off the top rail in center field, almost going out of the park.

Dad wasn't there for that.

I knew that fathers were flawed. I knew that I was flawed. But flaws were something different from a father sticking a gun in his son's face. I couldn't imagine how Luke felt as he sat in my recliner, on LSD, having to bear that burden. In the quiet dark, we passed the joint back and forth, the walls trembling in unison with Young's voice.

Foachman was right. Nothing was the same.

Brian Simoneau

Each Pleasure

I used to work
with a guy

who'd stick
his pinky in the vise

and crank it
till sweat popped

from the pores
on his forehead.

When I asked him why
of course he said it felt

so goddamn good
when he stopped.

He'd smile despite
the spite, spit on the floor,

mutter fuck me
when he meant fuck you—

screw it all, it's
all of it shit—

but still
he'd buy a round—

bury me upside down
and kiss my ass,

    stick with it long enough
enough's enough,

    it's rough but not so bad,
it's not so bad

    besides, two weeks
at the beach, each

    bite of a wave, the breath
when a breaker breaks

    against your belly, balls
like pebbles

    shot through your gut,
got to admit

    it's pretty good
and the rest of it

    who gives a shit,
just give me this.

    A hand cramped
around a handle

    (hammer, blowtorch, broom)
beckons

    the late-night longneck
bottle, becomes

    a way to grip
the world, grasp

    what you have
wherever you head

    when the workday
ends, bends itself

    around each pleasure
that passes your way.

Angie Macri

Spoon Flat, Ash Flat, Big Flat

span empty land. The controlled burn
turns the bluebird like stained glass
above the queen and her lace, strung
along every highway with her blood,

a pinprick in the center of each, so many drops
she must have stopped counting by now.
A boy rides a four-wheeler with a dog
under one arm, no shirt, just as any man

on summer afternoons. Any story
is fair game in the dull space to get the girl
to sleep when creeks aren't safe to wade.
The places have been marked where not

to swim (E. coli) so that she can't step
on the river stones worn smooth on themselves
by her father's side, hand in hand until she says
Pick me up, daddy, which he always does.

So many days without rain, we've stopped
counting, and summer just begun.
The boy rides on the shoulder in full sun,
dog pressed to his side like a friend.

Gary Leising

Hot Tub Scene

action*: to clear up a terrible misunderstanding.*
as if*: I were sitting in a hot tub nude with a female friend,*
and her boyfriend walked in and thought we were fooling
around. I then explain to him that nothing was
going on behind his back.
    —*An exercise from* A Practical Handbook for the Actor

For much of the world, something is going on here,
and no telling of details excuses a thing—
what could make it better? Say there are bubbles
and you both slouch so we see nothing below the shoulders:
it's like you're both swimsuited, conversing.
But the bubbles (like their tiny cousins in champagne)
could pop gooseflesh on the nape of your neck
despite the heat, and everything is lighter, less serious,
so she laughs at your joke, though you both know
it is not funny. (And didn't your parents tell you
making a nude woman in water laugh
was the first step toward pregnancy?)
And if the joke is a pun, she's so bubble-drunk
she closes in on you to touch your shoulder—
"I'm laughing so hard I might pee!"—
and her hand drops beneath the bubble blanket
and you don't know how close it is to touching you or
herself. And she laughs softly as if coming off a high
and the visible part of her arm shifts and the mere thought
of her hand has you so, well, in such a state—
thank God for the bubbles—you shouldn't stand up
and her boyfriend walks in, the only person in this scene

fully clothed. You want to say the bubbles were there already,
you closed your eyes while she undressed, kept them closed
until she slipped beneath their modest, whippy-cloud layer,
but you can't say anything, because you're telling yourself
to think unsexy thoughts, think potted meat, think boot black,
think marching bands, think sheep shearing and raw wool,
think the seeds and stringy stuff inside of a pumpkin.
The scene gets worse because everyone sees the bubbles—
she must have scratched her nose—
the bubble mustache clinging but wavering, about to fall
on each of her exhales. It comes
clean off when she says, "Hi, hun."
He stands above you, his steel-toed work boots
level with your eyes.
He could break your nose with a kick.
He looks down at both of you so long,
his features lengthened from below, an illusion
like the tiny top-story windows made large
in a Georgian house, so you can't tell which way
the corners of his lips move. His hands
hold the edges of his hips, and fear, excitement,
willingness to fight, resignation to fate,
readiness to run, bubble-hidden erection and all,
perverse joy at the anticipation of the inevitable
next scene in this drama pin you
to the molded plastic seat. Will his hands
come together around your throat
or undo the snap of his jeans?

Gary Leising

The Girl With the JAKE Tattoo

When I see some girl with a boy's name tattooed
on her arm, along her calf, or above her breast,
visible when she's wearing a tank top, I think
of the two possibilities: She's with him still,
and he's happy she's in that tank, showing off
her butter-colored skin and his name on it
in blue, always those tattoos are blue, so dark
I think of newsprint smudging my sweaty hands
in summertime. Thus the other possibility:
she wishes it were newsprint, smeared,
because he's gone, that bastard Jake, but
she's happy with some Mike, Brian, or Sam,
and he has a little twinge of jealousy when
she fastens an anklet below the Jakey heart,
or when they're at the pool and everyone
suspects he's Jake as he lotions up her back.
Someday they'll discuss it, how much removal
would cost, if it's worth it, but they haven't
been together long enough. And when she
pulls on one of his T-shirts after they've made love,
covering the JAKE on her shoulder, her wrist,
or the rose-wreathed JAKE hanging above her ass,
Sam will wonder if they'll ever get close enough
for that conversation, and how he'll bring it up,
awkwardly asking her to change her body
for him the way—is it the same?—she did for Jake.

Bobby Ross

Stories

Contradiction is the principal theme in my work. Good battles evil; harmony dances with discord; truth confronts lies. Questions posed are not answered.

Politics, popular culture, the environment, and, as I get older, aging and mortality are issues that interest me. I try to make my pictures clear and accessible, but not overly explicit.

I employ an illusionistic narrative form to convey my ideas. The images are compiled in an additive process analogous to collage, unplanned yet reconciled to an internal logic. Often two different story lines are blended to create a more complex end product.

My paintings are done in a highly detailed, multiple-layered oil technique on linen. The drawings are executed in graphite on bristol board.

Life demands great efforts, discipline, honesty, and sacrifice. Making pictures is the theater in which I struggle to act this out.

—*Bobby Ross*

Destiny

Collateral Damage

Jane and Eddy at the Park

Sanctuary

Evolution

Soliloquy

Sand

That Old Time Religion

Amanda Marbais

Bottle Rockets

"I've watched *Invasion of the Body Snatchers* sixteen times," says Jon as I knead his back. "Does that mean something?"

I don't answer but skim his spine's notches. I'm a terrible masseuse, but he asked for a back rub, so he's getting a dangerously bad one.

"Sci-fi movies are a turn-on," he says.

"I believe it," I say—in that, I believe they turn him on. Last week we visited his parents, and in their basement he wanted to make out during *Aliens*, groping during flashing images of one terrifying puppet just after we'd eaten a robust turkey dinner. He was also undeterred by Alex Trebek loudly posing answers, as upstairs his parents watched their favorite show. "What is Madagascar," says Jon. We keep making out. It definitely says something about him, but it isn't something bad.

Jon prefers bodily invasion, Hollywood cashing in on people's collective nervousness about being consumed: *The Thing*, *Aliens*, *V*, *Breeders*. We don't have this in common, but the last ten months have been good. I've been less of a hypochondriac, felt less raw and guarded during nights out. And, I barely think about mortality, which seems healthier. Still, I only have a single drawer in Jon's apartment, where my underwear lie in a small pile.

We finish nectars, salt-spiked umami cakes, sunken on a couch under a bay window in sunlight while our thighs still touch as we eat. With other partners, I have ridden bikes through windy corridors and blinding cliffs of high rises. Virtually sedentary, Jon and I eat salty, oily snacks, creamy food from deep bowls, adding thick adipose layers. Still, despite this, my body climbs to triage-worthy temps in the winter, and I make Jon bear the burden of shoveling. In the snow, he howls from the porch.

He knocks on the window, a warped icicle gripped like a snow cone fashioned of crooked bone, droplets clinging to mitten's weave, his nose coppery with aggravated rosacea. He gestures, runs around the porch, slips but recovers, and returns to taunt me with his shovel.

He went to school for film but now helps narcissistic jack-offs sell medical supplies, mainly needles. There's a hideous abstract sculpture in his building's lobby, a genderless person befriending a needle, but it looks more like the figure has taken a Jesus-spike through the hand. I don't like to visit him. There are too many actual needles in the office where he manages spreadsheets: three-edged, filiform, thirteen-millimeter needles, 130-millimeter needles. They also sell customer information, sometimes to dubious medical companies. This last company they sold to supplied illegal bath salts online. So in addition to feeling badly about the work, he questions me over his own ethics.

He has the least seniority, and in the bathroom, he heard someone refer to him as the Carpet Square. That's a good reason to quit, but also a needle may accidentally enter his eye, stabbing him through the dilated pupil, one smooth pointless shot in the cornea.

"How would this happen?" he says. "Bodily invasions of any kind are rarely accidental."

"Needle-factory brawl," I say. I can obsess over this if he can watch so many movies with elaborate puppetry that gets him off.

"I wish we had more of a medical background." But then I would probably be more phobic. For instance, I have a terrifying mole. It has deepened from shale to nipple-pink, coincidently the color of my urine, and my bowels are giving me trouble, maybe causing the change in my urine. It might be a stretch to think my bowels changed my mole.

As we shovel the sidewalk, Jon returns to a reoccurring discussion— he wants to replace Paul Reubens, my deceased bulldog. For him, my hypochondria stems from missing my mush-faced dog. Everyone feels their dog is genuinely intuitive, but Paul Reubens got me. When Zooey Deschanel came out with that annoying commercial, Paul Reubens always barked, sharing my irritation, his mouth as frothy and salmon as I felt, as he nipped at the screen and at Zooey Deschanel's ukulele-strumming hands. Saturday, Jon again mentions getting a new dog, which at first causes me to balk at the potential destruction of the empty space Paul Reubens has left in the apartment, a space his chew-toys and bristle bones still populate, like a surrealist landscape about dogs as a concept.

That night, in the bathroom, after fondue, my weight is twenty pounds greater, explaining the general softness of my stomach, which now obsesses me so that I run my hands over it in bed, while hoping Jon doesn't think I masturbate with him under the covers. I would wait 'til he was gone. I had expanded beyond my most expansive point, at eighteen, when my diet was pizza, a year I became what friends would describe as Plasticine. "Plasticine" leaves my mouth as Jon evicts me from the scale. He too has gained twenty-five pounds, and he makes a mewing noise like a wounded snow leopard in a ravine.

If we were basset hounds, the vet would prescribe a special diet like Nutritional Nuggets or Raw Dog, and if we were elephants we would die in a quagmire. In a moment of conflated ego, we both agree: relationships are all about each other's bodies, beginning with obsession, moving to comfort, finally, the bulking up after postcoital calm. Now he's closer to my way of thinking. My hypochondria doesn't seem so disjointed.

My metabolism has sunken into a glacial period: iced-over explorers slowly traverse my intestines shouting, "Smoke ahead," their pickaxes driving into a lip of tissue. That's not true. The intestinal travelers are quite silent because it requires so much effort to move through the permafrost of my bladders and veins, a Yakutsk, supplying its diamonds but remaining frozen.

My first breakfast-salad is late February, and it prompts Jon to say, "Asparagus?" and raise one eyebrow, but I remain silent. In my mind I immaturely shout, "I CANNOT HAVE A BOWEL MOVEMENT, "and it reverberates in my pulmonary, internal jugular and diploic veins, but stops short of the intestines frozen beneath my stomach.

"Jon," I say. "Do you want to travel someplace really dorky, but out in the boondocks."

"A trip?"

"In other words someplace I'm ashamed to say I want to go," I say.

Copper Springs' invasive pop up ads have made me want to get a massage, take the waters, slough off bad skin. I think of this as I drag a dagger icon into my I-hate-zooey-deschanel tumblr. I have made a gif of her barfing small stringed instruments as an adorable puppy barks at her. I call it Bark-Barfing, and suddenly realize I'm not good at naming gifs, and it depresses me.

Jon stops stamping a squid on a birthday invitation for his six-year-old niece, Candice, his hand suspended above the squid's immature, yet threatening tentacle. Candice loves squid, not knowing squid slither through the water, rotating their hooks just the size for boring a hole in a child, an image so disturbing I can't finish my breakfast.

"Where are we going?" he asks, his fingers poised mid-stamp, his mouth a straight line.

"Are you reluctant or tired of that squid?" I honestly can't tell.

"No. I want to go on a dorky trip with all of my muster."

"How much muster? Enough to call you a colonel?"

"You beat me to it!" he said. "No. I Poupon anyone with more muster."

"Love it," I say and deflate onto the shoal of the overblown cushions, and stare out the window at the elderly couple shuffling down the street. The flip mention of this bodily habit depresses me. The elderly likely can't have bowel movements, either. So much in common. So, so much.

We schedule a couples massage and drive to Michigan, a series of events which seem a little dorky until the throes of the check-in process reveal them to be ridiculous. In matching robes, we read *Dwell*, in a waiting room where furniture is positioned at protractor-worthy ninety-degree angles, and a wood-burning fireplace spans twenty feet of the room. I'm not even exaggerating, twenty fucking feet. If someone took a photo of us right now, it could be used for *Dwell*.

Birds weave an accompaniment to a quartet of soft pan-flutes, as through the windows, a grayish older man, in a billow of steam, tests the dark waters of a hot tub. His tentative actions suggest a tub filled with a flesh-eating virus, and he turns at the last minute, offering a view of his butt through the sixteen-foot windows, mesmerizing me with his body's intricate creases. Through the folds, his skin appears long and pliable, closer to loose-fitting pants, yet his buttocks emerge from the slack like an apple. I study his lack of self-consciousness and admire him.

A girl arrives, in a vapor of sandalwood, hands us cucumber water, and with non-threatening gestures introduces herself as Zoey, which elicits a sigh. This also brings on a renewed need to relieve myself, and revives the feeling of possessing a marmot in my gut. Imagining the happy colon pictured on the package of *The Garden of Life* not only does not bring relief, it annoys me.

We swish silently in our robes through low-lit rooms filled with ferns and callas, when a guy dressed in a smock appears, joins Zoey, and introduces himself as Rod. Not even kidding. Rod. It now feels like a sex party, a phrase that elicits the internal berating remark, *Liz*, how about "orgy?" What's the matter with the precision of that word? *Orgy*. Orgy? The glowing purple tub engulfed in fake ivy announces sex, in healthy, comforting, burning, burning oil. I project the aura of not being weirded out, but am weirded out.

Cloying sandalwood does not bring on legitimate relaxation. Home remedies haven't helped. Though I am fortified with Garden of Life products: colon cleanses, probiotics, St. John's, psyllium powders. Often I have asked Jon to leave me in productive solitude with excuses like a need for croissants from Sweet Cakes or my sudden concern over carbon monoxide poisoning, and the need for detectors from Ace.

As Rod works under the keen of whales, I imagine he massages everything from me, and wonder if being an agent of expulsion disturbs him. In his oblivion, he hums whales' songs. Or it could be Jon. No. Thank God. It's just Rod.

At home, we sing constantly, especially Magnetic Fields' *69 Love Songs*, which suddenly enter my head and swirls around to the whales' accelerated moans and clicks. Daily, I sing these songs to Jon, prompting him to make requests. "I'll hear that again," he says. Yet, he hates live music, and when we walk two blocks to the Empty Bottle, he buys the earplugs from the bar, under a sign that reads: "Take care of your ears. The band won't."

Once, for me, he stood through a noise band, growing the orange plugs, like giant skin polyps coming from his ears, yet smiled. He napped, balanced with one arm baring fulcrum on his bag, pushing away, as damp, bearded dancers swayed around us. He brags he can always be comfortable, and is a candidate for apocalypse survival leader, an image eliciting visceral dreams about strength, images of a healthy liver and spleen.

After the massage, amidst a rhythmic popping of overhead racquetballs, Rod and Zoey stare at the oil bath, and following an uncomfortable silence, retreat through the room's bamboo door. This facility doubles as a club. The closing door brings a feeling of nakedness, of me in the center of the court, balls popping me in the hefty stomach.

Jon's half-drunken eyes fluttering, he rests against the hot tub and dozes. He has conquered a recent interview, been hired for a better job, and will no longer be called Carpet Square by a band of Neanderthals maximizing search engines and selling pharmaceuticals. Earning this, he rests. The seat slopes like the shoals of a baptismal river, and in the purplish glow our skin appears bruised, like we've traveled far, are exhausted and broken. I am reminded of the song "Big Rock Candy Mountain," where the lakes are a panacea for hobos, with waters of whiskey and stew.

I ask Jon if whiskey and stew comfort him. "I've never had a good stew."

He is serene and naked, his ass jackknifed toward me. He asks, "Should it be this hot?"

"It depends. Do you mean the water?"

This is our first trip after months when my former roommate made it difficult for us to be alone. She complained of depression, wrapped herself in a three-wolves blanket, and sat on the front porch chain-smoking. We lived on Ashland Avenue, and my roommate left the door open. It was an accident, Paul Reubens' death, but I didn't leave the house for weeks. I broke up with Jon; I got back together with him.

You can't lock doors or windows or control your space, so you're basically screwed with a roommate, and then it's up to you to blame yourself. But, if I thought of it as a fluke, I might feel even worse.

Jon and I lay in the shallow tub, leaned against each other so we wouldn't go under.

"It's starting to cool down," he says, but I'm not sure what he means. For minutes, we don't speak.

He says, "Let's adopt one tomorrow. I've wanted a dog. Bloom, Brawny and Blake are all good names."

"Who names a dog Bloom?" I ask. "Blake is a frat name."

"True."

I'm not going to cry because I'm not at home, but I mew a little and someone immediately knocks on the door.

"They think we're having sex," he whispers, and raises his eyebrows.

"Or maybe there's a fire?" I say.

Jon grunts, screams, "Yes?" and smacks his arm provocatively until I whisper "Jesus! Stop." The door seems thin, and my adrenaline pumps, because whoever is listening hasn't moved. We are all silent as if in some kind of decency standoff. Finally, the person retreats in a rustle of sheets. "Yeah, I'm sure I know what they're thinking."

"So?" he says.

He sings "Big Rock Candy Mountain," and I settle on thoughts of hobos getting what they want and the railroad men tipping their hats. Much better. "Rod wouldn't tip his hat."

"No way," says Jon. "Rod's a Rod-bag."

"That makes no sense."

Jon says nothing.

One week later, I emerge from the bathroom where I had been tracing constellations of my potentially cancerous moles. They just sit there, in golden-brown treachery. Jon asks me to move in, and then "If you're cool with it, we could get married." Just like that. And, he's holding a plunger as if it just occurred to him.

A few months later, we've rented a house, and Jon has taken to making short movies again. The lights are low in the neighborhood when Jon shoots a long take of a bicycle crash. He has chosen this location for his bicycle-action short, about pod people who when angry, transform into Teletubbies. Murderous Teletubbies. (It's half animated, so it actually makes more sense.)

It's dusky, someone has a fixie, but the tires on the gravel and the huffing and puffing are only a little nostalgic. Lenny Kravitz jumps and barks, his chest hitting my calves. I have to bribe him to be silent with something called a Pig-Wrap.

Hands on my hips, I watch Jon goad people into semi-believable behavior. I think of how the old hymns ingrained in our psyches are about comfort, escapism, and reward and almost never about enjoying life. I resent my religious background. A friend of ours, on camera, sings a familiar song.

On cue, the pod-tubby leans and lights the bottle rocket as another person films. The traffic is a solid noise, ticking smoothness, in unbearable heat. A man comes out to water his lawn. Sometimes I feel inexplicably sad, despite being comfortable. Jon is laughing.

I lift my hand to shade my face from the fading sun, and the bottle rocket in a smoky line nicks my pinky, explodes, breaking the pink half-moon tip, singeing it, bringing blood. Later I find out it missed my nose by a centimeter. Jon's face appears above me, still calm. *I think it went right through,* I say. At least I imagine I say this. Kind of amazing.

Kellie Wardman

This Yin and Yang
Is Good for Something

You wouldn't understand P-Town: kaleidescopic queens
on electric scooters, Prince Albert and a pink flamingoed yard,
Jubilee Drag Bingo on the UU church lawn.

You're more of a Chevron guy with a basement
full of power tools. If you were here, and someone at the cabaret
brushed your booty, you'd say, "Get off me, fucker!"

Or you wouldn't. They'd never touch your ass anyway,
you're too unwavering and deliberate
for tomfoolery. Working long days while I'm away
pursuing the art. What did I do to deserve you and our light-

flooded house on Twist Hill? You built a perfect shed
with the Pythagorean theorem, edged us with leaf-free gutters.
You keep the azaleas watered, cars washed, wine rack full
of malbec, though you drink gin. You ask about poetry—

as foreign as cross-dressing—but you ask.
Four sisters and a hypochondriac mother served you well.

But what about the kid? He's mine, sixteen, a hobgoblin.
You want to shepherd him into something.

He makes us a perfect triangle; he and I are the legs
to your hypotenuse. Most days, half-scared to love you.

Emily May Anderson

Daughter

In *King Lear* it doesn't matter
what a daughter does—there's no
winning. She can put out
a man's eyes in his kitchen,
or she can remain loyal
beyond all reason, and she
will still be dead
before the curtain falls.

In the audience tonight, I will reach
for another man's daughter
and hold her hand—knowing
neither of our fathers would approve,
knowing that sometimes
no one wins.

Noel Sloboda

Hollywood Cemetery (Richmond VA)

Unmoored from the satellite, the car stops
        speaking and without another
    left or right, we find ourselves

trapped in this necropolis,
        forever repeating a loop
    passing landmarks merely confirming

lack of progress: the crumbling Celtic cross
        that reminds you of your roots
    but bears dates from an American war

and the onyx dog that pointlessly guards
        somebody else's long-cold
    child. I try to reassure you

we have not already gone
        past the exit—yet you can't stop
    worrying the lettering might be

obscured like so many stone legends
        here worn away by something
more persistent than weather

and I can't keep from reminding you—
        once again—I never wanted this
    holiday among the dead.

Kirsten Hemmy

On Considering Whether to Live in America: A Love Poem

for Ansoumana

Would you like to survive on sadness?
—Gil Scott-Heron

One day, in your country, you tell me it's unimportant
whether a person is Black or white (black or white) &

that you always look past this. You don't even
graze your tongue on *look* or *past*. We decide to go

to the U.S. for a few years, an opportunity for you
to experience my world & for our family to live in both.

We fill out visa forms then wait, taking your daughters on trips all
across the continent, my belly growing

every day with our two brown sons. At a beach in Senegal
a man asks me whose children these are, your girls, & when

I say I am their mother, he says *ohhh, adoptive.*
He recognizes they can't truly be mine, no matter

how profoundly I love & worry & raise them. I am
too white for their Black & therefore, can't really be

but soon we will arrive in the United States where
someone will do it for you, resting place of Trayvon Martin,

Emmitt Till & Amadou Diallo, men killed over matters
unimportant & yet grave. In the city where we will live

there is an active KKK & the comments in our city's
papers will rest like stones in your chest & deeper

still for our lack of humanity & for our children—
ours & theirs. When we travel further South

you will see roads that make your pulse harder, slower, sadder,
gravestones with no markers & no names, stories

that compose our untaught history & more than once you will dream
of trees in terror, not only their strange fruit but

also scars of trees which grow across ancestors' backs.
Road maps of evil truth, things our children will never

learn at school. On our way to work we will drive
past plantations & every day you will come to understand

girls will notice their black skin seems blacker
on an American playground & we will do whatever

is necessary to make sure they understand how
lovely & amazing they really are. We will find ourselves

working against America, what it does. You will be surprised at the
number & hue of people who will remark upon

the attractiveness of our boys; if you listen carefully you will
understand the subtext in the breezeless silences that follow

casual conversations about our family. When you go to work I will
worry about broken taillights &

every other reason police could have to stop you.
You will learn what DWB means & later you will learn

to redirect your anger so as to save your precious life. One day, you sit
down to teach our children all this, too.

Allison Doyle

Who You Are

"So you're a teacher?"

She asked the question while she scanned the one-page form I'd filled out. I needed the TB test so I could continue volunteering for a local non-profit that worked with elementary and high school students, and I'd written "Teacher" in the occupation line. That's where the lies began.

The pharmacist wore glasses that flashed in the harsh, fluorescent light. Her office was in the back of the store, next to the bathrooms. The small waiting room reeked of Lysol and industrial-strength cleaner. Thankfully, she must have had air freshener hidden away somewhere, because with the door closed, the room only smelled faintly of lemons.

I studied the woman as she flipped through my paperwork. Her hair was pulled back into a loose ponytail, and it hung down one side of her face in a stylish way. I could never pull off that ponytail. She was Asian—Korean, if I had to guess—and she seemed very content.

I was not. I had recently quit my job at a production studio and was applying to graduate programs in writing, working part-time when I could. When I began volunteering, I'd been surprised at how much I enjoyed helping the children. So when they told me that in order to continue, I would need to take a TB test, I readily agreed, despite my fear of needles.

"Yes, I'm a teacher."

I don't know why I lied. I guess some part of me had always wanted to be a teacher, or at least thought teaching was a commendable profession that sounded better than "volunteer tutor" or "aspiring, currently unemployed, writer."

"That's wonderful," she said. "Teaching is so important." When she spoke, her eyes lit up behind her glasses, and her accent became more noticeable. I felt a warm feeling in my stomach and knew we had made a connection, and I wanted more.

So I continued to lie.

"It is," I said, trying to sound humble.

"What do you teach?" She was preparing the needle, taking it carefully from its sterile packaging and examining the tip. I looked away quickly.

"Writing," I said. Which was, technically, true.

"Writing?" she asked. She rubbed a damp swab on my arm. "In English? That's wonderful. I was going to ask you about that, because you speak so well. Your accent is almost perfect. It's one of the best I've ever heard."

I winced as the needle pricked my skin.

"Thanks," I said, trying not to look at the small, foreign bump slowly forming under my skin. "Yours is good, too."

But she wasn't done. She pulled a stool up close to where I was sitting and crossed her legs delicately, as if we were in a cocktail bar and not a small examination room.

"You're Korean, right?" she smiled. "I can always tell. You have such pretty eyes."

She was referring to their shape. My eyes curved, like small, perfect footballs. I was a teenager the first time some older Korean women told me my eyes were an enviable size and shape.

I took a breath. "Yes, I'm Korean."

This second lie was harder. It was more difficult because it was at once true and yet not true.

I'm not really Korean—not the type of Korean she was talking about. I'm an adopted Korean, raised from infancy in a loving household of Irish-Germans. The only accent I might have had was Midwestern. But what could I do? She had already made the assumption that I was just like her, and she'd bonded with me. It felt wrong to correct her. It would just be embarrassing for both of us. So instead, I kept quiet and waited for her to speak again.

The pharmacist took off her glasses and rubbed the bridge of her nose with her hand. Without glasses and without her doctor's pad, I realized we were around the same age.

"I'm Korean," she said, as she leaned in. "How long did it take you to get rid of your accent? It took me years, and I still hear it sometimes."

The warmth I had felt earlier disappeared as quickly as it had come.

"We need people in medicine," she continued, not waiting for my answer. "So many of us go into the field. But you're the first I've met who has gone into writing. It must be so difficult, but it's inspiring to think we've come that far—that we can now even teach writing in English!"

"It's great," I said, and I didn't know if I was talking about the achievement or my own experiences as a teacher.

She smiled at me again. I felt guilty for her confidence in me, her friendliness. I had to confess, even though I dreaded the disappointment and confusion I would see reflected on her face when I told her the truth. I was almost about to speak when she stood up. She had taken my silence as a desire to leave. My confession was not necessary.

She walked with me back into the waiting room. After she handed me my paperwork, I realized I had yet to pay.

"How much do I owe you for the test?" I started to dig through my purse.

"Oh, don't worry about it," she said as she motioned for the next patient to join her in the office. She briefly touched my shoulder. "I've got you covered. We've got to look out for each other, right?"

The first person to call me a Twinkie was a nine-year-old boy, who was holding one of the sugary treats in his hand when he said it.

The day was hot, and I was sick to my stomach. An overpowering smell of kimchi came wafting in from the kitchen. I was sitting with the boy and four other Korean-American children in the stuffy, windowless basement of the Korean Presbyterian Church in Omaha, Nebraska. The church was the epicenter of the tiny, insular community of first- and second-generation Korean-Americans who, for reasons beyond my understanding, had decided to relocate to Nebraska. This population was a fairly new phenomenon in a city that had under four hundred Asian families living in it in 1990. Aside from the Koreans at the church, I was one of only five Asians I knew, and three of us were adopted.

It was the beginning of my seventh-grade summer, yet instead of hanging out with my friends or heading to camp, I was stuck in a basement that smelled like over-spiced cabbage, practicing basic Korean vocabulary with children who still played with Barbie dolls and action figures. We were all learning how to speak and write Korean, and I was one of the worst students. The others, even the youngest, could understand some of the language and had a foundation to work from. I arrived knowing nothing.

"What did you say?" I turned to the boy who had called me the name. The other children in the room had quieted down, and the only sound was the low-pitched grumble of the air conditioner.

The boy was wearing a dark blue Power Rangers T-shirt and frayed jean shorts, his small body shaped like a water balloon. He clenched the unwrapped Twinkie in his palm, and as our eyes connected, he squeezed its spongy shell and the frosting erupted from a small hole in the top.

"You're a Twinkie," he said. He held out the cake so I could see the creamy inner filling and smell its heavy sugariness. "You're yellow on the outside and white on the inside. You're not really Korean. Not like us."

The four other children in the room laughed, but when I glared at them, they quickly fell silent.

"Who told you that?" I asked. At my tone, I could feel the other children shift uncomfortably in their seats. I wondered what else they'd been saying behind my back.

The boy looked defiantly at me. "My brother told me," he said.

I took a deep breath. The pastor of the church, who was also the head teacher of our ragtag program, had recently introduced me to three boys my own age. I think he was trying to be nice—helping develop friendships and all that—but the surly teenage boys wanted nothing to do with me, and I wasn't surprised that they'd been talking.

It wasn't worth it, getting upset at a nine-year-old boy, or even being upset with his brother. They were right anyway. I wasn't like them.

There are communities in Korea for the abandoned, orphaned children that don't get adopted or sent away overseas. I visited one during my only trip back to the country. I've heard them called, "rainbow communities," but they're more like adult orphanages—places where children are sent as they grow older and are less likely to be adopted. The communities, which are often run by adult orphans, take care of these children. They are educated, housed, and provided for, and oftentimes the orphans end up staying in the community as adults because there's nowhere else for them to go. I remember meeting some residents of the community and feeling embarrassed as they touched my clothes and marveled at the short length of my hair. They asked me what it was like to live in America in a tone that made me think what they really wanted to know was what it was like to be free.

The largest wave of international adoptions out of Korea came after the Korean War. The mixed-race and illegitimate children of Korean women and European and American soldiers were not accepted in Korean society—single mothers received no government assistance and a stigma arose around adoption that still pervaded the minds of the second-generation children I met in that Omaha church.

I was a specimen of something they had only imagined, but never met—a Korean raised by whites. They asked me questions like, "What do they feed you? Do you get to watch as much TV as you want? I heard white people don't care what their children do at all! Do they make you work for them?"

They had no concept of what adoption meant and only had a vague sense that I should be pitied. This belief was fortified by their parents.

A young girl at the church told me that her mother had instructed her to apologize for the way the Korean government had treated me.

"Apologize for what?" I asked.

The girl looked surprised that I needed clarification. She looked at me, and her eyes grew wide.

"Because when we sent you away, you lost your heritage!" she said. "You never had a chance to grow up like us."

It was true. And there were many more like me out there.

From 1953 to 2007, an estimated 160,000 South Korean children were adopted overseas, the majority sent to the United States. Korean adoptees comprise the largest group of transracial adoptees in America and—by some estimates—account for 10 percent of the nation's Korean population.

During that fifty-four-year period, the sheer number of international adoptions from Korea had some critics even comparing the practice to human trafficking. In their view, adoption was a business, and the Korean government was systematically and effectively exporting its unwanted population overseas, and making a lot of money doing it.

Many Koreans I met, especially adults my parents' age, seemed to either be ashamed of their country's treatment of me, or defensive of its cultural traditions, like its adherence to the family registry.

A woman who helped cook kimchi in the church kitchen was one such adult. She stopped me one day as I walked past the doorway. Her hands had bits of cabbage stuck to them, and her eyes were watering from the heat and spices in the kitchen.

"Your birth mother misses you very, very much." She wiped her hands on the corner of her apron, and nodded as if she was talking about a good friend, though I was a stranger to her. When I didn't speak, she frowned. "I hope you know she did not have a choice," she said. "It is not up to us."

"I know," I said, wanting to find a way out of the conversation. And then, for lack of anything better to add, I said, "Thank you." She gave me a tiny bow, bending slightly at the waist, before turning around and heading back into the kitchen.

Korean family registers, or hojus, as they are called, were and still are an essential cultural aspect of the country. A registry is how the government tracks genealogical information, life milestones, and a citizen's official status in the country. Births, deaths, birthdays, and marriages are all reported and tracked. Only males can be the household heads, and only males can sign off on official documents. When a woman marries, she is removed from the registry of her father and added to the registry of her husband. If you are not added onto a Korean family registry, in many respects, you do not exist.

Only in the last decade has there been a push to encourage Koreans to adopt their own. The rate of adoptions to the U.S. has been on a slow decline since 2005, and in the last year or so, Korea formally apologized to its adopted children and tried to mend fences by offering dual citizenship to all adoptees who desire it.

I have yet to apply.

One morning I left my apartment too early from the peaceful, tree-lined roads of Hancock Park and arrived in downtown Los Angeles thirty minutes before I had to be at work. I had planned on driving slowly around the streets, looking for the perfect parking spot, but on this particular day, I found one quickly—a large, inviting space only a block or so away.

I sat in my car, listening to the end of the BBC World News, watching the disheartened trail of students make their way towards the nearby USC campus. The dashboard clock blinked. I still had twenty-five minutes to burn.

This is stupid, I thought. I guess I'll just be early.

With a sigh, I joined the unhappy procession, still vaguely hopeful that something would distract me and eat up the extra time.

I was walking past a small strip mall that sat just a few feet away from the crosswalk I was headed towards when I paused. A tired-looking security guard, uncomfortably squeezed into a tight-fitting black uniform that looked like it had been borrowed from the set of a cheesy cop film, was watching the procession of walkers with languid interest. She coughed and reached down beside her to pick up a coffee cup.

That's what I'll do, I thought. I'll go get coffee.

The thought sprang overeager and excited into my mind. I don't even drink coffee, but that didn't matter—it was something to do. I knew there was a small café in the strip mall, and I headed there without glancing at my watch.

As I walked into the café, a small bell chimed and a middle-aged Asian woman walked quickly out from the back kitchen. Her eyes lit up when she saw me, and she began speaking in a foreign language.

"Um, hello," I said. I could hear the static murmur of a television coming from the back room. Now that I was standing near the counter, I could see that there was a middle-aged Asian man sitting in the kitchen, watching the television as it chattered away.

The woman frowned and stopped speaking, so I took the initiative and ordered a tall hot chocolate. She frowned again, but nodded and began bustling around behind the counter, making my drink. She never took her eyes off me, even as her hands stayed busy. I pretended not to notice and instead examined the laminated advertisements for different drinks taped onto a glass divider that ran the length of the countertop.

Now, I am usually not someone who orders hot chocolate at cafés, but I knew as I watched her that she was taking a long time to prepare the drink. I thought about saying something when the woman spoke.

"Where were you born?" She carefully poured hot milk into a small cup and then glanced quickly toward the back room, and I followed her gaze. The middle-aged man was watching us with the volume turned down on the television. As soon as he saw me looking, he returned to watching his show.

"You're Korean?" she asked.

It is a question that has followed me for the eighteen years I lived in Nebraska and the eleven I have spent in Los Angeles. I have heard it so many times that I have devised multiple answers, one to fit any occasion, each of varying length, tone, and complexity. And yet I'm not satisfied with any of them. But it was early on a Monday. She was getting the shortest answer I had.

"Yes," I said. "I was born in Korea." I stared at the cup of quickly cooling milk in her hands and wondered how rude it would be to cancel my order.

She gave me a thin-lipped, satisfied smile and nodded, her eyes flitting around my face, appraisingly.

"But you don't know Korean," she said. I shook my head.

"My children have friends like you," she said, turning the steamer back on. "They know no Korean—no language, no writing."

She dumped the milk into the cup. "They have given up their culture."

She began stirring the now lukewarm chocolate.

It was time to go. I began to open my purse. "How much?" I asked.

"One dollar," she said, but continued to speak. "I have taught my children how to read and write in Korean," she said. "They speak both languages very well."

She handed me the cup. As I reached for it, she momentarily placed her hand on my arm.

"You need to learn," she said, and her eyes held my gaze for a moment. "It is who you are."

I nodded, not knowing what else to do. I could get upset, explain to her that I wasn't like her children, and I didn't need to learn her language or her culture. I wanted to tell her she should stick to making drinks and not handing out advice to strangers. I wanted to tell her to mind her own business. But the clock on the wall told me that I only had three minutes to get to work. Without thanking her for the drink, I half-sprinted out the door and across the street. When I finally sat down at my desk at work, I took one sip of the now cold hot chocolate and threw it in the trash.

I blend in with the people around me, cloaking myself in their assumptions and indifference, yet when my disguise is questioned, I never give a straight answer. I'm Korean. I'm American. I'm Korean-American. I'm sometimes even Amer-Asian. It happens more than most people believe. When I do decide to tell my friends about my latest mistaken identity, their eyebrows raise skeptically and they ask, "Why do they always assume you can understand them?" and "Why don't you just tell them you're adopted?"

Of course I've done that, too. There was an old Korean woman who used to hobble down the street I lived on every afternoon. She would wait for me to pass and reach her hand out to pet my dog. She loved my dog, which was surprising because many people, especially the elderly, are scared of the black German Shepherd that trots confidently by my side. Yet this old woman, easily eighty years old, would lean over her walker and show no fear as we approached. She'd give me a wide smile, and I'd lose her eyes in the deep lines of her face.

On our first encounter, she began speaking to me in what I assumed was Korean. I can now pick out some vocabulary and sounds if I concentrate.

"I'm sorry," I said in English as she hugged my dog's head. "I don't speak Korean." Of course, she kept right on talking. In Korean. I tried again, slower. "I'm sorry, but I really can't understand you."

That got her attention. She stopped speaking and looked at me the way adults do when they're about to scold naughty children.

"You Korean," she said in halting English, pointing one of her knobby fingers at my face.

Then she pointed at my dog. "That Jindo."

Jindos were one of the original Korean hunting dogs, and they were also common street dogs in many rural Korean towns. The solid-colored ones were traditionally considered lucky. My neighbor, a twenty-something second-generation Korean living with his mother, owned an all-white Jindo. He'd told me they also came in all-black.

I didn't want to argue with the old woman about my dog and my heritage, so I picked one, writing the other off as a loss.

"Well, yes," I said, wondering how well she could understand me. "But I'm adopted." And then I did something that I knew wouldn't help. I repeated the same word, only slower, and louder, as if the volume of my voice would help her understand what I meant. "A-DOP-TED."

For a moment, she was silent, and I stupidly thought she had understood me. But after a pause, she began chattering away in Korean, looking at me as she did, so I would know she wasn't talking to my dog. What else could I do? I started nodding and smiling at what seemed to be the right moments, concentrating on her words, as if just hearing them enough would help me transform the sounds into a language I could understand.

There have been times when I could have explained my adoption to people who probably would have understood; but instead, I chose to pretend, to be the person they assumed I was. I could say it was because it's not their business, so why should I have to correct their assumption? It's exhausting to explain a complex topic to a stranger, who then usually has several follow-up questions of a personal nature. There are still so many assumptions people make about what being adopted means.

One of the first bosses I had working in California once admitted to me, after I had worked for him for several months, that when I applied for the position, he assumed I was going to be, as he put it, "a blond, white Midwestern belle." He referred to my resume, which mentioned that I was once a Nebraskan debutante.

"Your name was Allison Doyle," he said. "So when you came in for the interview, I was shocked."

"Why didn't you bring it up?" I asked, adding that I was glad he had still hired me, despite the racial surprise.

"Because that's not something you ask," he said. "Besides, I just assumed you were half."

The maps they sell in the seedy trinket shops on Hollywood Boulevard don't exaggerate the average Nebraskan's view of California. We actually do think that Hollywood takes up a considerable chunk of southern California and that palm trees line pristine, wide streets, and everyone is beautiful, tanned, and in the movies. What I didn't realize about California until I visited was that many of those people were not white. And in fact, a large percentage of them were Asian.

Once, when I was around eight years old, my family traveled to San Francisco. My father took us—my sister, my brother, my mother and me—to visit Chinatown. When we walked into one of the smaller alleyways, I was stunned. I couldn't understand what I was seeing. The crowd spilled from the sidewalks onto the street. People were walking quickly up and down the sidewalks, pushing past each other and going about their business, completely indifferent to me or my family. The crowd was, for the most part, Asian. I had never seen so many before.

I remember thinking that, for the first time in my life, I could completely blend in and become lost in the crowd. And yet I felt detached from the people bustling around me. I knew I wasn't like them. I was sure they would be able to spot me as a fraud in no time. Yet when I turned back to my family, I understood that I was also not like them. Not fully. I watched them, standing on the street corner, pressed up against a wooden stall filled with fruit, cheap plastic fans, and incense, and they were the ones who stood out—not me. My mother held my father's hand, watching the rush of people pass by. My sister and brother, biological to my parents, were also intent on watching the crowd, though my brother, six years my senior, was trying to hide his interest by slouching up against the brick wall and half-shutting his eyes. Together, they were an All-American, Midwestern family—Irish-German, blonde hair, green eyes, full features. My sister, everyone always said, looked like my mother. My brother was more of a blurred mixture of both my parents, but the genetic connection was still obvious. They looked good together—like a family should. I wondered if I grabbed the hand of the nearest passerby, would we look good together, too? I knew I should walk back before my mother noticed I was gone. But some part of me wanted to test her. To see if she could recognize me in a crowd of similar-skinned, dark-haired people. So I stayed where I was, in the middle of the street, and wondered who I belonged with more.

Richard Newman

Gift Shop at the Gates of Hell

The rows of coffee mugs, each saying *Hot*
enough for ya? The shackle keychains. T-shirts
(*My parents went to hell and all I got …*)
and roasting sinners ash-globes (*Just desserts!*)
or charred-edged cards that read *Wish you were here!*
The pens that write in our own bloody ink
for the nose-, lip-, tongue-, and eyebrow-pierced cashier.
Pictures to prove it so everyone can think
what fun, great place to visit—lies freely bought.
But I am sick of feasting on my losses,
mothered in sadomasochistic sauces.
The monuments were smaller than I'd thought.
Sorrow no longer seeps. The rage won't foam.
Here, friends, are trinkets I've brought back. I'm home.

Nancy Carol Moody

Coffeehouse

Because I am not in love
with the barista

he does not paint pretty pictures in the foam of my latte.
The barista is accustomed to people
falling in love with him.

I know this.

I know this because I am not a person
with whom other people fall in love.

Phone numbers are not scritched on cocktail napkins,

a nickel a good day in the tip jar of me.

The woman at the next table
twirls the stem of a single white rose.

An oak leaf swirls at the top of her mug.

Even this kid, gangly in his khaki shorts,
was gifted a happy face to float in his.

My cup, it's growing cold.

Lips to the rim, I draw my first sip.
There is nothing here to lose.

Nancy Carol Moody

Faith

The boy who wanted to be an agronomist
also wanted to take me

to supper. Before the meal
he slipped his warm hand over mine
and tried to lead us

to a State of Grace.

I'd been content with Illinois.

Some women drive men to drink.
I drive them to God and end up paying for the gas.

The first time it happened was at a cafeteria table.
"Excuse me," he interrupted, and I set down my fork,
gazed straight up into the question of
"Would you like to know Jesus?"

Another promised me a pretty dress
if I'd wear it to his immersion.

That jigger of Jack directly to his lap?
The one baptism that was mine, all mine.

I believe there's a saint floating around up there,
advocating for me
and my cold cold soul.

Dear Lord, he prays,
please find someplace warm for her to go.

Gabriel Welsch

Faith

The e-mail lets me know there are
Horny Housewives who apparently
Want to Have Sex with me *Right NOW!!!*
Well, I should think they could do better.
Mild eczema, speedy about my business,
prone to coughing fits, often adenoidal,
games in bed an act of faith
my maladies won't drag themselves
in tattered clothes to the fervid party.
But people tell me, you have to ask—
who clicks, who responds with
Sign me up, that mix of cynicism
and impossible hope—enough to buy
that so many women want to fuck around
and yet he has not met any of them.
This is a man who knows hope
like a rich friend, faith in the ends,
ignorance of means. The man who clicks,
grabs his crotch the way some tear
at a calendar—tomorrow not yet inked,
the last day a waste, an affront to the prayer
he whispers again and again, the sacrament
of *You never know.*

Amber Sparks

Prayer For Very Thirsty Souls Who Are Out of Beer After the Liquor Stores Have Closed

O Father of mercies and God of all comforts, our only help in time of need: We humbly beseech thee to provide for us just one more beer. Look upon us with thy mercy; for surely our own mortal eyes have been too weak to see the Miller Lite logo hidden behind the milk jug. Surely in your infinite abundance, O Lord, you will lead our erring hand to the crisper, wherein we forgot we had stashed away a bottle of milk stout, or even just a lowly can of PBR. O Father, preserve us from the temptation to drink from the bottle of ouzo that some joker gifted us at the white elephant Christmas exchange; O Lord please spare us from having to drink that weird gooseberry flavored ale that our friends left here after their stay and that has gone unopened for many seasons now. Lord, if there be beer, then let us by the good grace of thy unwavering affection find it now for the love of you; or else please give us the patience, the good humor, and the steadfast temper to endure these infernally lingering party guests with nothing but a glass of champagne which, O Lord, is not to say that we are turning away the good fruits and beverages of thy vines but rather, O Lord, that it tries the patience of thy humble servant mightily to hear these endless stories about the twins and their diaper mishaps without a brew in hand, Jesus Christ dear Father dear Holy Father Our Lord. In thy good time, restore our refrigerators to full and our glasses to overflowing and enable us to live our lives, O God, without the absence of one of thy most precious gifts. This we do pray, in the name of hops and yeast and dry malt, for one more beer, AMEN.

Amber Sparks

Prayer for Video Game Characters Who Are Running Out of Hit Points Right in the Middle of the Last Boss Fight

Holy Trinity, one God,
Have mercy on your humble servants who are just trying to defeat this last boss.

From all evil, from all new attacks, from all glitches and freezes,
Good Lord, deliver us.

With special attacks undiscovered, with super weapons yet unused, with potions yet undrunk,
Good Lord, deliver us.

By your glorious Resurrection and Ascension, may we similarly be resurrected, may we complete this game, may we not perish in this very last fight after many days and weeks and months of constant battle,
Good Lord, deliver us.

We sinners beseech you to hear us, Lord Christ: Cannot you see that even now he is turning red and flashing? That even now he is temporarily weakened and we could totally finish him if we just had more HP? Dear Lord, may it please you to deliver the soul of your servant from the power of this boss and from eternal video game death,

We beseech you to hear us, good Lord.

Jesus, bearer of our items:
Have mercy on us.

Jesus, bearer of the world map and compass:
Lend us your strength and then roll the final cut scene.

Bryan Merck

Fiery Chariot

Elijah Dewrite, apostle, pastor of the New Sharon Fire Baptized Holiness Church, shepherd of the recently miscreant flock at the Jacob's Ladder Rescue Center, bane of demons, hammer of Wiccans and New-Agers, takes a seat on a bench beside the Five Points Fountain, the one with "obvious occultic symbolism."

Lon and Tony skateboard past the fountain, down the sidewalk, and vanish into the First Baptist Church parking deck. Elijah can still hear the clacking and banging of their boards. The fountain's pumps switch to high mode, and jets of water from the mouths of five bronze-green toads arc up many feet into the air, collide and splash down onto the turtles, rabbits, and dogs and storyteller goat-man. A fine mist tickles Elijah's face and triggers an early and pleasant memory. Our apostle travels back into time at the speed of reverie. He leaves his body by the fountain.

This is great, the slip-and-slide when the sprinkler hits just right. I go all the way down the hill in our yard. And I've got that new Green Lantern comic book in my room. The water smells clean. If Mama would just leave Daddy alone he wouldn't drink so much and hurt Mama. This is great.

Elijah returns to his present moment. Some goth teens gather around another bench nearby. They wear black. They have black hair. The girls wear black fingernail polish and lipstick and gray eye shadow. They all have a pale and sickly cast. One boy wears a T-shirt with "Antichrist Superstar" on it. Elijah waves at them and smiles. They ignore him.

Something spooks the crowd of pigeons on the church's lawn. They speed into the morning air with indignant cooing and a synchronous rush of wings. In a tight pattern, they circle around Five Points a few times and then return less noisily to the trimmed grass.

Once, Elijah wanted terribly to die. He prayed for this to happen. The skies were brass. He was too afraid of judgement to end his life.

Elijah has a controlling vision, an eye seeing beneath and above and within, relentlessly reading an imbedded text. He is often tired. He does not consciously know that this is what drains him.

Across the street, a few pigeons land on and around the statue of Brother Brian. He kneels and intercedes for Birmingham, hat in hand. Very early mornings, Wanda Lyn wipes the pigeon poop off Brian's head and torso as she leaves work.

Elijah goes too often into apocalypse mode. On a deeper level, he somehow realizes that joy matters, that it underlies material reality. He does not know that he already knows everything. He still sees existence as a trap. He teaches a hot hell and a heaven hard to make.

Elijah will soon be involved in a study on how non-invasive electric brain stimulation enhances altruism.

For a month or so he will be paid a hundred dollars for a Tuesday a.m. hour's worth of electronic sloppy love. This will push him into a positive mindset. The resulting changes for the better in his life, in his people and circumstances, will at first accrue unnoticed. The tipping point will be reached one morning in Advent. He will experience a marrow-level understanding of God's willingness.

Matthew Fogarty

We Are Swimmers

Something got stirred up between us here at the bottom of this great lake. A minute ago the water was blue-green and we could see each other through it, see our blue-green faces and hazel eyes. But now there's dirt floating free up from the lake bed, a cloud of particulate mud, this cloud cumulonimbus, Loch-Nessian, and we're down here straining for breath within it. Both of us rathering to drown in the mire than float to the surface and see again. Both of us rathering to grow gills, to grow fins, to mermaid and merman ourselves, to transform our human bodies and spend our stardust lives swimming this silty freshwater necklace of glacial lakes. We think that'll solve it, that neither of us'll see the other cry if our whole together world is wet. Like we'd look only forward, ignoring the four brackish streams tiding back past our estuary tails.

Matthew Fogarty

Meteors

We drove through a meteor shower in the dark of the early morning as she tried to catch a flight. She kept pointing them out, squealing each time she would see one shooting across the sky. I missed them all except the last—a long galactic trail of brilliant fiery orange and yellow that arced above the horizon. It only lasted an instant before vanishing and I panicked. I reached down to grab her hand, to make sure she hadn't also disappeared in the atmospheric fuzz that seems to snag all good things that dare try to cross through it.

KV Wilt

The Dump: Bermuda, 1960

The dump smells of seaweed and smoldering tires when we approach in the black Morris Minor, windows down, fishing-pole antennae sensing the salt air. It's the isthmus between the eight-to-four and four-to-twelve shifts. No one's there when we walk up the gravel trail with our rusted bike frame, green toolbox lacking its latch, and three-legged table and put them on the exchange place, a sort of coral altar. We see what others left—a bent shelf, a crusty anchor, a flat-head burnt umber shovel whose split handle is splinted with electrical tape. All things not good enough for the thrift shop. With his hands, Dad imagines them remade. After we carry the shelf back to the car, we return with our poles, tackle box, bucket with a Bowie knife, frayed towel, and a box of half-frozen squid. We scramble over the coral thumb like mountain goats over cordilleras. To the ledge, the edge of the unknown. Where sun sets and humpbacks leap. Where I'd be dizzy without the anchor of Henry Lee. When we sense something bigger than speckled hind, we use steel leader and a silver hook larger than my thumb. If the current is strong, we clamp on an extra square of lead. Then we weave half a squid on and around the hook, pray we catch something worth keeping, stand, swing back, and fling the tip's anticipation, our trigger finger strumming the monofilament that parabolas, then sinks in our imagination.

Brittney Scott

The Weight Aurora Carries

It splits me open knowing
I couldn't pull him

from his violent burning.
How the world spun in fury

to me, as if I were responsible
for letting my brother die.

And how my sister's face eclipsed
upon knowing her favorite sibling,

who always brought the perfect gift
wrapped in carbon paper,

was lost. In this new eternal dark
there is nowhere to travel.

Now my mother tilts
to no one, her life buckles

under the starry cloak.
But I was the one

who heaved herself over
the horizon to retrieve him.

I was the one that made him rise
after night's long ruin.

Couldn't anyone see me? I was there,
I was standing just in front of him.

Timothy Geiger

The Labor

for D.L.M.

Because your brother
can no longer speak
you spoon cold oatmeal
into his gaping mouth.
Since the accident
his hands are wounded birds.
On your bedside perch
littered with *OK*
and *Lifestyles* magazines—
you hold the wineglass
with both hands now,
realizing out loud,
"*This* is what
my life has become."
From outside, sparrow song
and everyday traffic
pour over you
like scalding water,
and you think seriously
about brutally throttling
your own brother.
What, exactly, is he
supposed to do about it?
And what voice,
like a transistor buzzing, tells
the clock to run backwards,
makes you think because
he's like this
he doesn't want
to be loved?

Keegan Lester

Numinous

In the dream there's no heaven here,
                     just our hands.
I'd like to tell you someone's ribs
                   had rusted over.
That two birds were singing vespers inside—
                   that I don't know if I could ever learn
to forget that sound. But in reality, the dream begins
                   with you holding the cadaver's heart:
each secret nestled inside: the misshapen lung;
                   years of smoking in secret
at night on the back porch and hamburgers;
                   secrets we promised to take with us
to the grave. I'm writing them down, Edith. Filling a Mason jar.
                   Filling it full like a mouth of light.
Putting it into the ground where it belongs, with the sound
                   of someone else's ribs breaking beneath
the weight of my hands. At night, I'm still relearning
                   where my hands go, on the shapes
of a stranger's body when I try to sleep.

Eve Strillacci

Superstition

I used to hold my breath as cemeteries
reeled past, their bright statuary gleaming

through the picture frame of the Toyota's
windows, a florid jungle, replete with curling

fleurs de lis, the dark tendrils of a mourner's
hair stitching sorrow into the quilted morning.

Don't breathe, kids warned, *or they'll suck
your breath*, but it was awe that sealed

my chest like a canopic jar, the preservation
of wonder: The graceful stones pressed up

from the earth like teeth, ossified arches
bowed like the backs of saints, and somehow

the graveyard always seemed to me
the vast skeleton of a man, picked clean,

in hallowed ground where we laid our giants
to rest beneath an orbiting mobile of vultures.

Years later, watching crosses stream by,
I searched for a giant in the foothills

of the Blue Ridge Mountains, sensed his eyes
on me, hungry and sharp. *Fee fi fo fum,*

he hummed, or maybe it was only traffic, but
I was on my way to my father's, already late,

trying to recall the other reasons not to trust
what's beautiful. *Feed us,* the dead cried,

but I held my breath all the way to Greensboro,
where the sweet air, studded with pollen,

cast a gauze over my eyes, and the bees waded
through it, smelling of sea salt and honey.

Eve Strillacci

Patrick Kane Dreams
a Night Garden With Wild Horses

Not one of the horses knows his name,
he is sure of it, but he hears
in their thunder shared syllables, and he hears
stems snapping under hoof, a bone garden
powdered with the marrow of sorrow. Name

it *next year*, huff the horses,
call it *snow moon, hunger moon,*
stiff season of blue wind and ice.
He skates the dream into home ice,
drags furrows for planting: here

iceberg bulbs into nebulous moons,
here snow peas in shallow graves. He gardens
while the puck teases the horses
to run, rink air stirring their manes
into ridges he will not name,

knowing only the spine of ice
that rises like a brand on the flank of a horse
when he stops just so, pausing here
and there to admire his glorious garden,
fruits hanging like ripe little moons

waiting to be plucked, moaning
their ripeness—it sounds like his name,
as if his body were a garden,

limbs the rivers running to it, ice in their voices,
ice the place on the map reading "You are here."

Where are you racing to? ask the horses.
To the cup, he answers, and the horses
see that to him the puck's a dark moon,
dowsing light as it travels a heroic
journey over the north, renaming

the continents Shadow and Ice,
tilling dreams' dense soil for a garden.
In this garden, the hero buries
ice in the ground so the moon will rise: dark cup
of proud voices, the namelessness of horses.

Alex Mattingly

Alfred, Lord Pennyduck

After he showed up in the tub when Benton went for bedtime bath, an emergency Council of Cousins was called and we took a Unanimous Opinion Vote. Before my family left Michigan for home, the Council decreed we would dismember and distribute Alfred, Lord Pennyduck into trash Dumpsters all across Carleton.

Lord Pennyduck was a twenty-five-year-old stuffed and stitched mallard, Uncle Gene's first try at Grandad's trade. Lord Pennyduck had no legs, and his body was stuffed in a peculiar way so his neck and tail was all bulgy, and his belly was all small. He had raggy feathers and his beak was broke open at ninety degrees, which everybody knows is the worst way. But even worse than that was his eyes.

Uncle Gene took a long while to learn how to taxidermy eyes, how to pluck the little jelly globes and replace them with glass. Lord Pennyduck got it real bad. When Uncle Gene tried to take his eyes he crushed them all up, and the sockets broke out huge, too big for the glass eyes he was supposed to use.

"So I glued on pennies," Uncle Gene explained, any chance he could. "Good as new."

It was not good as new. Nothing about the duck was good. The duck was evil and hate and fear and it gave us every goose bump we ever had. We messed up telling that to Uncle Gene. That same night after we told him, Alfred, Lord Pennyduck turned up in my pillowcase.

Then he got everywhere, that bird, at all the worst times. After a whole year of it, we couldn't stand it hardly ever again.

Benton and I were at this time detectives. Nobody paid us, but we got good at figuring clues out of gum wrappers, cigarette butts, and flickering porch lights, and we had our shows to watch so we learned more. It made sense the Council picked us to find the duck.

"I want his head," said my sister Natalie. "You do what you want with the rest of him."

"We have to find him first," said Benton. He was right, that was the main thing. We'd thought before to try and hide him, stick him in a sack and stash him in the crawl space or something, but none of us knew where he lived. Alfred, Lord Pennyduck would just appear, and then we screamed, and then Uncle Gene came bounding into the room, giggling and sweeping up the mallard and running away again, and we got so wound up we'd just tear each other up.

"I can't believe you screamed," Janie said, after the bathtub incident. "That was our big chance."

"You screamed last time, Bozo butt."

"I wouldn't have screamed this time, ya pansy. It was so obvious."

"Well, thanks for the warning, Paul Revere."

"Quit it," said Natalie. "This is the oldest trick in the book. Split and conquer. We have to stick together."

Janie and Benton glared another minute, then pinky hooked. "Agreed."

We listed hiding spots, ranked by danger. Uncle Gene and Aunt Patty's closet was low on the list—we weren't allowed in their room, but we snuck in there every year at Thanksgiving to peek at unwrapped Christmas presents, and if we got caught the worst we got was a thump on the butt and chased out.

More dangerous was the trunk of Uncle Gene's Celebrity. We weren't allowed to play in the car, so we wouldn't get heat stroke and die, or kick it in neutral and roll into the street. That would get a few swats and no TV, and you got real embarrassed when you cried after the swats in front of your sister and cousins. You probably wouldn't want to play the whole rest of the night.

Second Biggest Danger was the underwear drawer, where Uncle Gene kept his naked girl magazines; that one time Benton saw by mistake and he had to wash his eyes out with soap and got spanked and had to go to church four times that week. I asked what the naked girls looked like and Benton said he wished he didn't even know, and I believed him because gross.

But the Number One Big Danger on the list was the garage where Uncle Gene practiced on dead animals and where he kept his power tools and propane and had his own private fridge that Benton said was nothing but beer. Benton got spanked just for touching the padlock on the garage. If we got caught in there, I didn't even know what, but it would definitely be the end of our careers, and probably our spy case with the magnifying glass and the baby powder for fingerprints would get taken away forever. And probably Benton and I would never even see each other again, which would be the worst, even if it meant I also wouldn't ever see Alfred, Lord Pennyduck.

You don't leave your cousin alone to live a life with Alfred, Lord Pennyduck. You just can't.

Since we had all the training, it would be me and Benton to go in the garage. But we needed help. We had to be sure not to get caught. So that's why Natalie and Janie had to come up with the best distraction of all time, and fast—my family only had the one more day in Michigan. After that, there wouldn't be enough of us to do even one single thing about Lord Pennyduck.

Janie planned that it had to happen at dinner.

"Everybody has to be all together for the snakes," she said. "It makes maximum chaos."

We figured out to do the distraction at dinner, and we figured out to do snakes, because Natalie and Janie weren't scared of them and knew about a secret nest of where they lived.

Dinner was the four of us kids and all four adults, Mom and Dad and Uncle Gene and Aunt Patty. Uncle Gene was making his famous chili. It really was famous—it was in the Carleton United Methodist Church Cookbook three years in a row, right at the beginning of the second section, "Stews and Chilies." We all sat down in front of empty bowls, the table set with cheddar cheese and oyster crackers and hot sauce and sour cream. There was also yogurt, but that was by Mom, because she's the only one that likes it so she gets it to herself.

"Hope you're hungry," Uncle Gene said from the kitchen, ducking so he could look at us through the space over the sink and under the cupboards. We heard the wooden spoon clang against the pot and I looked at Janie and she just nodded real slow, her hands under the table where she had her backpack full of snakes. You couldn't tell if you didn't listen, but real quiet she was unzipping the bag, and me and Benton got ready. Janie's the best snake catcher you ever saw because she thinks they're pretty, and Natalie was ready to scream real good and knock things off the table and Make Matters Worse.

We'd already sneaked the garage padlock key from the junk drawer and not got caught by anybody. Benton had it in his T-shirt pocket.

Uncle Gene came in with the pot, one hand on the lid and the other holding a big towel against the bottom.

"Soup's on," he said, and pulled off the lid, and we all screamed and screamed and couldn't stop because Alfred, Lord Pennyduck popped out of the chili pot and crashed into Benton's bowl.

"For Christ's sake, Gene," said Mom, who was his sister and got away with cussing at him. Then she looked at her feet. "What ... oh Jesus!"

Mom kicked away from the table and fell backwards off her chair from where the snakes were loose. Dad, Uncle Gene, and Aunt Patty noticed them next, and Dad and Aunt Patty screamed while Uncle Gene jumped up onto a barstool. Benton grabbed the duck, and I was still screaming and my sisters were still screaming and maybe even Benton was still screaming but he had the duck, and so me and him ran like hell, out the kitchen and down the steps and then right out the door.

It took us awhile to catch our breath. We ran all the way to the park and hid in the trees on the far side of the creek, which you can cross if you know the right stones, which only me and Benton do.

"Had to spring-load that duck," said Benton, panting. "He had to of."

"You got our spy case?"

Benton shook his head. In our hurry, neither of us remembered. We sat there awhile, deep in the woods, telling each other what poison ivy looked like so we wouldn't get too much a dose, and after a minute we were sure nobody followed us. On a patch of leaves and dirt between us was Lord Pennyduck.

"Guess we should smash it up," I said.

Benton looked real serious. "Dad fixes stuff up all the time. Remember when Janie kicked Lord Pennyduck across the room and his beak came off? We could break him in a million pieces and he'll get stitched back together."

"So what do we do?"

My cousin frowned. "Hafta burn it up, I think."

Made sense, I figured, and then I got mad again we forgot the spy case. We kept a box of matches in it, even though we're not supposed to, because we saw on TV once how a detective burned up a secret letter because his client was guilty, but beautiful. That taught us a thing about justice and the law, and how sometimes they aren't the same thing.

"Maybe Janie will think of that," I said. "Or Natalie. Maybe they can figure out where we are."

Benton didn't say anything, because we both knew how that wouldn't happen, but we could both hope awhile that it would.

Then a whole while passed, and it was starting to get fireflies out, and we knew we'd have to go back soon.

"I should leave now," I said, "maybe get the spy case and get back without them seeing me. Maybe they're still chasing snakes."

Benton glanced around the woods, where it gets night extra early. "You'll need an escort."

"We can't take the duck," I said. "Uncle Gene will take it back."

"Can't leave it here," said Benton. "Dog'll get it. Or a coyote. And if it disappears, you know what happens. It'll come back. It always comes back."

Benton was right. We knew a thing or two by then about Lord Pennyduck and how it was an evil thing. We knew, too, how an evil thing can always find you again, when it wants to.

"So we go back all three of us," I said, and neither one of us wanted that to be true but we both knew it was. Benton took up the duck and we started back toward the creek, back along the stones. The secret is you don't step on the big gray middle one that looks like Montana, cause it's always got a green moss that makes you slip and roll your ankle. If you step wrong, you're Done For.

Benton hid out with Alfred, Lord Pennyduck on the far side of the garage, so he couldn't be seen if someone looked out the kitchen window. He still had the key, and there was all that gasoline, but before he snuck in for it we had to know the coast was clear. Otherwise we'd get cornered, and then it would be Curtains.

I came up to the house from the side that's got no windows because it's real close to the neighbors. With the metal fence there Uncle Gene can't even fit through with the mower, so it's just weeds and the garden hose. I figured I could get real close to the house that way, then crawl around and peek in the windows and find out where everybody was, just so I didn't walk into a big mess.

The front door was open, I saw, but nobody was holding it. I guessed they thought some last snakes was still inside and would go out on their own. I got up close enough I could listen, but I didn't hear talking, and then I saw a car was gone from the driveway. That meant at least one grown-up was gone, and maybe more, because they were unpredictable. The fewer the better.

Uncle Gene keeps some matches in the same junk drawer where Benton got the key, and I wished he thought up this idea sooner about the fire. We could have been more prepared. But it was my fault too, because I forgot our kit, and because we're a team.

I still didn't hear any talking, so I got up the courage to get low and peek around the bottom of the door. You can see the staircase and through the front hall into the kitchen, and after that it's a straight shot through to the back door. If I was fast, even if I got spotted I could get out, I thought. But I still didn't want to get seen.

I moved in slowly and hunched down like I was doing my old man impersonation, which cracks everybody up. I peeked around the door frame and still didn't see anybody, but that close up I thought I could hear somebody talking upstairs, our sisters, maybe, sent to their room for the snakes. Whoever got in that car probably went to look for me and Benton, or, if it was Uncle Gene, to look for Lord Pennyduck.

I took off my shoes because the floors are wood and I could skate along quietly that way. I shh-shhhed my way down the front hall, where there was nobody, and into the kitchen. You can see in the kitchen just a little, under the cupboards and over the sink, but obviously you can't see a lot or we'd have seen the duck go in the pot. I got real low and crawled along until I got to the drawer. I checked all around, and nobody was there so I reached up and slow as I could pulled the drawer open.

"Come here, kid," said Uncle Gene. He must have been still at the dinner table, which I couldn't see in my crawl. I don't know how he heard me. I was in full stealth mode.

I froze. The I heard a chair slide back from the table, and I took off running toward the front door, since it was still open, but Uncle Gene was faster and he snagged me by the shirt.

"You got the duck," he said. I nodded.

"You don't like the duck," he said. I nodded again.

Then we stood a while, Uncle Gene maybe trying to think of more questions, and me trying to think of escape. Finally he sighed and pulled me into the living room, kind of pushing me toward the couch in a way that didn't knock me down but could have if he meant it more. I knew I was supposed to sit, so I did.

"I want to introduce you to somebody," he said, and then he went back toward the dining room and got a box up from where he'd been sitting. I could have run again, but Uncle Gene was so fast, and if he came outdoors he might look around and find Benton. Plus I wanted to see who was in the box, even if it was snakes. I don't mind snakes.

Uncle Gene came back in and he sat next to me and he set the box on the coffee table. I waited for him to open it, but he didn't. Then he slapped it with his palm, and told me to take a look.

I pulled up the flaps. Inside was, well, I didn't know. It was a taxidermied something. It was a chicken, I figured, but instead of a head or a neck on top there was like a little alligator face, maybe a caiman. I know some reptiles, that's how I know about caimans, which are like little small alligators and I think they'd be a good pet.

I took it out of the box and Uncle Gene scooted away a little bit. I saw all the hairs on his arm go up and his face got real pale like he might get sick.

"That," said Uncle Gene, "is Crocadoodle."

"What's Crocadoodle?"

"One part little crocodile, one part rooster," he said. "You know who made that?"

"You?" I asked, though I could tell he didn't like it.

He shook his head. "My dad made that for me. I was five years old. He always wanted me in the business, and thought that might get my attention. I liked unicorns, but he couldn't taxidermy a whole horse for me, not just for a birthday present, so he made up a mythological animal and that's what I got."

I pushed my finger against the different teeth, and petted its rough skin nose. "It's very beautiful," I said, and I meant it.

"Scared the shit out of me," he said. "My dad didn't like when I cried. Said, Crocadoodle will toughen you up. Then he took it back, and I got him again for Christmas, and my birthday, then Christmas again, every year like that, until one day I didn't cry, and he got proud of me."

I didn't understand how he could be afraid of something so perfect. It wasn't missing any legs and it didn't have pennies or quarters or anything for eyes but what was supposed to be there and it was like a miraculous wonderment from God.

I cradled Crocadoodle a minute, then looked at Uncle Gene. "It still scares you."

"Sure does."

"But. OK. So you know how we get scared, but you still scare us. You should know better."

He moved a pillow from behind his back and put it between him and me. "I got to know, Michael. I got to know how old before you don't get scared. My whole life I wondered, was it normal to be scared so long? Of something like that? Is it normal to still get scared of it, even a little? So what it is, I got to see how old you are when you stop being scared, you and Benton and Janie and Natalie. If we're all the same, or if there really is something bad or wrong in me."

"But you should stop scaring us."

He got real quiet, and then just whispered, "I got to know."

This was worse. This was worse than getting scared and him laughing, because before I thought he was just stupid, but now I thought he was mean. I guess he could see I was trying not to cry like a big pansy, because of what he said next.

"But even though I got to know," he said, "I can make it a little more fair. I'm giving that to you. You take me out to get the duck, and I give you Crocadoodle to do with as you wish. You turn me down, I take back Crocadoodle and hide him so good, and then I make another duck, meaner and uglier than Lord Pennyduck, and you got nothing."

"That's my only choice?"

"That's your only choice."

I carried Crocadoodle in its box and led my uncle out to where Benton was hiding. Benton did not expect my betrayal, so he was relaxed at first when he saw me, and then Uncle Gene came around the corner a little behind and before Benton could run my uncle grabbed him around the waist and picked him straight up. With the other hand he retrieved Alfred, Lord Pennyduck.

"You tell him the deal," he said to me, and then he set Benton back down on the ground and went to go back inside. I told Benton everything he'd said, and then I regretted it, because nobody wants to hear what his own dad gets scared of.

"Fine," said Benton, and he spat on the garage. "Let me see this stupid thing."

I set down the box and peeled up the flaps. Benton tried to look mad and mean but you just can't look that way at Crocadoodle, because he does something to you on account of his beautiful nature.

"Dad's afraid of this? This is a miraculous wonderment."

"That's just what I thought," I said. "Word to word."

"We talked how we should get a Doberman," said Benton, and I remembered how we saw sometimes good detectives have guard dogs or Animal Partnerships. "But I think this is better."

I agreed. And then we talked awhile about our plans, and we talked awhile about grown-ups, and we gave Crocadoodle a secret name to make him ours, and if I could tell you it I would, because it is a name that fits so well, and if I could tell you I think you would agree that the secret name that made him ours was just, exactly, perfect.

Meg Eden

The Excavation

When my father ripped out the hallway,
he found a snakeskin stretched over the door.
I can't help but think of Passover and how
once, fathers protected their doorways
in blood, so no angel could mistake them
for being anything but chosen.

Instead of lambs, we get serpent
tempters. For being Gentiles.
And while those first lambs had no desire
to be slain, this snake chose to shed
what he could not cling to, which Jim
Elliott once said is far from foolish.

As Dad pulls out the skin, I wonder
where the snake is now, if he hears
my lusts under the bedroom floor, or if
he sustains my kitchen gluttony. But I know
that even if all the walls were split open,
his body would never be found.

At night, I listen to the creaks that come
from inside the walls. I say a whispered
prayer, as a covering above my head.

Cynthia Marie Hoffman

[I sing the alphabet]

I sing the alphabet because there is a needlework of the alphabet in the nursery and the baby seems to be looking at it. Because it is written into the song, I ask the baby to sing along. When will I feel like a mother? The baby looks at the light that hangs from the center of the ceiling like a bellflower. I ask her what does she see. She bats at my wrist with her open hand, a little sound of smacking skin. Her eyes are a clear gray and do not divulge their intentions. What does the willow say to the wind, wobbling its branches at the air? What says the wind, stroking the snow across the lake? All day, I carry her up and down the stairs. I feed her. I wipe her skin with cotton. I rock and sway and shift her. I am biding my time for something recognizable, something studied and willful to break from her open mouth, perfectly formed, to declare me who I am. Until we speak, we are merely creatures. The cat who sits on the nursery floor and stares at me hard.

Hali Fuailelagi Sofala

Clearing

Back then, when I never thought of myself as a girl,
I spent long days clearing brush, skinning
thin branches from trees,

my father cutting the wilder paths
and me, machete in hand,
whacking whatever was left behind.

My sisters were too small-bodied
for the job and whined whenever
brought out to the far acres.

I was the only one of the three
that laced up my work boots regularly,
the only one that welcomed the bite

of heat in the clamp-jaw of July.
And I remember waking one night—
my arm and shoulder throbbing

with a burn that would turn
to the most delicious soreness by dawn.
My father awake too but silent,

flipping through 3 a.m. rugby matches.
I remember thumbing the lid of a pill bottle—
the thing wthat had brought me out in the first place—

and deciding to put it aside instead.
And I sat with my father until morning,
pain strumming down the skein of our bodies,

both of us unwilling to give it language.
Unwilling to admit we were anything
but real men.

Hali Fuailelagi Sofala

Answering

It happens just once at your first job
when you've been pulled from the seclusion
of the box office to guard the ticket line
while the boys clean the cleared-out theater.
The crowd of kids there to see the show
push up to the velvet rope, crane their necks
so they can see down the hall—tired of waiting.
It only takes one girl, the leader of her clique,
to shout out from the crowd: *Are you a boy or a girl?*
It only takes one giggle before it's infectious
and suddenly every teenage mouth is split in a grin,
laughter erupting, the sound spewing onto
whatever you are. And you blame the bow tie
that you have to wear and the vest that fits tight
across your chest, leveling the small mounds
of your breasts; you blame the darkness
of the corridor that stops them from seeing
the ribbon you tie in your ponytail to prevent
events such as these—always dropping clues
for strangers. You blame your body for failing
to be frail and small and feminine. And you stand
there for a long time never speaking and for years
you blame your whole self for staying silent, for letting
them see you cry, for having to answer at all.

Matthew Vollmer

Academy Girls

after Rick Moody

And then there were the girls: girls we loved, girls we liked, girls we loathed, girls we were not—under any circumstances—to touch. Girls short, girls tall, girls round, girls slim, girls in between. Girls Korean, girls Mexican, girls Guatemalan and Filipino, girls black and Indian and white. Girls with glasses, orthodonture, droopy eyelids, thin lips, knee braces, faces birthmarked by port wine stains. Girls with curls, with bobs and braids, with cascading sheets of long and lustrous hair, with boyish Peter Pan-like cuts and bangs that obscured their vision. Girls reed-thin, girls lumpy, girls unendowed.

But also: girls who lived their lives inside voluptuous, fully-grown-women-shaped bodies. Girls with thick lips and spaces between their teeth. Girls angel-voiced. Girls wheezy. Girls afraid, girls shy, girls forward and backward and long-legged and jerky.

Girls signing papers, pledging to uphold the rules, promising never to cheat or haze or steal or gamble or possess incendiaries or listen to rock music or smoke cigarettes or drink alcohol or do drugs or wear jewelry or use profane language or undermine the denomination's beliefs or disrespect faculty or engage in improper social conduct or meet in a deliberately planned and secretive manner or toy with the occult or enter buildings by any other means than their regular entrances or conspire to degrade others or destroy school property or ride in unauthorized vehicles or leave campus, ever, without proper permission.

Girls partnering with us in chemistry, fixing the errors in our calculations—we who failed to solve for X or to remember essential elements of the periodic table. Girls in Bible class pretending to be our fiancées, computing the costs of our fake future weddings, so that we'd be taught pragmatic lessons about what we might be getting into, so that we wouldn't try to go too far too fast. Girls rushing to P.E., changing into gym shorts and T-shirts, lifting miniature barbells while "Eye of the Tiger" blasted from the gymnasium speakers. Girls taking notes in anatomy, on anatomy, laughing at *coccyx* and *gluteus maximus* and *latissimus dorsi*. Girls daydreaming, drowsing while rain smattered panes. Girls drooling, but only a little. Girls leaning over desks, whispering messages, their warm breath on our necks, our ears. Girls asking dumb questions, asking better ones than we ever could. Girls getting As and Bs and Cs and Ds. Girls failing. Girls promising parents they would do better. Girls raising hands, asking for help. Girls buckling down.

Girls taking breaks, taking it easy, playing foosball and footsie and basketball. Girls totally juking us. Girls shooting granny-style in games of H-O-R-S-E. Girls laughing and losing and winning. Girls trash-talking. Girls making faces, sticking out tongues. Girls—much to our collective delight—hooking their feet around their heads and rolling across gym mats, inspiring us to say *whoa*. Girls inflexible, refusing to move or be moved. Girls on the sidelines, cheering for us as we engaged in intramural sport— never interscholastic, because competition was dangerous and could lead to inflated egos and Satanic self-importance. Or, more likely, and more frequently: girls totally ignoring us. Girls playing paper, rock, scissors with each other. Girls piggybacking on other girls' backs, riding best friends from one place to the next. Girls flipping pages of fashion magazines, thinking, *Oh, that's cute* and *Mm, I want that.* Girls spending way too much time determining their next day's outfits, not to impress us, necessarily—or ever—but because they wanted to look good, their absolute best. Girls in all black. Girls in paisley. Girls in boots. Girls borrowing clothes they'd never return. Girls losing underwear. Girls with shoulder pads and girls without, girls who got away with wearing makeup and those who were asked by their deans to wash the paint from their faces. Girls shaving their legs and pits and—in some cases—upper lips. Girls in big, baggy cable-knit sweaters. Girls in tank tops. Girls in their boyfriends' jackets, hats, sweatshirts, trench coats. Girls poor, girls rich. Girls wearing Liz Claiborne pantsuits, worrying that Liz Claiborne contributed frequently to the Church of Satan, and that wearing Liz Claiborne endorsed, if inadvertently, the Prince of Darkness.

Girls rolling their eyes.

Girls working hard, girls hardly working: for extra cash, to pay off their bills, and because they had no choice, because everyone at the academy worked, because Christians must learn to serve happily and often, and idle hands were—or so it was understood—the Devil's playthings.

Christians must learn to serve happily and often, and idle hands were—or so it was understood—the Devil's playthings. And so: girls serving in cafeteria lines, washing dishes and trays, cursing those who'd pooled leftover lunches of lentil loaf and mashed potatoes and peas and carrots and packed the resultant sludge tight into juice glasses. And so: girls at the dish station firing shots of hot water at offenders. And also: girls on their knees, weeding flowerbeds, scrubbing floors. Girls—the lucky ones—soldering the wings of stained-glass hummingbirds at the campus' stained glass factory. Girls grading quizzes for the Spanish teacher (a mustachioed young man whose unselfconscious enthusiasm for all things Spanish inspired swooning) and tests for the English teacher (a white-haired lady whose sun-worship had granted her flesh a distinctly raisin-like texture) and exams for the math instructor (a greasy-haired fellow who, while standing in the cafeteria line, would open his mouth and, like a snake preparing to swallow an egg, lower his jaw, and, with his tongue, dislodge his partial, a set of four porcelain teeth, stained and spit-slickened, which he clicked from his mouth to his hand).

Girls thinking: *Gross.*

Girls thinking: *Gag.*

Girls thinking, *If I don't hurry I'm gonna be late to class.*

Girls passing notes to us in hallways and cafeteria lines, answering letters delivered by other girls from those of us who were desperate to be theirs. Girls who had never been available, who would always have boyfriends who were not and would never be us. Girls whose names we'd scrawled in the margins of our notebooks, on the surfaces of our defaced desks, the letter sequences tried out for size, for eternity. Girls we hoped—but never prayed—to kiss before Jesus returned and ferried us away to a sexless paradise or left us here on Earth, to be consumed by fire for having so frequently and unabashedly employed these unkissed girls in our private fantasies, casting them in roles they would have turned down in a heartbeat, would have been mortified to have played, if only hypothetically. Girls saying "yes" and "maybe" and "no thank you" to invitations to events our school referred to as "banquets," where, because our denomination frowned upon rock music and dancing and flesh foods, we pinned foul-smelling corsages to girls' dresses and rode buses to local hotel conference rooms, to eat vegetarian lasagna and drink flutes of sparkling grape juice and bask in the non-offensive light of G-rated movies. Girls riding beside us afterwards, hopefully in the dark, or behind seatbacks tall enough that we could slink below the sightlines of rearview mirrors.

Girls rushing back to their dorms to undress, to don pajamas and gossip, to tell tales about our failures and successes, how we slipped them the tongue, let them unbutton our slacks. Girls peeling back the lip of a turtleneck, revealing a hickey in the shape of the United Kingdom. Girls wide-eyed. Girls jealous. Girls like *so* grossed out. Girls requesting other girls to stop talking, for real, because they absolutely had to finish their geometry homework. Girls slinking away.

Girls hungry! Girls who missed having kitchens and who, given the chance, would have liked nothing more than to bake a tray of brownies and serve them to their friends and families, with sides of popcorn and apples and root beer floats. Girls eating hot noodles with chopsticks. Girls stuffing beach towels under doors so other girls wouldn't complain about the smell of kimchi made by Korean grandmothers—old bent women who dipped their pizza slices in ketchup and, upon finding pictures of their granddaughters with their arms around white boys, tore them to shreds. Girls sad.

Girls devouring entire boxes of Little Debbie Swiss Cake Rolls, to fill the void, to fill their stomachs, to lose themselves in the thought-obliterating joy of consumption. Girls gazing into mirrors, thinking *I'm gross* and *I'm fat* and *No way, I am not breaking out right now* and *No boy will ever like me.* Girls panicking. Girls sticking fingers down throats. Girls—girls who you'd never in a million years think would—throwing up discreetly and often. Girls smiling, pretending nothing's wrong. Girls calling home, missing parents, shedding tears, wanting to leave, wanting to stay.

Girls adjusting.

Girls not.

Girls inventorying their contraband, trading Dr. Pepper for Diet Coke and Metallica for Bell Biv DeVoe and Marlboros for fantasy novels and earrings for mood rings. Girls striking matches after lights-out, tossing flames into sinks, watching them sputter and burn. Girls restless, wanting to do something fun. Girls peeing in the sinks of their rooms because—no joke—they were too lazy to walk down the hall. Girls rinsing. Girls spraying peach air freshener. Girls running—for shits and giggles—topless down corridors before lights -out, shaking their boobs in the faces of other girls and asking them if they liked it. Girls pouring conditioner into a sleeping friend's hair, shaving cream into a sleeping friend's hand. Girls resetting alarm clocks, staying up, watching other towel-wrapped girls shuffle, at 3 a.m., to the showers. Girls sneaking out of the window in their friend's ground-floor room—a window that, unlike any others they'd tested, opened all the way. Girls giggling. Girls lighting cigarettes, coughing, imploring each other to *Shut up, you wanna get busted?* Girls navigating darkness. Girls knocking heads against knots in low-hanging tree branches. Girls thinking they heard something, saw something, felt something. Girls spooked. Girls returning to rooms, hearts beating wild and fast. Girls relieved.

Girls playing the flute. Girls in white gloves ringing handbells. Girls singing.

Girls teaching us new songs with complicated hand gestures, crooning about panting deer and living water and the redemptive properties of the blood of the lamb. Girls harmonizing. Girls praising God, girls lifting Him up! Girls testifying. Girls standing beneath stage lights holding microphones, claiming to have given up alcohol and drugs and rock music and the occult, explaining what God had done in their lives, how he'd touched their hearts and made them whole. Girls who'd been reading their Bibles—like really reading them, for the first time—and could now see the errors of their ways. Girls nodding, girls closing their eyes. Girls frowning, to signal that they got it, that what had been said was of the utmost importance.

Girls in their beds, alone in the dark. Girls—those who had promised not to touch themselves—touching themselves. Girls escaping. Girls feeling good, then great, then bad. Girls brimming with anguish. Girls not knowing where to turn but to the Lord. Girls turning away. Girls saying one thing and doing another. Girls in love. Girls devising plans. Girls falling for those of whom their mothers would never approve, white boys and black boys and boys with lazy eyes, boys dull and drab and dangerous. Girls cheating. Girls worrying about blemishes and the numbers on their scales, about tan lines because we told them we preferred bodies without them. Girls tanning topless at the old airstrip. Girls sunburned, peeling dead skin from their breasts in garish strips.

Girls sending us treats during Pony Express, the nights when dorms exchanged letters: Hallmark cards, M&Ms, photos of themselves, gift bags containing candy and notes and Duran Duran cassingles. Girls writing, "I love you" at the ends of their letters and meaning it, or "Love ya," without thinking and certainly not meaning it, but fueling our hopes nonetheless. Girls reserving spaces in yearbooks, writing "Reserved for" in the white spaces reserved for autographs, followed by their names, then drawing a box, a border that signified that space as theirs, and nobody wrote in that space out of spite, nobody took these spaces they'd claimed. Girls employing—without abandon—the exclamation point. Girls finding all the pictures in which they'd appeared, even if—and especially if—their faces were only one blurry circle in a photo of a hundred others, and signing their names as if the letters were sprouting from their heads. Senior girls revealing favorite memories ("Ski trip '89!" "Staying up late with Paige!"), pet peeves ("Granddaddy longlegs," "Sloppy lipstick," "my wrists being touched"), favorite sayings ("I'm not conceited but I have every right!"), and secret ambitions ("To become the world's best wife and mother … when I'm ready, that is!"). Girls wanting to express themselves, to be understood, to communicate affection without being misinterpreted, wanting to flirt without us getting the wrong idea, wanting to play, wanting to hang out and laugh, wanting to sit by us on bus rides without us—just for once—trying something.

Girls wanting it. Girls wanting it bad, feeling bad for wanting it. Girls looking this way and that, to see if the coast is clear, to make sure no faculty were in sight. Girls kissing us quickly with mouths closed or (so dangerous!) with mouths open, slipping us tongues, letting us slide our hands under their shirts to sample the miraculous softness beneath. Girls—the brazen, the brave—with their hands in our jeans. Girls exclaiming, "Oh!" Girls wary. Girls reclining on beaches during senior trips, on beds in bedrooms during home leaves. Girls thinking and girls saying, *Maybe we shouldn't be doing this.* Girls saying, *OK.* Girls worrying. Girls assuring themselves. Girls coming and girls going. Girls who—it was said by people who claimed to know, people who had heard from reliable sources—were nymphos. Girls who'd given blow jobs in the equipment room of the gymnasium, hand jobs in the back of school vans. Girls who could describe exactly to other girls the shape of a boy's penis. Girls who couldn't believe what they'd heard.

Girls waiting for periods. Girls anticipating bad—in fact, the worst possible—news. Girls making promises to God. Girls losing their minds. Girls finger-painting self-portraits as creepy clowns. Girls writing us incomprehensible letters, referring to what we had done in veiled and symbolic language and saying, no, no, no, never, never again. Girls saying, "Don't worry … you'll be better off without me." Girls assuring us that everything would be OK, even when—especially when—it wouldn't. Girls lying. Girls apologizing. Girls telling us we had no idea. That no matter what happened, please know one thing: We were so, so special. Girls promising to write, pledging we'd be friends forever. Girls wishing they could be ours. Girls assuring us that someday, we would make someone very happy. Girls with sad faces waving good-bye, good-bye—to us, their biggest fans.

And us waving back, we who were—as always—so very sad to see them go.

Jody Reale

There's No Telling

I was going to kill Lou. That's what I told him anyway, just moments before he started wiggling his little nub of a tail, head cocked, ears up. "No, you little shit," I told him, slapping my hand over my eyes, "I said I was going to kill you, not feed you a steak, you damn mutt." I stalked off to the linen closet, mumbling under my breath, trying to decide what to do with a dog skilled beyond his species in knowing how to make me so mad that my brains melt and ooze out of my ears.

That was the night that Lou had decided to sneak up onto the bed, which was—and still is—strictly verboten because of a certain pesky habit of his. When left without an activity for more than a few moments, Lou decides to worry his paws, chewing on himself until either a family member intervenes, or some unsuspecting stranger has the nerve to ring the doorbell. And so he had slinked that night, unnoticed, onto the bed, to perform the extended dance remix of such a session. He had to have been up there forever—the length of one Allman Brothers song, at least—long enough for every ounce of saliva in existence to soak through a down comforter, two flannel sheets and a mattress pad to the mattress, which is probably still wet today. It was nine o'clock by the time I discovered the invisible mess. Actually, my feet discovered it, the moment I sunk them down to the bottom of the bed, and plunked them right into the cold slime Lou left behind.

It was late at night for me. I was pregnant and cranky from commuting for two an hour each way to and from work. Ordinarily I would have flipped the mattress and changed the bedding without blinking, but that night I sank to the floor, sobbing and cursing our spotted friend with the offending paws and the saliva glands that had just deposited the volumetric equivalent of the Dead Sea right there in our bedroom.

"Hey," Alex said, quoting the immortal lyrics from a Frankie Goes to Hollywood song, "relax. Don't do it." He added, "Let's just put a towel over it and go to bed." He told me it would be OK, that it was like, "a little ecosystem down there." Think of it. The flora, the fauna! Our own little indoor Everglades; it would be romantic. "I've always wanted to sleep in Biosphere Lou." I said bitterly. But I changed the sheets anyway, and skipped all the flipping and fussing and fighting, and I vowed to kill the smiling mongrel some other time. "To think I rescued the little bastard," I said.

Lou came from a town of fewer than a thousand people in south-central Colorado called San Luis. It's Colorado's oldest surviving settlement, founded in 1851, just off the New Mexico border along the Sangre de Cristo mountain range. More than 25 percent of the population lives in poverty, and the county unemployment rate hovers around two or three points higher than the state average. I met Lou there in 1998 while my parents and I were visiting my older sister, Gayle, and her husband, Don, who had moved there a few years earlier from the Bay area.

At that time, his name was Dingo. "He's a purebred blue heeler," Gayle told me. I eyed his black-and-white spotted coat, the complete absence of blue markings, and suspected he was mixed up with some other breed or two. "A rancher offered us good money for him as a working dog. He's bred to herd." He was two or three months old and untouchable. He darted away from all my random acts of friendliness with his ears back and his body lowered almost to the ground, but like all puppies, there was something irresistible about him, and I made it my visit's mission to pet him at least once.

While I was gradually drawing him closer using a trail of hot dogs that led to the inside of my parents' RV, I asked one of Gayle's friends, a heavily tattooed man by the name of Chief, about Dingo's stub of a tail, and the stubs of tails that seemed to plague all the other dogs I'd seen there. "Everybody cuts off their dogs' tails," he said. After not a lot of probing, I learned that the job is usually carried out by the owner, with whatever's around that's sharp. There is anesthesia, but it's for the guy doing the axing, and it's usually a six pack and a joint.

It was the man in the trailer next door who had docked Dingo's tail with an axe, before handing him over in one kind of shady transaction or another.

There was an even more potent story about how Gayle's husband, Don, accidentally ran over Dingo with the car while backing out of the driveway. "His guts squished out his butt," someone told me. And then a friend, who was the EMT in town and who happened to be nearby, stuffed Dingo's intestines back inside his body and put an oxygen mask over his muzzle. "Saved his life," Gayle said, pointing to a dog that ran without a limp or any other sign of momentary or prolonged disembowelment.

These were the kinds of stories I heard in rapid succession over the next few days of meeting friends and neighbors, so that by the time I had been there two hours, I had no idea what to believe. Everything sounded like hallucinations. There was the story of a man who walked through a pit of angry rattlers, unharmed, because he had meditated and fasted for days beforehand. "He was in the zone," Don said, waving one hand in the air. There was some sort of home improvement project on the premises that took the form of materials all over the yard, the completion of which had been delayed long enough for weeds and thistles a yard tall to grow up through the chambers of the scattered cinderblocks. "I've got to put the pencil to that one," Don said, pointing to the splintered plywood and then staring into the middle distance. According to all sources, drinking and driving around town had been decriminalized; there were acres of free land to be had if you could prove you were of a certain ancestry, not that the land there isn't cheap. "You paid more for your car than I did for this house," Gayle said, at top volume, scratching and picking at the open wounds that covered her face. And if you needed dental work, you went just down the dirt road, where "a guy with a really good pair of pliers" would fix you right up. That last part I believed, since most of the people I met had what I call "summer teeth," as in, "some are here, some are there." I was retreating to the immaculate quarters of my parents' RV when someone asked where I was going. I pointed to my mouth and said, "To floss."

What interested me most—and what remains unsolved to this day—was the shooting two years earlier at an acquaintance's home that had claimed most of Gayle's right arm. Don was airlifted to one

Denver hospital, Gayle was rushed to another. No other witnesses were present, and nobody's stories matched. Even the police, who made no arrests that night, were unconcerned with the event. There were no investigations, no convictions, no questions asked.

There were miles and miles of nothing but sagebrush in San Luis, interrupted by piles of junk cars, abandoned trailers, and scrap metal. So much metal. If space aliens wanted to move the Earth, dangling a giant magnet over Costilla County would do the trick. And then there were the little living things that were also everywhere.

Dingo looked lean to me. It was a hot summer, and when I went to fill his food and water bowls, I couldn't find them. I asked for the Puppy Chow, but there wasn't any. I put out plastic bowls of food and water the four days we were there, much to his confusion. He backed himself into a corner under a rickety bench on the porch, and growled the day I surprised him during a nap. I laughed and said, "You come here, you little ferocious beast."

"You better be careful," my dad said. "He looks scared enough to bite. He's liable to grow up mean, that one."

I had adopted my first dog the previous year, a big one, and had stuffed him into my little townhome in Denver. I knew I was asking for trouble, but I couldn't help but fawn over Dingo with the missing tail and the cowering body language. He went to lie down under the old school bus inhabited by the gaggle of Gayle's friends who were passing through town on their way to the next installation of some show. It was hand-painted and adorned with a ship's mast and giant solar panels that Chief told me were purely ornamental. I met the young woman of the bus; she went by the name Wednesday and made her living making and selling hemp bracelets. She was soft-spoken and delicate and never drank anything but root beer during her visit. When Chief, Dusty, Wednesday, and Earth would eventually drive away to attend the next Dead show, Dingo would have to find shelter from the sun elsewhere. I begged Gayle to let me take him home with me.

"You hate dogs," I reminded her, and it was true; the one thing I knew about her was that animals had always frightened her, and her track record with them was as pocked as her skin, but she had lots of them anyway. The horses all had worms, the goat had been mauled to death by a pack of dogs, and the conspicuous absence of food and water for any of her animals made me want to either take them all home or put them all down. Even the garden area looked ravaged by some rogue band of vicious bugs, and there was trash and junk strewn everywhere. The whole landscape bore a resemblance to a late-night commercial in which a tearful actress implores you to consider setting aside thirteen cents a day.

"Oh, no," she said. "The baby would miss him too much." It was a story I almost believed, even though her son, I'll call him Jay, was only two. Gayle was pregnant with him the night she was shot, and I watched the boy and the dog, two survivors, run into the field together. They looked only joyous for each other's company, the puppy nipping the boy's bare heels to herd him across a field of dirt, felled barbed wire, and rusty nails. "He's a purebred cattle dog," she said. "A rancher offered us good money for him."

Somehow, a few days before we left, Dingo let me put my hands on him, and eventually hold him. He was filthy, and smelly like a Cheeto rolled in tuna carcasses. "Ugh, Jody!" Dad said again. "Don't kiss him. You're going to need antibiotics." I shared at least half of each meal with him, and by the end of my stay, Dingo trusted me enough to take a snooze on my lap. I rubbed and scratched him within an inch of his life, and everyone said, "It's a miracle," as if amputating an animal's body part shortly after he's born isn't really the ice-breaker it's cracked up to be.

The morning we left, I watched Gayle bully Wednesday out of what was probably her last ten dollars and my head started to ache. Before I got in the car to leave, I slipped Wednesday a twenty. With tears in her eyes, she gave me a hug that almost knocked me over. Minutes later, I looked out the rear window as we pulled away from the crumbling adobe home. There was Dingo, lying in the dirt, panting and darting his eyes every which way.

A week later, my mom called with news. I suspected some catastrophe, but instead she said only, "Dingo disappeared." I didn't respond; I only imagined young Dingo being lured into the dark by a coyote, or tangled up in a nest of rattlers, while he was most definitely outside of the zone. In my imagination he was stepping on every nail that had ever rusted; the highway wasn't far from the house. Anything could happen to a young dog like him. I thought of the fates that had befallen most of Gayle's other animals, and figured my hot dogs had gone to waste.

A few weeks later, Mom called again, this time to report that she'd spoken to Gayle again; Dingo had been living in town, and was found casually dining on garbage behind a restaurant. "Do you want him?" she asked.

Dingo arrived, skittish and far from house trained. He'd endured four hours in a car, and the moment he leapt from the back seat, he ran inside my parents' garage and let go with a stream of urine that could have dowsed the Great Chicago Fire. I took him home and, in some small act of distancing him from everything that had come before, changed his name to Lou.

I introduced him to my dog Boris, gave him a bath, and bought him the local PetsMart's entire inventory. He shook and shuddered through all of it, even his first walk in the park. Although he insisted on eating every stray turd on the ground, the only way to get him to eat dog food was to start feeding him by hand and then transition him to the bowl. Never having seen a collar or a leash before were cause for considerable alarm on his part; the ensuing bouts of bloody diarrhea were cause for alarm on mine. I bought ID tags that said "Mr. Lou Reale," took him to the vet for vaccinations and a checkup. I wrote on his questionnaire, "I don't know anything about this dog, except that he's terrified of everyone over the age of two." A side note: If a statement like that doesn't generate obscene amounts of sympathy from the staff, you've either accidentally walked into a slaughterhouse or the taxidermist's quarters.

Shortly after arriving, Lou began what I like to call his home renovation series, in which he "modified" my home drastically enough to warrant a deep discount by the time I decided to sell it. The trench he dug in the carpet from dining room to front door was my favorite, with chewing the length of one kitchen wall coming in a close second. The day he had his way with a couch cushion was the day I learned that it was best to hide my horror upon discovering these acts. Any outburst at all at these damaged goods, and Lou would loosen his bladder in fear right where he stood, so that not only did I have couch stuffing to clean up, but also a gallon of urine.

It took Lou six months to surrender himself entirely to a good petting, an act that revealed he is one big tickle spot. Any scratching at all yielded involuntarily leg spasms the likes of which resembled kick-starting a motorcycle. With his tongue flicking the air, his leg jiggling wildly, and the remains of his tail wriggling and squiggling, he became the modern major general of pleasure. His separation anxiety died down after the better part of a year, and after paying the veterinarian the equivalent of her student loan, so did his colitis. He stopped scratching holes in his own skin, but kept up with the paw licking, which I considered a considerable improvement as habits go.

And this is how it becomes clear to me the difference between me in my twenties and me in my thrities and beyond: During my twenties, I was thrilled to have him, mostly because his black legs and white spotted torso gave him the look of having donned a pair of trousers. In my thirties and forties, my careful guardianship over Lou became more resolute, mostly because I could love him, I could save him, I could end one tiny little story from San Luis happily.

I met Alex shortly after adopting Lou, and maybe a nanosecond or so after I declared to everyone I knew that I didn't need or want a man in my life. I had dogs, which were not only cuter, but were physically unable to use my credit card without permission, or hack into my voice mail after we had spent a solid twelve hours breaking up. As an independent woman, I had to ditch my plan to become the canine variety of the crazy old cat lady, because the first time Alex and Lou met, it was like watching Batman meet Robin or Fred meet Ginger. Actually, it was more like watching Butch Cassidy meet the Sundance Kid, because despite all my efforts at correcting them, they were both hell-bent on breaking all my laws and ruining everything I owned in the process.

As it turns out, Lou is a one-man dog, with the emphasis on "man," as he seems to have no use for humans of the female persuasion. He would run away from me every chance he got, and would come back only for Alex, an event that happened frequently the year we all moved to the mountains. They were the best years of Lou's life, during which he proved what we knew all along: He was designed for the outdoors with his sturdy and strong physique, his bull neck and broad shoulders betraying his sweet disposition and fragile ego. He's chased every manner of wildlife through the woods—including coyotes and foxes—and scared off a mountain lion just beginning to disassemble a four-point buck laid open and steaming in the snow. The memory of the day he caught two greyhounds running afield in full sprint and then body-checked them into oblivion is a keeper. We dubbed him president of the Nub Tail Club for that, but now that he's graying and slowing down, and refraining from ruining everything we own, he's the Elder Statesman or the Mayor. Yes, his belly is getting rounder, but we like to say his head's just getting smaller, because when life only lasts a decade or so, I say you don't have to spend it all on some damned diet. When we brought home the strange, wailing new human, he shouldered his demotion like the consummate professional he is. He rewarded himself by sitting under the high chair during mealtimes.

One day I told Lou, "You've known me a lot of years now, just a few months short of your whole life, so you can believe me when I tell you that the vacuum cleaner is not going to kill you." Despite my testimony on the safety record of the vacuum and all other household appliances, Lou still becomes very nervous when I vacuum. He becomes very nervous when the washer begins its spin cycle. Likewise when the dishwasher door swings open, and ditto in spades with thunder and fireworks. In fact, about the only thing that doesn't make him nervous is when I leave the room with dirty dishes on the coffee table, but he re-ups on the anxiety once I reenter the room to find him with his little spotted snout all but impaling a plastic container, his tongue dislodging every last molecule of flavor from it. He cowers under the dining room table when Sophie digs the little broom and mop out of her toy box and pretends to clean house. And there's something especially frightening about living entities walking by or opening the mail or inhaling or exhaling within a four-mile radius of the water bowl while he's drinking. But nothing, apparently, is as frightening to him as the sound of his own gas. Even the slightest little fart sends him scooting out of the room, checking his backside for the stalker who must have sneaked up on him. And then there's the relief, the discovery, that the only deadly thing in the room is the smell.

But woe is the well-meaning fund-raiser who comes to the front door to sell candy bars, Girl Scout cookies, or memberships to one environmental organization or another. And despite all of his shyness, he used to think that attacking my head while I slept was the best possible way to spend a Saturday morning—pre-dawn. I thought of this little habit he'd outgrown while I was doing the floors one day, and told him, "If I were going to kill you, Lou—I ducked down under the table to explain—it would have been then, and by the way, I wouldn't have used a Swiffer to do it." Then just moments after my persuasive speech, a wrinkle.

The smoke alarm batteries were dying, and the intermittent warning beep was enough to convince Lou that the sky was falling. Shaking and cowering, he ran outside and hid practically inside the prickliest bush he could find at the farthest corner of the back yard. It almost took a T-bone to coax him back into the house after I'd spent a whole day changing every smoke alarm battery in the house. Two months later, my sneaker squeaked on the wood floor. It sounded just like the smoke alarm. "Uh oh," I said, watching Lou skittering along like a cartoon character on the tippy-tips of his nails, out to the safety of his favorite prickly bush. Jimmy Dean himself could not have extracted him. I realized then that the cruelest fate that could befall Lou would be attending a basketball game.

It only took Lou six years to figure out that a bath is just like a massage, only with soap and water between the two of us. His body language has gone from revealing his all-out terror at such abuse to something more along the lines of "I would prefer this to having my tail cut off with an axe pretty much any day of the week."

He remains a mystery to me. I don't know if he's proof of randomness or the philosophy that there are no accidents, no coincidences. I don't know if he's the product of nature or nurture. I only know that, in addition to being a part of our little family, he's impressive on paper, especially after adding "porcupine-quill cushion," "groundhog hunter," and "cancer survivor" to his CV. To date, Lou has outlived two of my other dogs, and the sister and brother-in-law who delivered his quaking, spotted little body to me this many years ago.

Five years after meeting Lou for the first time, I went back to San Luis, to close the door on Gayle's life. She'd been widowed since my last visit, after Don drove himself off the highway one night. She and Jay had moved since then, to an even smaller, poorer town down a dirt road from San Luis, and into a trailer with Gayle's longtime extramarital boyfriend, Sam. I didn't know much more than that; nobody did. All we knew was that Sam had discovered Gayle's dead body at about 5 a.m. on a morning in June, when he awoke on the couch and went to bed.

The drive with my parents was one speculative conversation after another. "Maybe she had a blood clot from that time the horse bucked her off," my mom said. "Remember that?" I did, and dreaded the assortment of pets and livestock that may or may not be waiting for us, or anyone.

Driving up to the dirt lot with a trailer on it, there was no way for me to imagine that this was a family's permanent residence. I saw the twisted frame of a bicycle leaning against one end of the trailer, the hunk of metal rusting into the siding. There were plastic grocery bags strewn about. Car parts, corrugated sheet metal, pots and pans, carpet samples. Empty food cans covered the ground in random layers. There was once a garden outside the front door, maybe, since that was the only litter-free section of dirt with any sense of organization. That's where seven-year-old Jay was playing in his bare feet with other children his age. They were the grandchildren of women inside who were maybe two years my senior. Everyone wanted to know where my children were I said I didn't have any yet. "I just have dogs," I said. They looked confused.

I took a deep breath before going in, and was relieved to find that it was nicer inside than out, save the smell of cigarettes. Sam's sister greeted us wearing a pair of yellow rubber gloves that barely came off for the rest of our time there. She'd been cleaning and straightening everything up since Gayle's body had been taken to the funeral home, and she had made great strides toward the illusion of order in the house. I was warned about the soft spot in the floor between the living room and bath, which was where the whole structure was apparently falling in, and then I found that it was best to avoid the bathroom for other reasons, too. There was a load of clothes going sour in the washer, and Gayle's grown daughters took everything to the Laundromat to re-wash, dry, and donate to the Salvation Army. Literally two hours later, we saw people in town wearing the same stuff we had just dropped off.

We cleared the shelves and cupboards of mouse droppings, jars of dried beans, broken glass, dust. The next day was my dad's seventy-eighth birthday, and we spent it settling up small debts at places like the gas station, where Gayle bought most of her groceries, and notifying the government agencies that wrote Gayle's aid checks. We ate Chinese food in Alamosa and made birthday toast with our tea. "Happy birthday, Dad," we said.

Going through her things, I realized she was more mysterious to me than Lou, a creature who couldn't speak and owned no possessions. She kept a thorough register of her checkbook, yet her workbook from the court-ordered drug treatment center she attended for twenty-six days was as blank as the day she received it. Every TV she had ever owned had been stolen, but never her computer. And who really owned the dust bowl of a lot with the collapsing single-wide trailer on it? Although some money changed hands, there had been a dispute over the title the year before, and it was anyone's guess who belonged to the property. "You get a receipt when you buy a pair of pants," I said, leafing through reams of loose documents, "but there's no deed here, no proof of any legal transaction." She owned a closet stuffed so full of women's clothes that there was no way to close it, but all I ever saw her wear were men's T-shirts and jeans. "She must have moved this thing a hundred times," I said, finding my grandmother's antique sewing machine. Mom said, "I can't believe she still has it." As I was sipping a soda outside, considering it all, two little dogs scampered out from under the trailer.

Lexie, a tiny Chihuahua mix, and a similarly bred puppy named Brownie were the newest pets on the scene. They came from nowhere, and were kept for their willingness to live under the house. I knew the dogs' fate, even if the stories about them were as fabricated as they sounded.

Lexie, Brownie's mother, was reportedly impregnated by a Rottweiler, thus ensuring her death during labor and delivery, if not sometime during her pregnancy. The truth is, she looked sickly to me, but I guessed at the time that I was probably projecting. It buoyed me up, though, that Brownie, Jay's latest in a long succession of dogs who came and went, was about as old as Lou the first time we met, but dramatically less anxious.

Sam saw me playing with them, gave me a look, and asked me to take the dogs home. I explained that I had just agreed to adopt Mona, an adult black Labrador mix with blue eyes, a thorough veterinary record, and a certificate from obedience school. "I just started a new job an hour away from home," I told Sam, and I couldn't quit to house train and coddle a new pup and its pregnant, possibly ailing mother. What I really meant was that I had just entered a new era of my life, one in which I was committed to an adulthood that was more deliberate. As I told a friend the last time she invited me to shop the yard sales, I wanted "no more furniture by default."

There would be no more designing my life around what I could get because it was there. I wanted to be more conscious about my fate. What I didn't know was how difficult it would be to turn down the unwanted. It pained me to decline, but I did many times. "They'll be fine here," Sam said, winking the cigarette smoke out of one eye "but I see how much you like them. Why don't you take them?" Later, I was explaining the waves of terribleness that were washing over me when my mom said, "Sometimes you just have to just look away and forget it."

Soon, in similar fashion, but without the hard sell from anyone, I turned down Jay. "Consider Alex and me your safety net," I told my parents, who were worried about having to raise him themselves. "We'll adopt him, but we really wanted to start our own family this year." But Jay had lots of relatives, and one of his dad's eleven children quickly agreed to take him into her home of a husband and two sons. Jay became the member of a household in which dogs had bowls of food and water and lived to be old. And also for the record, as it turned out, Mona, the dog I chose on purpose, became a total nut job. But she was my nut job.

When I think of orphans, I never think of Jay. None of us do. I think of orphans as young people taking illegal factory work, their skin and their nightgowns the same color battleship gray. But he is technically an orphan, one who is growing up to look a lot like his dad, long before his dad's skin turned purple and his liver bloated into the size of a two-bedroom bungalow. He's an orphan because his mom, after a few weeks of clean and sober living, went to the carnival that came to town, which was probably where and when she scored the cocaine. The coroner called her death an accident, but there's no telling what was an accident, what was a mistake, and what was deliberate. She died of an overdose, on a mattress without any sheets on it, in the bedroom just past the rotting floorboards. She died alone on the other side of her young son's bedroom wall, the room where he slept in a bunk bed crammed against a window that faced the Sangre de Cristo Mountains, and the mountain of junk on the ground just outside.

I drove my parents back to Denver and myself back to my own tiny town of Nederland after five days in San Luis, where Lou was waiting behind the front door, barking, as I turned the key, as if the four horsemen or the UPS man had come; he went back to bed after realizing it was just me. The house was quiet, hot. Smelled like dog. "Who wants to go for a walk?" I asked, ditching my purse, and changing my shoes. I stepped out onto the deck, smelled the air, pointed my face toward the late afternoon sun. We walked up the dirt road and into the trees, where Lou looked back at me, grinning, and sprinted off into acres of national forest. I knew it would take me at least an hour of walking and calling his name to find him, and another to convince him to come home with me. I pressed my fingers to my temples and whispered, "Goddamn it."

C.D. Albin

Cicero Jack Contemplates the Heart-Stays People

My daughters worry with words, more so than
sons who fence hearts, won't transgress boundaries
without invitation. The girls fled

these hills to wed city men, but now fret
raw nerves over me alone on this ridge
kin have dwelt three generations.

I spoke an hour just yesterday, the phone
numbing my good ear while I sought fit words
to tell my eldest about the Osage

and their little band that stayed, wouldn't part
from sacred soil like the rest but planted
themselves on the spot of ground they loved, till

kin began to call them Heart-Stays, meaning
mock or praise, I do not know. Often my
daughters' tones go soft, seem full of plea, but

behind my back I fear they use words like
stubborn or mule, frantic I quit ridges
steep enough to tilt tractors, or sell the

roan mare who kicks hind heels like a show bronc
that won't be broken. I surely wish those
girls could shut a door on dread-fears, let their

eyes remember pastures they've known since birth.
They learned to walk stony ground. Their children,
like the Osage, were meant to stride this land.

C.D. Albin

Endgame

In memory she arrives without sound,
ghosting into my office while I scan
yet another essay, but as I lift
my gaze she is there, weeping, her left eye

bruised blacker than the coffee I've just poured.
This time I'm leaving him, she rasps. *I won't
be in class anymore.* Nodding, I try
to gather my thoughts, hope something worthy

sneaks past my lips, but before one word comes
she turns, pads down the hall. I wait too long
to rise, am late getting to the exit
and can spot her nowhere on the grounds when

I burst outside, staring at the now-strange
faces of students, a few of whom call
me by name. Wind moves among maple leaves
as I walk this softly autumned campus,

my bruised pupil impossible to find.
At the street corner I stop short, note a
curled condom on the curb, marvel at how
chancy the endgames of human embrace.

Doug Paul Case

The Old Queen Has the Gym

figured out. The pool closes at 10
so if he finishes his walk by 9:50
he'll make it to the lockerroom just
before the water polo team comes
in from practice. And what you've heard
is true. They holler. They slap towels.
They talk shit about the competition,
about the coach, about their bitches,
about the rest of us who happen to be
in there at the right time,
who happen to be in their sight.

Never you mind where I'm looking.

But they ignore the queen, perhaps
put off by his paunch—larger
than their fathers'—or otherwise
his gaze, lingering on their asses,
perfectly round even outside
their Speedos. To him,
to them, nothing matters.
It's delicate complacency.

Then, all of us in the shower room,
and my attention on neither the team
nor the steam, but the old queen
and his obviousness—terrified
that'll one day be me.

Dan Lambert

Stone Disguise

The meteor will be here
tomorrow. A baby is born
wishing to be a bell
that has meaning when rung.
Back yard, my brother, we fire
bottle rockets at a pile of pine
brush, while our wives are left
to argue with themselves
over the possibility of escape.
It is impossible for all of us
to be with both our parents.
What if the destroyer comes
early in the night? It is the one
thing we can't sleep through
together, though we wrap
the house in a blanket made
with smaller blankets. We fill
our mouths with the largest
stones we can find, hope
the meteor swerves away
in arced mercy, and mistakes
our family for hers.

Dan Lambert

The Gospel According to Rain

It is appropriate that the ruins of Eden,
the dried husk of what is perfect,
long dead in the lap of the Euphrates,
would entertain a day where it rains only people.

Men bring down the sky in gray thuds
and are hushed quickly in the treads of wheels.
I listen close to their quiet
seething, listing ways to open:

They are balsa wood,
snapping soft like an invitation to come,
they break on the head of a child,
know the length of one Earth's breath.

Men land on the banks of the river,
flail like wet bandages in the back
of mouths. Saying, two hundred years,
we did the math while we fell.

Khanh Ha

The River of White Water Lilies

We were staying in the base camp that was once a French fort during the Indochina War. From the rear of the base, looking west, you could see the U Minh forest beyond the perimeter of barbed wire, the leaves of the forest green at first light and turning a dusty green during the day because of the heat haze. But the forest was always beautiful in the early morning when trees flowered white, and soon the flowers would wither and fall in the heat and then in the monsoon rain. From the base looking east past its gate you could see the little Viet town, the red-dirt road that ran through the town and the spreading crown of the chinaberry that shaded the refreshment shack.

Beyond the town the river glinted like a mirror. The Trẹm River. That's what the Viets called it. The river took us north on our patrol until it bisected the U Minh forest into Upper and Lower U Minh, where we would stay out for a week at a time guarding the villages that lay hidden in the banana and bamboo groves along the river, and one of them sat beyond the riverbank and back into the forest so that on a quiet evening you could hear from inside the village the sound of waves coming from the western sea.

That village, Mamma, was a Catholic village which we protected against the enemy. The villagers were northerners who had escaped the Communist terror in 1954 when Vietnam was divided by the Geneva Accords into North and South. They were anti-Communist and would kill any of them without remorse. We were friendly with them, and they liked us. The mammas and grandmas would bake dumplings and steamed buns and we'd eat them and thank God that we wouldn't have to eat our ham and lima beans and in return we gave them our C-ration cans. The village militia had lookouts in the forest and along the river, and they communicated with one another using

Morse code through their handheld radios. They had M1 Garand and carbine rifles and though underarmed and undertrained they had no fear of the communists. We gave them M-16 rifles and mortars and they were quick in putting them to use. One night their scouts spotted the Viet Cong's movement toward their village and sent their men the coordinates through Morse code. They fired their mortars. Mamma, they got the Viet Cong just as they were crossing the river. When it was over, what floated on the water were the canteens, rubber shoes, and bodies of those that had refused to sink. In the morning the river had carried away the blood but the blood had soaked the mud along the riverbank and the fish now fought one another for the human flesh caught between the battered-looking paling.

Mamma, I want to tell you about the Trẹm River. It runs north-south through the U Minh forest, cutting it in half. One day on a river craft patrolling the river near a creek called Ra Ghe, which flows into the Trẹm, I saw white flowers afloat along the riverbank. From where it meets the creek, the river runs straight for some ten miles and all you see are myriad rows of flowers whitewashing the edges of the riverbank. They float on their round-shaped leaves, and the leaves notched deeply down the center look like the heart. The breeze smells fragrant and the fragrance then follows us upriver 'til the river bends and the white flowers and their scents all disappear. Someone on the river craft said they were water lilies. When I asked the colonel many days later he said, Do you know what the Viets call that stretch of the river? *The River of White Water Lilies.* Mamma, I was up and down that river as far north to its mother river, the Cái Lớn River that empties into the ocean, and far south to where it extends itself into the Đốc River, and the whole river changes its colors, brown-red during the monsoon season when creeks and canals with their wombs in the cajeput forests carry peat-brown water into the river, and then opaque white during the dry season when silt at the river mouths comes inland with saltwater. At night when we patrolled the river we would often see fishermen out on the water in their sampans, each hung with a lantern on the stern and on the bow, brightly lit, and the river would smell of smoke and glow afire with the lanterns' reflections. I asked what they were doing and was told that they were out to catch prawns, not the ordinary prawns but tiger prawns. Mamma, they are at least ten inches long and plump, rusty-brown with black-and-white bands across their humpbacks. But if you ask me what I remember most, Mamma, I remember the floating lily pads and the river that runs long and white with water lily flowers.

Good old Ian Vaugh.

He was a good boy, Mamma.

He caught my eye one day. That day we were out at first light on patrol outside a Viet village. A hazy morning. We were wading single file across a canal that hugged the side of the village. Hedged by water hyacinth, the bank was thick with a barrier of bamboo and aquatic reeds bolstered against water erosion of the soil. Where the hedge ended you could see the soil so fretted away by water the roots of eucalyptus and water palms stuck out, dangling in a jumbled mass. Brown thatch huts, at times only their roofs, peeked out between the green leafage. Suddenly a figure slunk out behind a clump of reed. A kid. He was lugging a rifle. Ian, our point man, hollered, "Hey! Who goes there?" The kid turned, looked back. Then he bolted. A gunshot rang. The kid fell. Sergeant Sunukkuhkau lowered his M-16 as he climbed the bank and walked into the tall reed. The kid lay prone. His nasty-looking wound still leaked blood like bright red paint spattered on the back of his short-sleeved white shirt. Sarge picked up the gun. An old battered Thompson submachine gun. Its walnut-brown buttstock, badly nicked and chipped, had a faded look you thought it had been buried in the paddy since World War II. The first man Sarge lay his snake-eyes on was Ian.

"Did you really say that?" he asked Ian. "'Who goes there'?in the name of God?"

Ian looked down at the kid's lifeless body and back at Sarge who stared unblinkingly at him until Ian's batted his eyes. "He was just a kid, Sarge," he said as if apologizing to the dead kid.

"And this?" Sarge thrust the old Thompson against Ian's chest. "A wooden toy?"

"Maybe they made him do it." Ian looked down into Sarge's eyes then quickly looked away. "Told him to shoot at us."

"And what happened if he did empty this on us?" Sarge tapped the twenty-round box magazine. "May I ask?"

Ian said nothing. He stood hunched like a loneliest heron. A tall boy, his hair, flame-red in its root, was straight like the Viets', with only a patch on the top, and the rest was shaved all around down to the back of his neck. His freckled face looked boyish, like someone had just pulled him out of bed one morning, slapped the fatigues on him, and said, "We'll make a man out of you."

A devout Catholic, brown-eyed and innocent, he once said to me, "LT, I don't want to kill."

"Then you'll get killed," I said, "if that's your choice."

Once we were moving into an enemy territory and everyone went to lock and load. The man next to Ian doubled back and talked to Sergeant Sunu. Before long, Sarge came up the line and poked his finger at Ian's M-16.

"Remove the magazine," Sarge said.

"Why?" Ian said.

"I want to see it," Sarge said.

Ian pressed the magazine release. The magazine fell out and before he could feel it in his hand, Sarge seized it. One peek into the magazine and he grabbed Ian by the collar of his shirt. "This," he said, shaking the empty magazine in Ian's face, "is unthinkable. Someone from our side could've paid a dear price for this. You don't want that on your conscience, do you, boy? You kill the slopes or get killed. Simple as that."

Slopes, gooks, dinks. Ian remembered every war slogan inked across a banner hung in the barracks back home had one of those words. The "Kill-a-Cong" posters were favorite among the new recruits—it portrayed a Viet wearing a coolie hat. Here in Nam, he was told, you get a three-day pass if you kill a Cong. A body a day will get you three.

In this Catholic village Ian met a girl. We were stationed on the riverbank and he would go into the village during the day, the free time he got before his night guard duty. Sometimes he had the girl up on the ten-ton thunder truck, sitting on its bed mounted with a quad-50 machine gun. The kids would wave and smile at the truck as it rolled through the village and the adults stood in muted admiration at the sight of the quad-50 draped with an American flag in red, white, and blue. Late afternoons sometimes the men would test the fire range through an exercise and Ian would sit with the girl on the bank while the quads roared like thunder and the twilight glowed with myriad streaks of red tracers and every living Viet in the village would come out of the hooches, watching the fireworks in awe. But then, he told the girl, who was the village schoolteacher and spoke good English, that it always pinched your gut when the quads went into action. She asked why and he said that it meant some souls in the bush were in trouble. She said he had a good heart and he told her he always carried the Bible with him, even when he was out on patrol. Being a Catholic herself, she studied the Bible with him. He taught her English and she taught him Vietnamese. When he felt confident enough to speak Vietnamese to her, he asked her if he could teach English to her students. She was happy to hear that. The children would perk up at the sight of the red-haired American who stood hunched in the low-ceilinged classroom, speaking words in English to them and hearing them repeat in chorus. The lanky young American made them laugh with his sometimes off-tone pronunciation of the tricky Vietnamese words and their teacher, the girl, would cover her mouth, giggling. *Say khúc khủy. Mazy. Say ngoằn ngèo. Zigzag.* The children guffawed.

Ian laughed too. Those were words he felt impossible to pronounce. "Your jaws must relax," she'd say. "Let your lips form the sounds."

"Tough words," he said. "How about saying that backward?"

She cocked her head. "Mr. Ian," she said, "if you have an iron will."

"I'll count on that," he said. "My father used to drill me on spelling and multiplication when I was a kid. The only child, so it was pretty hard not to get my parents' attention."

"So was I, the only child."

"Did you grow up a Catholic?"

"Yes. My parents' whole village was Catholic in the north. And what are you?"

"Presbyterian."

"*Giám Lý?*"

Ian laughed. "I have the foggiest idea what that is."

"That's where I get confused," she said. "I heard that the sects are split into black congregations and white congregations in America."

"We have Presbyterians, Episcopalians, Baptists, Methodists, lots of others. Of course, the Baptists are divided into sects of their own. We have Shakers, Quakers, Mormons, Lutherans, and only God knows how many more."

"Stop!" She laughed, touching her brow. "I've already forgotten all those names."

Sometimes after school he would follow a kid's parent home and, sitting on a rush mat on the packed-dirt floor, ate their food. First he worked his feet out of his heavy boots so he could sit like them with his legs cross-folded painfully into each other, so his left foot rested on his right thigh and his right foot on his left thigh. Over time his limbs began to adopt such posture with less pain and his tongue acquired a taste of boiled vegetables, poached fish, and rice. They ate a lot of fish, cabbage, and sweet potatoes, and every meal there was a crockpot of *canh*, their soup, with pumpkin and baby shrimps. With *canh* was *nước mắm*, their fish sauce, the pungent smell of which soon became inseparable from the food he ate. A few times he ate with them before it got dark and, the river now rising with the moon, he could hear the deep-throated *cu-ckoo-cu-ckoo* of the birds echoing mournfully across the water and the swamp and shrubs and trees. Every dwelling was built of cajeput wood and thatched with nipa palm fronds. Evenings they would burn cajeput leaves and the bitter-smelling smoke made his eyes teary; yet it kept away the mosquitos. Every dwelling had chickens roaming and feeding happily in its garden, and the bright red of a rooster's comb was the red he'd see in his mind when he thought of the village, and the clucking of hens and the calls of cuckoos would bring him a peaceful feeling.

Sometimes he'd bring with him the C-rations and took pleasure in showing the kids how to open the cans with his P-38 can opener. Then he sat and watched the kids eat ham and lima beans with rice, and most of them would pause when they first took a mouthful of spaghetti and meatballs and some would spit them out and some would swallow with such difficulty it cracked him up. He made her try the beans and franks. She took the hot dogs, cut them up, and fried them with onions, and ate them with the white rice. It tasted much better that way when they shared a meal, and the beans were cooked with the porridge, steeped in chicken broth, and afterward none tasted like the C-ration food anymore.

He went to her house on several occasions. The first time, upon her invitation, he remembered what she told him and removed his boots before entering the anteroom. Her father was the village chief, a cultured white-haired man who came from a Mandarin family in the North. With her sitting beside him, both conversing at ease with Ian, he noticed that the man sat in the chair with his feet planted on the floor, his hands resting on his thighs. He never crossed his legs. Ian considered himself fortunate that he had sat like them, for later she told him that one of the Viet protocols on mutual respect was never to cross your legs with your foot pointing toward your guest. Do not sit like a cowboy, she said. And do not touch their heads. The head. He had rubbed many Viet kids' heads, he told her. That was all right, she said. But you are doomed as classless if you pat an elder on the back or rub his head. He started feeling like an alien. Yet gradually he opened up to their culture and began to realize that once he put away his biased mindset, he no longer felt arrogant toward them. Nothing they did, nothing they had to offer in his daily contact with them, would take him aback. Once she asked him after the class what "full of piss and vinegar" meant and showed him an editorial in the *Stars and Stripes* that he brought with him. "In Vietnam," he read what she pointed out, "poor bastards had been at war for fifteen years. And here we come, full of piss and vinegar, wanting to win the war in six months." He explained that it meant "full of youthful energy," and she, not contented by the answer, said, "Why can't it be some refined words instead of these crude words to express the same thing?" He almost wanted to tell her that his country's culture was unrefined, that the cowboy mouth usually got the better of him before his thoughts came through. But it was too much to try to explain that to her, so he just laughed and she, too, broke out laughing at the peculiar expression. And if you ask me, Mamma, was there anything from this people that might have shocked him? I must say the sight of their black-lacquered teeth. It shocked me, too, the first time I saw their elders smile. I'm sure our men, also. Especially those from West Point. Those with a brilliant mind in physics, mathematics, understanding how the B-52's all-metal skin worked from a wrinkled appearance of the fuselage's forward section to expanding and becoming smooth when the aircraft gains altitude. Those who carried out Samuel Huntington's credo on how to defeat a people who struggle against foreign intervention: "Dry up the ocean so that the fish don't have any water." What would these men think when they first interact with a Viet whose teeth were all black? But, Mamma, Ian understood this people. He ate their rice, rice that we burned so the Viet Cong wouldn't feast on it, rice soiled with buffalo dung that they brought home and sifted through with care because rice was their staple of livelihood, rice that grew in paddies where we killed the Viets sometimes indiscriminately and later the farmers would bury the bodies and harvest the rice and by then the bloodstains on the rice stalks had turned to the color of paddy dirt.

Then one night the Viet Cong attacked our platoon outside the village. It was half-past three in the morning. We held our position, but when dawn broke we could hear gunfight in the village and knew they had punched through it by holding us long enough at bay on the riverbank. At first light a pair of jetfighters showed up, dropping low, almost skimming the treetops still wet with dew. They spotted the Viet Cong in the canal, the long canal that flanked the village and flowed into the Trẹm River, and unloaded napalm bombs on them. From the river we saw flames and smoke and soon the wind brought a foul smell of petroleum. We could hear guns roaring each time the jetfighters came swooping down and drew fire from the enemy, and we could hear the trees burn, popping loud, and the air felt hot on our faces, the downwind fumes reeking so bad we had to cover our faces with our hankies. When morning came the bombings had repelled the attack and now with the mist having burned up we moved into the village.

There was a long line of men and women frantically digging a trench between the side of the village and the canal. The wind was fanning the fire that licked the brush on the canal bank and people started cutting down cajeput trees. Ian found the schoolteacher. He had prayed that he would see her again and when he saw her, spade in hand, dirt-smeared face hardened with a muted pain he saw so often on the Viets' faces, he crossed himself and took out his entrenching tool and joined them. They chopped, they hacked away climbing fern and tree roots, and the severed roots of milkwood trees dangled white and dripped sap like leaky faucets. They dumped dirt from the trench into the raging fire, the peat soil so porous it was easy to dig so that each stab of a spade would bring the soil crashing down. An elder told her to dig quickly but not to swing her arms too high so she wouldn't tire out too soon, and she told Ian that. The fire roared past the canal bank and trees shivered and crackled and Ian could see the shimmering water and knew why they didn't use it against the fire, for water only helped the napalm fire gain its strength. He could see through the smoke her back and the backs of the people ahead of him. At times they were just vignettes. The heat grew, the air soaked with a gasoline smell. Then the trench grew longer, deeper and wider until the fire came upon them and its heat breathed a murderously hot air on their faces. Some slow-footed women and kids got burned and people had to pull them and as they pulled they brushed the skin, the clothes with their hands and the jellied petroleum stuck to their skin and they and the victims all screamed in agony.

Evening came and the fire had stopped at the trench. The sky was a hazy yellow from the smoky treetops and the heat of the day and that of the fire had waned. She stood leaning on her spade, her face blackened from dirt and soot, her blouse stained with sweat, and as she gazed at the ruins Ian took out his canteen and gave it to her. "Drink," he said. "Things will get back to normal."

She took a sip, coughed, said, "This is the worst I have seen." Her voice was soft. Around her people stood contemplating the charred landscape, their eyes like glass eyes, their figures soon darkening into silhouettes as dusk came. They followed the canal home, walking in tandem, some wrapping their heads with an elephant-ear taro leaf for heat relief, and the last glimmer of sun cast a glow on the water and there were bodies lying in all sorts of positions on the banks and in the water where they got caught under the felled trees. The dead by the napalm bombs looked like human-shaped slabs of meat, just scorched flesh and bones. Along the bank she picked up a tortoise as it tried to crawl downwind away from the heat still simmering on the ground. She patted its dome shaped shell. "Poor thing," she said to Ian. "Let's find a cool place for him." When they reached a grove of cajeput, she placed the tortoise in the grass and suddenly they heard the frantic calls of storks and herons deep in the harbor of tree crowns. Wings beat on and on and the harsh calls didn't stop. As he looked up into the inky black vault where the birds were marionette shades of pale white, he could see them hovering like hummingbirds and none touched down. He heard her exclaim, "Heaven!" and in her words that told him the birds now lost their roosts he knew the petroleum heat from napalm bombs had made their colony inhabitable.

It took over two months for her village to rebuild. He often helped when he could. One day before he went on his seven-day leave to Singapore, he brought her a gift: a paintbox and a notebook with handwritten poems. The paintbox was enameled white with two deep mixing wells. The notebook, pressed together by two faded brown cardboards, had drawings and poems written neatly in Vietnamese on the ruled-line sheets. She asked him where he got them from and he told her from a dead North Vietnamese soldier's rucksack. He couldn't throw them away after he saw that it was filled with what he thought were love poems. Each was illustrated with drawings of flowering twigs and solitary blossoms, of floating clouds and a full moon. He could never imagine soldiers like him would have a mind to write down their thoughts, their feelings. Words. Drawings. Now he saw the drawings. Read the words. Not that they let him. But after they had died. Still, nothing was real anymore because they no longer had an owner. It was like smelling a dead flower. What he said moved her. "You have a mind of a poet," she said. "And these are love poems written by a soldier yearning for home and his sweetheart."

"Where did it say that?" he asked. She put her finger under two words, "Yêu em." *Love you.* He mouthed the words. Loud enough for her to hear. That made her blush in the face and she broke out laughing. "You silly silly silly oh silly you," she said, still laughing and he, too, laughed. Like two children.

In Singapore on his recreation and recuperation leave, Ian bought himself a three-piece suit for fifty dollars and a long sapphire-blue silk scarf. He settled on the scarf because he didn't know what else she would like. She always wore indigo or sapphire blouses. He imagined her wearing the silk scarf. He imagined its translucent hue, its intense blue. He wrote the words "Yêu em" on the back of a card and put it in the gift-wrapped box.

When he came back to the base camp, his platoon was still out in the bush. But it wasn't guarding the Catholic village. They were pulled out right after he left on his R&R and the following night the Viet Cong overwhelmed the village defense and walked every living villager to the Trẹm River where they shot each of them in the head and kicked the body into the river. They said the river turned red in the morning with bodies still floating downstream and from those snagged on the aquatic palms along the riverbank. Those who hid away survived and were later taken to the New-Life Hamlet, a free-fire zone. He found out there were fewer than twenty in that place and she wasn't one of them.

When he left the ruins of the village and rode back on the 10-ton thunder truck mounted with a quad-50 machine gun, the truck went up along the Trẹm River. In the bright morning the deep green of cajeput was breathtaking, the river white with water lilies along the edge of the riverbank, and the scents of water lily flowers perfumed the air. He watched the river go by and couldn't make sense of what had happened. It did not add up. He watched the storks taking flight from the river, going going until they reached their roosts in a cajeput grove beyond and he thought of a home.

Then he started crying.

Santiago Vizcaíno

The Storm

Which of the two writes this poem
Of a plural I with a single shadow?
—Jorge Luis Borges

On the skin,
the disturbing touch of an insect
senses the timid pronouncement of fear.
I can hear someone quickening the movement of my blood,
I spit,
I'm so disgusted by the liquid in my marrow.

The lights swing back and forth like the balls of an old man
dancing on the pavement.
Don't bother to worry about the fluttering coming from your muscles.
What's needed is to scrutinize what is scarcely pulsing between your
    fingers.
Eyes widen with the impossibility of pleasure.
What remains is the trembling of an eyelid: the chill of a young dove.
Outside,
only stillness heralds the storm,
air slipping through and muddying the breathing of the other.

We are two,
his voice comes down like a morning squall.

To say death now pretends beyond our ken,
but he gazes at me motionless, from the other side of night.

Translated From the Spanish by Alexis Levitin

Benny Andersen

To a trap

Even when you're not smoking
you regularly brush off your jacket and tie
as if you had spilled ashes or embers
fix your gaze on a low-flying fly
pinch your nostrils together with two fingers
let go only after the flush is bulging to excess
and snicker: "All right,
that's enough about that."
Regardless of what is being discussed
Christiania, gender roles, childrearing
Beethoven's fifth
or insomnia
for you it always ends at odds on some
unfathomable obscene point
that you won't grant to us others.
And still you say:
"We'll have to get together again
there's so much we didn't get to talk about!"
and brush the last scorpions from your tie.
But what can a curious victim do
with a trap that has no entrance?
And maybe it's not obscene at all
but something quite beautiful you're keeping hidden?
As generous as you are with bait
that's how stingy you are with yourself.
I always come away from you famished.

Translated From the Danish by Michael Goldman

Salgado Maranhão

Sea Drift IV

The rare comes from the borders,
skittish, barbed with moons,
hooking itself on the plain
of the eyes.

And the music the gesture
foreshadows

         strips bare
the color that bursts forth
from the stain. Highways

open themselves
with a willingness like nectar;
         there gathers

at the garage-heart
all of suffering (and a feint) and/or
remains of what is harvested
though never planted:

they are codices, voices, waves
that flood my hydrants

so that, in the end, the abyss may sing.

Translated From the Portuguese by Alexis Levitin

J.T. Robertson

The Dodo, the Balance, and the Bee

Jeremy looked down at the pistol gripped shakily in his hand and pondered the implications of extinction. He imagined a sort of standoff between the last dodo bird and a hunter with an archaic rifle, staring each other down across a small clearing. If the man had known, would he have pulled the trigger? If the doomed bird had known, would it have run away? He pressed his forehead against the cool, protective glass of the climate-controlled enclosure. It had to be done to save them. Nothing else would work. He was the only one who could, the only one with the ability. The pistol was heavy in his hand, heavier than he remembered. He held perfectly still as Greg, the night guard, passed by on the lit asphalt path, the keys on his belt jingling their location with every step. Jeremy waited in the shadow of the enclosure for Greg to get out of range and wondered what his life could have been. None of it was really his fault. He'd always had the best of intentions.

The greatest thing in Jeremy's life was Sarah, his girlfriend for the past three years. She was really the only person who understood his predicament. They'd met when he was working as a cab driver. It had been a good gig for someone with his condition. If things were shifting too far in one direction he'd just run through a deep, grimy puddle and soak someone walking down the sidewalk. If things were going downhill quickly, he'd take all the right shortcuts or turn off the meter for a while. It worked really well, at least until the cab company was bombarded with complaints. They'd let him go after that, but that was OK because he'd moved in with Sarah. That meant he was able to look for work without worrying about being on the street again. He would have just stayed in a shelter, but he'd been banned from most of the local ones years ago for starting fights.

Sarah was fairly well known in the local art scene, particularly for her paintings of what she called "selfless people." They were all done in crimson and burnt orange oils and featured the great martyrs and self-sacrificing saints of history. Once she told Jeremy she thought there was no greater way to die than in the act of saving others. He figured it had something to do with her dad, who had been a firefighter. One night their house caught fire while her father was on duty at the station. He got Sarah to safety, but succumbed while trying to rescue her mom, who also died in the blaze. Sarah had made paintings of her parents surrounded with fire, but refused to show those to anyone but Jeremy. He didn't know why.

He never went with her to her gallery shows or sales, though. She asked him to come along, but he always declined. Honestly, he was afraid the balance would tip while he was there, and he would have to embarrass her by rubbing cake in an important critic's face or drawing silly mustaches on the people in her paintings with a permanent marker.

"I care about you, and I don't want to put you in danger," Jeremy told Sarah one night, while they watched a *M*A*S*H* rerun, all snuggled up on her faded green couch.

"You won't," she answered dismissively, kissing his nose.

"You don't understand," he said, pulling back so he could see her whole face and show her how serious he was. "It's hard to control."

She sighed and turned off the TV with an over-exaggerated point of the remote. "Look," she said, in her best no-nonsense voice, "I get it. You're convinced you have 'reverse instant karma.' You do good, bad things happen. You do bad, good things happen."

He started to say something, but she stopped him with a finger to his lips.

"The thing is, I believe you. Call me crazy, but I do. I've seen the weird stuff that happens around you if you're too bad or too good. I really do get it. But if you think I'm going to let that keep me from being with the one guy who's treated me right, and who I'm ninety-nine percent sure is the perfect man for me, then you're sadly mistaken."

He didn't bring it up again after that. It was like he had some disease that they chose not to talk about. He was OK with that. It seemed like the only time he didn't constantly worry about the consequences of throwing something in a recycle bin instead of littering was when he was around her. It had been nice to have someone to share it with, even if they didn't talk about it.

For the longest time, he hadn't told anyone, or honestly even known what was going on. The first time he really started to add it all up was when he was eleven. He had stepped proudly onto the stage at the state spelling bee, and spelled out S-E-N-E-S-C-H-A-L. His mom had been with him every letter of the way, quizzing him with flash cards, and telling him how proud she was when he studied. As he pronounced the last letter on that winning word, his mom slumped over in her chair on the front row. The doctors said it was an aneurism, and there was no way anyone could have known about it beforehand, but even at that age, Jeremy had started to believe that something was very, very wrong. How could something so bad happen during something so good? Why then? Why her? Why him?

Dr. Brady told him it was perfectly normal to ask those questions, especially at that age. Jeremy had been seeing Dr. Brady since he was thirteen, when his dad decided he needed to be seen. He was acting out at school and constantly in trouble. It didn't make any sense. He'd bring home an A-plus project about helping the needy in Nicaragua, and then the next day he would get in a fight with half the football team. His dad couldn't understand, so Jeremy didn't blame him too much for sending him to talk to someone. Dr. Brady had always been very kind, and Jeremy was still in touch with him. In fact, he'd talked with him on the phone just a few hours ago.

"Hello, there Jeremy," the doctor had said, his voice soothing and pleasant as ever. "What's on your mind? Cathy said you tried to call me four times this afternoon."

"I did, Dr. Brady. Did you see the news? About the kids trapped downtown?"

"Yes. But Jeremy, you know you had nothing to do with that, right? We've talked about this kind of fear. It's impossible for you to control the world around you by doing good things or bad things. You know that, right?"

"Yes," Jeremy said, switching the pay phone receiver to his other ear as Tammy from the zoo's big cat zone came into the break room. She smiled at him and grabbed something out of the refrigerator, then went back out into the bright sunlight, leaving behind the scent of foreign manure and dusty fur. "I know it's not my fault, but what if I could help?"

"What are you suggesting, Jeremy?"

The conversation hadn't gone much further than that because his break had been over. He didn't think Dr. Brady would understand, anyway.

Plus, Jeremy wanted to make sure he kept his job. With his criminal record and spotty employment history, it had been more than a minor miracle when the local zoo had offered him a job. He was mainly in charge of the "Wild Wings" concessions stand in the exotic birds area, but he did other things, too. Every morning he came in promptly at 7 a.m. and helped Scott, the bird handler, feed all the birds in their enclosures. By nine when the zoo opened, he was ready for business in his little stand with the hotdogs roasting on their rotating metal bars and the Slushee mix dancing red and blue behind the machine's round glass porthole.

It was a great job. It wasn't hard to deal with his condition in the zoo, surrounded by so many people and animals. The best indicator he'd found was the flies that perpetually plagued the zoo, constantly hoping to procreate on the massive amount of manure output the zoo created every day. If he'd been a little too nice to his customers, flies would begin to die for no reason, falling lifeless to the ground mid-flight. That let him know he needed to be a little rude for a while. He might even shortchange some customers on purpose, for their own good. It was all a matter of keeping what Sarah once called his "karmic balance." If he didn't keep careful track, things went south in a hurry. Like the time he made the mistake of chasing down a customer that had left his wallet. Ten minutes later one of the zoo's oldest and most beloved macaws, Ginga, fell off his perch, dead. Jeremy felt bad about that. It was all his fault, even if Dr. Brady didn't agree. At least Sarah understood.

"You know, sweetie, you're just going to have to learn to control it," she said one afternoon when they decided to go for a walk in Westchester Park. "It's like you're a superhero who just got his powers or something. You've just got to figure out how to channel that energy, harness you chi or your aura or whatever it is."

"Karma?" he suggested.

"Sure, your karma. Whatever you want to call it. If you think about it, it's a big deal." She led him behind one of the big bushes by the lake and sat on a stump, lighting her afternoon joint. "I mean, yeah, it's kind of wild to try and control, but you can make things happen. You can control the future! Influence the lives of those around you!"

"I can?" he asked, taking a quick hit and then handing it back to her. Sarah said smoking made her artwork come to life and got her creative juices flowing. He didn't like to smoke much, himself. It could upset the balance, considering it was technically illegal.

He had no complaints about the legal system, though. It had been really helpful at times, especially back when Jeremy hadn't been able to maintain a very stable balance. Jaywalking had been particularly useful. If it was officially posted somewhere, he could use it: No U-turns; no right on red; no shirt, no shoes, no service. It worked for doing good, too. With a little premeditation if things got desperate, he could announce he was going to make a U-turn out loud, then consciously not make a U-turn, and it seemed to work in his favor. Sarah said she figured it was a loophole he'd found. By planning to do bad, then not doing it, he was actually doing good, even if he was being bad by cheating the system. That was just how she said it, and he'd had to make her repeat it slowly three times before he could get the words to make sense. She'd laughed so hard she snorted.

Looking back, it was amazing to him that he hadn't swept across southern Illinois like a plague as a kid. He'd been a stand-up, sitcom-good kid before his mom died. He'd played baseball and basketball, had a decent number of friends, and always did well in school. After the spelling bee, he started to get into fights and his grades dropped like a dead macaw. He wasn't willing to risk ruining his dad's life or losing him like his mom, so Jeremy did as much wrong as he could. Consequently, (or coincidentally, according to Dr. Brady), his dad won a million-dollar jackpot, was promoted three times at work in under two years, and actually started growing back hair that had been claimed by premature balding. When he was eighteen, Jeremy stole a car and drove it to Texas, and that same day his dad met his new wife, Christine. They were a match made in heaven, facilitated by Jeremy's premeditated hell-raising.

"I don't want to see you anymore, son," his dad had said the last time Jeremy went to visit, a touch of contempt and sadness in his voice. His son was a bum, a criminal, a lunatic. "I love you because you're my son, but I never want to see you again. Is that clear?"

"I understand," Jeremy answered. "I love you, too." He'd known for a while that day would come. It was like Sarah said; he was a hero. He had made his dad's life better, but like all true heroes, it came with a cost. He was Spider-Man losing Uncle Ben, and Superman mourning Krypton. He was losing his only real family but for all the right reasons.

That had happened over a year ago. Today, he was at work when an urgent news announcement came on his stand's antique black-and-white travel TV, the one that some former employee had broken the antenna off of. He watched, horrified, as the announcer detailed a tragic accident downtown in somber, professional tones. Someone had bombed a building, but they didn't know who it was at this time. There were two adults and twenty-four kids trapped inside, way down in the belly of the rubble. They'd just been there on a field trip, but initial probing by the fire department had revealed a blazing fire down there with them, eating away at the precious oxygen, and creeping closer and closer to the kids and their teachers. The rescuers were doing their best, but it would take a miracle to get them out before the oxygen ran out.

On his lunch break he called Sarah, and explained the situation and his idea to her. As he spoke, he watched the closed captioning on the muted break room TV. A reporter was interviewing the daughter of one of the trapped teachers, begging the rescuers to do what they could on live television. She couldn't have been older than eleven or twelve, but she was doing her best to look brave through the tears that glistened on her cheeks.

"What do you think?" he asked.

"Yes," she said. "You have to do it. I love you so much, but you're the only one who can stop it, sweetie. You're my hero. My superhero."

"I love you, too," Jeremy said. He wondered if she would paint him someday.

He had a pistol, left over from his rough days. He'd purchased it originally at a pawn shop so he could rob a gas station and offset helping a little old lady across a busy street earlier in the day. It had been worth it because of her wrinkled smile once they got to the other side. That smile had reminded him of his mom, somehow. Of course, the money and free beef jerky had been a nice perk.

Jeremy was on his last break when he called Dr. Brady. That last hour at work he spit in every Slushee just to get things started, and when he got off work, he "forgot" to turn in his access key at the security office. On the way home, he spit his gum out on the sidewalk and jaywalked six times. Then before he went out again, he left a silent, three-minute message on his dad's answering machine.

Two days before today, Jeremy had gotten up and headed to the zoo early as always. He helped Scott feed the birds, one cage at a time. He always had to be rude and cheat his first five or six customers to make up for helping, but he figured it was worth it. Scott was a good guy, and Jeremy thought the birds were cool.

"What are those?" he asked Scott, peering through the thick glass of what used to be the pygmy-tailed cockatiel habitat.

"Those are emerald-hooded herons from South America, man," Scott said with a grin. "Sweet, aren't they? Real special, those. They're the last of their kind. Just five left in the world."

"Only five?"

"Yep. Three females and two males. Everyone thought they were extinct already, but someone stumbled on them in this little valley out in the middle of the jungle. Dr. Kuhlman's coming out in a couple of days to see if we can get them to mate, or if we can just do it with test tubes. Anything to save the species, right?"

"Save the species," Jeremy whispered, looking down at the gun in his hand, glinting in the lights from the path. "Extinction." He'd stopped shaking. Greg was well out of earshot now. It was time. He stood and took a deep breath. Sarah's voice came to him. "My superhero," she said, his mind repeating the words over and over. Those kids needed a miracle, buried under that burning building, and only a true hero could save them. A real hero had to be willing to do whatever was necessary. In his mind, he imagined himself engulfed in one of Sarah's paintings, staring down a defiant burnt orange heron, his finger on the trigger. He took one more deep breath, released it slowly like Dr. Brady had taught him, and then stepped into the cage, his finger on the trigger.

Katy Resch

Loss

My husband fears losing me. We're driving from Virginia to Missouri, to visit his—our—family, when he admits it in a road game: name your greatest fear, your greatest source of pleasure. His favorite thing is painting. Mine is to make metaphors. He doesn't ask my fear. I have already told him I fear in twenty years I will wish we'd had a child. I fear a regret I've grown powerless to amend. What he doesn't know is I will fear this in ten years, five, one, tomorrow. Because our fears hurtle towards us faster than our car can climb this West Virginia mountain: Up ahead, a rock face resembles a UFO, now a polar bear, now a man with a broken nose; now it is upon us and clearly, concretely a rock face.

The clarity of a concrete thing upon us: Maybe that is why my husband doesn't ask my fear. My husband has insisted he will never want a child.

Now, we enter thick fog. Fog is not a metaphor. It swallows the road and my husband must concentrate on driving. And so I don't ask him what shape loss might take. Online, in a forum where we curate our lives, his sister posts a picture of her nine-year-old daughter to represent her. This is who his sister chooses to be before the world. His mother posts her granddaughter's image in the space marked "Profile." *Mom, you look so young*, my husband has typed as comment.

Often, to think about my favorite thing, I take solitary walks in uncharted parts of the park. I turn off my phone. I have panicked, forgetting the markers for my return—left at the fallen bird nest? At the trunk robed in moss? Once, I came home before my husband expected me to. Music blared so loudly from his studio, he didn't hear me crack his door. He didn't sense me watch him. He was *painting*, a word that can't capture how he knifed pigment into an image, the pointed, determined gesture of it. How his feet pounded out the moat of sound around him. And his face—still, I struggle to describe it—how it had been reassembled into a face I didn't recognize. New muscles fixed his mouth and eyes; his jaw jutted. My husband—has he ever seen this strange man's face? Can we see our own expression of divine abandon? Perhaps this is why we make things, to call forth the hidden mind and give it a knowable shape. I could not wait to study my husband's painting, to catch the mark of his remote self. *Yes*, he said, *please look*, when he noticed me finally and the man I recognized returned to his body, pouted to signal sheepishness. *Don't look at me*, he was saying. *Look for me, in my painting.*

If I were to take my turn at our road game, I would not tell my husband I fear losing him. I have lost him; all the time, I lose him. *I fear not being able to find you again.*

In Missouri, we will visit my husband's grandparents, who lost their son to the Vietnam War. Each visit, they show us his photograph, say my husband looks just like him. I agree, he agrees, but privately, we don't see it. My husband's mother leaves the room. His grandparents peer into my husband's face. It's the brow, they determine, a certain way of saying certain phrases. *How you sit in that chair like that.* They bore through him. They are eighty-nine years old and aware enough to be furious at their failing memories. To feel the mind slip and to be afraid. They pray often; they will reunite in heaven. They will reunite with their son. If his grandfather goes first, as they suspect, his grandmother will be able to see him anywhere, if she looks hard enough, because God the father has poured himself into everything he has made. Do you pray, they ask us, do you believe?

My husband's brother, once again, won't show for this reunion. He calls us on the road—there's a good-paying gig, a studio session. And so their parents will fill the house with recordings of his music—drums, bongos, instruments we've never heard of, playing Afro beats learned in Ghana. How their mother worried all that could go wrong while he was there, unnamed diseases for which there is no remedy.

Their father will tap along on the breakfast table, describe the details he understands—where the songs were recorded and how, in a studio rigged with corrugated metal and the stuffing from old chairs. All day, strange time signatures jostle us; my husband's brother shrinks in our visions as a field of dry grasses expands around him. Dinnertime comes the classic rock station and his parents hum along. His sister will holler to her daughter and four stepchildren—young adults sleeping in former bedrooms—to come eat. My husband will remark that his sister has got that down, that mother voice with which she has never spoken to him. Her oldest stepson isn't there; he is in rehab again. No one mentions him. And her own daughter will get sick during our visit, a stomach bug severe enough to upend his sister's plans for the week. She will cancel our brunch date, when she might have told us how her stepson's addiction has re-routed her marriage. How her husband is paying, yet again, for his son's debts, for his treatment, despite her protestations and his former promises to let go, to stop. Her stepson is nearly thirty, an adult, a liar, she has claimed, whom her compassion has hardened against. She will not tell us—she will not need to; we will see it in the clumsy way they pass plates of food—that in relenting to his son, her husband has gone strange to her. *Where is the man I know?* she has wondered. *Where is he when he is searching for his child?*

On the road, we are spent. Winding through thick clouds, we tensed and braced our bodies and are grateful, now, for a clearing. We can see rock faces; they are rock faces. They are all upon us with pine trees growing from them perpendicularly. The trees appear precarious, impossible. *Would you include that in a landscape painting?* I ask. He says, *It'd be the best part.* We pull off onto a gravel lot labeled "Scenic overlook." Whatever conditions produce fog also produce an exquisite, enormous sky. Candy pinks melt over green ridges; wispy clouds feather the light. I don't believe in God—which might mean only that I have never feared immediately for my life, my husband's life—but I can imagine what it is like for believers to apprehend a sky like this. To gaze upon something mysterious and beautiful and think, if they look hard enough, they will unlock a secret about their creator, who has made us in his image; see a glimmer of the divine we fear is lost to us but is always present.

Phong Nguyen

The Story of Ill-Begotten

The Stoughtons

Technically, there was nothing wrong with Ill. No extra chromosomes, no missing fingers, nothing terminal or chronic or congenital. He was just Off. This, of course, was before the APA got wise to all the ways a child could be considered Off (or, at least, in need of good drugs), and came up with a whole secret language of acronyms to talk about all the "problem children" out there, even though in the end it amounted to the same thing: O.F.F., which Ill was for damned sure.

When Ill was six, he learned about recycling. In the eighties, the whole country was crazy about recycling, and so was Ill. He read it in school. He heard it on radio spots, PSA's. He even watched it on a cartoon show, "Captain Planet." He asked his mama about recycling and she explained the deal to him: You put stuff in the green bin so it could be reused and nothing would ever go to waste.

How can they use paper I already drawed on? Ill wanted to know. His Mama told him they used old paper to make new paper—he didn't know *how* they did it, but they just re-shaped stuff into other stuff, different stuffl, that other people could use. Ill never used the regular trash again.

Well, pretty soon Ill's mama, Harley, started to find things in the recycling bin that didn't belong: the broken toaster, the perfectly good lamp, photo albums, and, in a memorable discovery for her, their morbidly obese Siamese cat, Sonny.

Ill-Begotten—for that was his full name, Ill-Begotten Stoughton —had said that Sonny needed to be remade. He wanted to be a *new* cat, he said.

233

☾

The rumor was that Ill-Begotten's Mama had man-raped his pop for his genes. His pop Winstone was supposedly an Ivy League genius, internationally famous in the fields of applied science, mechanical engineering, and musicology. He was a Renaissance man, literally. He performed music of the Renaissance period, and collected obscure instruments from sixteenth-century Europe. He tried to rebuild Da Vinci machines in his spare time. His ambition was to produce something that, like the inorganic chemicals ammonium and cyanate, when combined in the lab made something completely different—an *organic* compound, urine. *That*, he said, was a *discovery*.

Harley first ran into Winstone at the Christian Science reading room. He was browsing in the kids' section, probably looking for a gift for a niece or nephew. There was something about him; Harley knew right away. She may have been uneducated, and unskilled at everything that would have helped her advance in the world, but she was excellent in this: She could smell good genes from across the room.

Hi, she said, and stood there like making introductions wasn't necessary.

Hello, said Winstone, who, in his distraction, had not noticed the woman staring in his direction for the last several minutes. Now that he saw her, it occurred to him to be frightened. She had an acorn shape, a front-butt that pushed out from her jeans, and the slightest layer of peach fuzz on her philtrum. She had light blue eyes, so wide and vacant they seemed to be the locus of all her sense—as though they could hear and smell and taste, as well.

But, as a Renaissance man, Winstone thought this woman had a certain Rabelaisian grotesqueness about her, which was oddly appealing to his classical sensibility. His aesthetic was, to euphemize, anachronistic. But Winstone's ideas about chivalry, too, were anachronistic, and had no idea how to go about courting a modern woman.

Harley made it easy. She put one hand on his bow tie, and the other on his crotch, and shoved him into the rear of the store, into the unisex restroom, where Ill-Begotten was ill-conceived.

Harley

Only a month before Ill-Begotten was born, Harley found Jesus. Or, since her new evangelical church said *He* was everywhere, you might say she *sought* Jesus, let Him into her life. As soon as she did, she felt terrible guilt over what she had done to Winstone, and she named her son "Ill-Begotten" to remind herself of her sinfulness.

She wished that she could be more like Mary, waiting for an archangel to plant a child in her instead. But, Harley thought, not every virgin was so lucky. Some got sacrificed. Some were just quiet and ugly, and that's how they lived and died.

She got involved with a group of abortion protesters, mostly men, who were so happy to have recruited another woman for their team that it didn't make the slightest difference that she tended to spook people away with her big golf-ball eyes.

Pregnancy makes some people hungry or nauseous or tired. For Harley, being pregnant gave her a sense of newfound righteousness. A stance in the world. She began to think bitterly about legions of theoretical people who were out to murder their babies.

They call it "justifying." You wait outside a clinic for a four-hour shift and talk at all the passersby, whether they are getting abortions or not. You show them pictures. You give them literature describing *the facts*. You *justify* them. They could go ahead and do what they came to do, but they couldn't leave without knowing what they were doing was wrong.

Once in a while, maybe twice in a year, the method worked. Harley would never forget her first and only success "justifying" a baby-killer. It was early morning, before her shift had technically begun, and she hadn't even got together her pamphleting material. A woman showed up ten minutes before the clinic was even open, and was forced to wait around outside. She had dirty-blond hair all the way down to the middle of her back, and a thin nervousness that put Harley in mind of her mother (and, when she thought about it, of a whole generation of thin, nervous mothers).

Harley didn't have any flyers on hand, so the woman went ahead and stood next to her, as though they were forming a line to get inside for their abortions. It was jarring to Harley—so different from the reaction to the method—to be treated like a normal human being, rather than as a woman who stands out in the cold for four hours every day with no pay just to impose her values on them, which is what she really was, I guess. But the situation called for a different approach, something more personal than the usual line.

"Do you know what techniques they use here?" Harley asked. The woman shook her head. "The vacuum," she answered her own question. "Or, depending on how far along you are, poison, too."

The woman looked visibly disturbed, but she didn't wince, or even squint. "Well, I'm only eight weeks," she said.

Harley could have recited the whole facts table without once consulting the flyer. But she thought the effect was different when you saw it on paper. She fished out a flyer from her bag and handed it to the woman. "You know, at eight weeks, your baby already has fingers and toes." Having fingers and toes, she thought, is something anybody ought to identify with.

The woman looked up with understanding in her eyes—relief, even.

"See this?" Harley pointed at her belly. "This baby was the product of a rape. But I'm going to *deliver* this baby, and I'm gonna *raise* this baby, because I *still* believe it's a blessing from God."

"You must be a very strong woman," the thin woman said. "Not everybody could do what you're doing."

"All women are strong. That's why God entrusted us to bear *His* children. They're angels, every single one of 'em."

"I agree with you," she said, without hesitation.

"What's your name?" Harley asked, then.

Her name was Jean Connor, and her baby, she said, wasn't the product of rape—it was the product of bad love. Her husband was a struggling actor who'd turned to drink. A living stereotype. And he said he loved her, and she was so young, and he lied so much. All of his *other* sexual conquests aborted *their* babies. Jean didn't want to be the only woman stupid enough to have his child. But she didn't like abortion either, she said. She was actually Catholic. At the mention of the C word, Harley managed to cringe and smile at the same time. A *lapsed* Catholic, Jean assured her, and Harley proceeded to invite the woman over to her house for a home-cooked dinner.

☾

Harley was vulnerable to "globe luxation," a rare condition that meant every once in a while, given the right sequence of events, an eyeball would pop out of its socket. The best way to handle globe luxation, she'd learned over the years, was to pop the eyeball back in and take a double dose of Tylenol. But it happened at the most inconvenient times, such as getting fitted for a dress, or while pleasuring herself in front of the TV.

Which is not to say there is ever a convenient time to lose an eye.

But the worst was the day Jean moved in to Harley's house. They'd become fast friends, and the sometimes over-bearing Harley Stoughton had found Jean—her quiet, mousily pretty companion—an easy conversion. As far as Harley was concerned, she'd saved Jean from hellfire, earning her a seat in heaven. And now she was even giving her a place to live on earth.

When Jean showed up at the door, suitcase in hand, she pressed the doorbell with her elbow. Then after a moment passed, she dropped the suitcase, and pushed the door open quickly, just as Harley was running up to answer it. Harley slammed into the swinging door nose-first, and both her eyeballs sprung out, like googly glasses. Jean, who was not easily shocked, staggered backward, her mouth turned down and open as though for a silent scream. She fought the impulse to cover her own eyes, now that she knew what could happen to them.

After pushing both eyeballs back into their proper places, and taking her painkillers, Harley apologized constantly, repeating it as though to herself rather than to Jean. The air was so full of "I'm sorry" that to say it now seemed like overkill.

Pretty soon, Jean's horror turn to awe, when she thought about how indifferent to pain Harley must be. It symbolized Harley to her —a woman who could take a hit and roll with the punches, whose eyes popped out of her head, and who stuffed them back in by herself, then went to the kitchen to finish breaking eggs.

They grew pregnant together, and gave birth a month apart, using the same doula and midwife. Harley insisted on a home birth for both of them. Jean followed Harley's lead and gave her child a name of significance. He was born Coinflip Connor, to remind his mom that there was half a chance he wouldn't have even made it out of the womb. At the tender age of fifteen, Ill-Begotten, an older boy named Red, and Coinflip (or just plain Flip) ran away to live in a glorified crackhouse in Soho.

Ill-Begotten

It was the nineties. Rock-starhair gave way to white-guy dreadlocks. Turtlenecks turned into lumberjack shirts, and jeans remained jeans but got bigger and baggier, while windbreakers became basketball jerseys, and so on. This wouldn't have been relevant at all, except that Ill-Begotten continued wearing wristbands and jogging outfits unironically, which tells you something about how Off he was.

Ill-Begotten is the one who got Flip into health foods. Those years, the two of them fought over Soy Yogurts and the last Tofu Square (a delicious finger-food Flip invented that Red referred to as "Toe-Food"). Ill would eat oatmeal for breakfast, then pop Quaaludes right after. Good health was something he hoped to achieve by starving himself and getting really high.

All this pissed Red off no end. He called them "little faggots" and "fairy-boys," or, when the situation warranted it, "the two stooges" (not realizing, perhaps, that he was the obvious choice to fill out the slapstick trio). Red just liked to smoke and play cards. It was the only thing that kept him mellow and his hands busy. Years later, he would be kicked out of this place for making bad deals, hit rock bottom somewhere in Boston, and then show up as the owner of a shady club in Providence.

Red had sort of a penis-head. He was one of those bald men whose head-shape made you wonder why they didn't just settle for a comb-over. And he had a cocaine sniffle. And he had just one angry-looking eyebrow that bisected his head, going straight across from temple to temple. He was the leader by default. He was older and more intense-looking than they were, and besides, the two of them had flunky names: Flip and Ill, like guys who got their lights punched out by Robin the Boy Wonder on the Batman show. *Wham! Thwack!*

One time Red caught them going on one of their trips to the health-food store, and he yelled out, "Hey, fuckers, take it easy on the soy. I heard that shit puts estrogen in your system. I don't want you boys growing tits." I guess Red was about as close to a father figure Flip or Ill would ever get.

Everyone in the old neighborhood knew who Ill-Begotten was —knew his story, and used his example as a stark warning against youthful error of any stripe: teen pregnancy, gang membership, shoplifting. Whatever it was, Ill was said to be the result, the example —for girls, that's how your baby would end up; for boys, that's you in ten years' time, if you keep it up.

What happened to Ill was unique, though; unprecedented, in fact. The truth was you couldn't meet a fate like his if you wanted to. To lots of weirdos then and since, Ill Begotten became a hero of the improbable.

The sad thing is that all Ill ever did wrong was try to find his dad. But, like ammonium and cyanate, each man alone had his separate use in the world, but once mixed all they could do is make piss.

Winstone

It was not hard for Ill to find his father. Winstone Normal worked in the labs at Brown University, day and night, and everyone knew about him. He was a campus eccentric—the subject of constant rumor and debate among the student body. Like the boy on acid who thought he could fly. Or the millionaire who gave up his money to go homeless. Or the janitor everybody said used to be a guerrilla warrior in some obscure South American dictatorship. Winstone Normal was the mad scientist who was building his own Frankenstein's Monster in the university laboratories.

Flip went along with Ill on his first visit. They took a bus from SoHo and got out at Burnside Park. By then Flip had gone scrawny from all the health food and grew a perfectly formed handlebar mustache for the Pawtucket Mustache Contest that weekend. But Ill swelled even bigger and let his chin sprout uneven patches of scraggle. He looked just like Harley had, the day she and Winstone first met in the Christian Science reading room. They even wore their hair the same way.

So Winstone's natural reaction to the sight of Ill was fear. He hid behind the particle oscillator and picked up a handful of lug nuts as potential projectiles. "I come in peace," Ill said, and it was so Ill —that freakshow alien, the near-spherical man holding his hands out like whole hams and pleading for his father to come out from behind his vaccuum unit.

"You made me," Ill said, relishing the *Batman* quote that was still fresh in the year 1993, and for a long moment, Winstone searched his mind for some renegade invention he may have unleashed on the world long ago, which could have gotten beyond his control and come back in the shape of a big man in a jogging suit.

Coinflip

When Harley showed up, Ill was already plugged into Winstone's machine, wires all flowing from the machine to his body, fixed by electrodes and intravenous tubes. The scan was said to measure the ratio of human and animal qualities. Winstone wanted to be absolutely sure, before acknowledging Ill as his son, that the boy's human/animal ratios demonstrated a capacity for higher thought.

Later, skeptics who doubted Ill's unique place in the history of science would speculate that it was a flaw in the machine that caused the incident. But Flip was there and he saw it happen with his own tripped-out eyes. Flip's theory was this: The first time Winstone and Harley were in the same room together, Ill was made; the second time, he was unmade. So God simply corrected His mistake, using those two as catalysts for His grand plan.

Winstone recognized Harley immediately and hid behind the particle oscillator again. Though Ill turned out to be harmless, he wasn't taking his chances with this creature of appetite with whom he had such a painful history.

Harley, morally reformed as she was, stood proudly in the presence of the man she had abused, the man she had borne, and the man she had saved from never having lived at all.

"Ma, go away!" Ill said, moving forward as much as his restraints would allow. "You're ruining it!"

Harley looked at him with a sympathy-for-your-soul face that only true believers make. "I can't, baby. I woke up this morning and the Lord guided my steps," she said.

"This isn't about you and the Lord, Ma. This is about me and pop." Ill had run away at that age when a kid can't tell the difference between talking and yelling. In the presence of his mama, Ill just seemed to pick up where he left off at fifteen.

"Sweetie, *everything* has to do with the Lord." Harley held out her hand, but not palm-up, as in an appeal, but palm-forward, as in a healing touch.

Ill looked to his pop for support, but only Winstone's hair was visible from behind the vacuum unit.

The machine started to blip and wheeze. Winstone crawled over to the readout, and after scanning the crests and valleys that map man's levels of instinct and rationality, shouted out: "It's mostly human!"

"Stand back," Harley said calmly to Winstone, and he complied, more than willing to move farther away from the crazy-eyed lady. "You won't be corrupting my son with your devil science."

Then Ill started to laugh. The thought that anybody could corrupt Ill beyond his self-made corruptions was a premise to be ridiculed. He looked around at his worlds colliding. Mama-world, doped-up Three Stooges world, and now the brave new world of science and his pop Winstone. Maybe he just couldn't stand the leaking of separate dimensions. Maybe his two selves split at the middle.

Fuck speculation. What happened to Ill was bad. No, "bad" is the wrong way to say it. Ill's fate was unbelievable, and defied physical laws.

His body ballooned first, bloating so big and lumpy that it tore the jogging suit from his legs and torso, looking for all the world like a swelling nut-sack breaking out of a pair of tight-whities.

Then there was a splashing sound, and pieces of Ill rained everywhere around them. When Flip opened his eyes again he found an ear stuck to his sweater.

"He's blown up," Harley said, because sometimes the most obvious things need to be said.

The headline appeared on the AP wire in the "curious scientific facts" section. He was posthumously honored with a Darwin Award, a distinction awarded only to those rare individuals who "leave the gene pool with style." But the most lasting legacy of Ill-Begotten was the way his story was tossed back and forth in religious circles and debated at scientific conferences for years afterwards.

Winstone seemed embarrassed by his association with this scientific anomaly. His personal account of the incident led to a loss of credibility and an eye-rolling toleration among his peers. So he buried his son mentally long before they ever gathered the pieces to bury him in the proper way.

Flip, on the other hand, spent hours trying to put Humpty-Dumpty back together again. By the time campus security rolled up, he'd found enough pieces of Ill to make a crude, two-dimensional body—some crazy Picasso-painting person. It's a sort of grieving, to honor the dead by making art out of pieces of them.

The incident made a perfect excuse, however, for Harley to go on tour. It was heavy ammunition, to be able to say, in answer to the question, "How can you be so sure about an omnipotent God?": "My son blew up! It was a miracle!"

Technically, a miracle is when an event occurs that has no scientific precedent—when the laws of nature are reversed for one moment, and it cannot be explained in any other way but as an act of God. But then you have to wonder: Is it a miracle when a man nobody wanted anyway is smudged away with an eraser? Did God do that?

Ken Haas

God's Widow

His son wasn't hers and the spirit never as holy
as biographers made out. Halfway through
the sixth day she told him he looked tired, said
nothing's wrong with free will, but coupling it
with the directive to have dominion could take
a bad turn; instead give more power to the whales
or trees, or the moon. But no. Then all those nights
in the basement working on his special project.

Not mother or minder, Thelma, Heloise, or the Virgin
Queen. She is the Other. Capital Oh. And now
I have to pray to her. She whose love was not
enough, whose dear I was never, whose green home
has been savaged, who couldn't care less if I believe.
My girlfriend says I might want to start on my knees.

Alan Michael Parker

Letter to the Buddha, Including an X-Ray of My Foot

So now you know even more
than everything, now you see
how little I am
in the little room
of my body.

There went Sue the X-ray technician
running to hide in her lead booth
like the Bodhisattva of Fear Itself.
And here is the body in black-and-white,
moonlight on a playground:

the twenty-six bones of the foot:
talus, calcaneus, cuneiforms I, II, & III,
cuboid and navicular. Five metatarsals,
two phalanges in the great toe,
three phalanges in the other four.

What does an X-ray X-ray?
The forty-two muscles,
the thirty-two joints, the more than
fifty ligaments and tendons, and the more than
250,000 sweat glands of the foot

seen through—as the Unknown
slams shut the door to the X-ray booth,

the sound on the intercom the sound
of Sue sucking on her teeth.
Hold still. Don't breathe. Good.

Master, I'm sending you a picture of my foot,
the one that hurts,
a foot made in the world, pain
you could teach me not to need.
There. Good. Done.

I am writing to say that I'm sorry
there's still stuff I want,
that the hospital smell of the chemicals
feels like it burns, that I hope
no human foot hurts again.

Yes, we both know that I'm not better.
But I am writing to say that it's OK,
you can let go of worrying about me,
Buddha, they took an X-ray,
Buddha, the X-ray was negative.

A Telephone Conversation
With Naomi Shihab Nye

San Antonio, Texas, and Springfield, Missouri
September 24, 2013

Naomi Shihab Nye is considered one of the most prominent poets of the American Southwest. Born to a Palestinian father and an American mother, Nye grew up in St. Louis, Jerusalem, and San Antonio. Today, Nye has written and edited more than thirty books, including two books from the Middle East. Her poems have appeared in numerous anthologies, journals and newspapers. She currently resides in San Antonio, Texas.

Missouri State University student Julia Greene spoke with Nye this past fall as she was about to visit Missouri.

Julia Greene: Hi, how are you?

Naomi Shihab Nye: Good morning. I'm fine. How are you doing?

JG: I'm well. Thank you.

NSN: Well, thank you so much for taking time to talk to me.

JG: Thank you so much for allowing me to interview you. It's such an honor, honestly. I'm a huge fan of your work.

NSN: That is sweet of you. I really appreciate it. I'm excited about coming back to my home state.

JG: I know. To Bolivar. I'll see you on Thursday.

NSN: I look forward to it.

JG: Okay, well, let's go ahead and get started. You were born in St. Louis. How long did you stay there before you moved?

NSN: I stayed there until I was about fourteen. And I loved it there. I've gone back over the years many times to see old friends, be in the old neighborhood. I love St. Louis, its sights and smells and historic buildings and parks and memories, very much.

JG: How would you say your ethnic identity as a Palestinian American has influenced your writing?

NSN: Well, it probably didn't influence me any more than everybody's background influences them, whether we have a bicultural or single-cultural background. I think we're all influenced by the context we grow up in. And I felt, even as a child, quite lucky that my parents were from two different parts of the world and had grown up with different traditions, different religions, different foods, etc., because it was almost like having a doubled experience. It was not a conflict for me in any way. It was like a richness, a feeling of, "Wow. You know, I have access here to different worlds through my parents."

JG: You've stated in previous interviews that your visit to, okay, I believe it's pronounced SAN-jile. Is that correct?

NSN: Oh, SIN-Jil! Where my grandmother lived, yeah.

JG: Oh, SIN-jil. You stated in previous interviews that your visit to Sinjil when you were, I believe it was about fourteen, had a profound influence on your poetics. Can you tell me a bit more about that visit, and how it influenced your writing?

NSN: Well, it was …. I was a freshman in high school at the time my family moved back to Jerusalem. And we lived on the road between Jerusalem where my father's family had lost their home in 1948 and then the village where my grandmother and other relatives had ended up living. So, it was sort of like being suspended between the past and current worlds of that part of the Middle East. And I think I became much more aware of transmission and expression, how people who didn't speak the same language could still communicate in profound ways that oral history was something, or oral expression was something very much alive, not only in my father which I already knew, but in my grandmother and in my father's brothers, just the whole spectrum of people who go on telling the old stories. And I felt that I had a sudden access to understanding my own sense of humor more because I think I could see it reflected now not only in my father but in his mother and kind of the way the family, the family attitude went back, not with a huge amount of bitterness, but with a quirky, resolute irony—"Look what happened in our lives. We lost everything. It's not great, but here we are." At that tender teen age you're still forming opinions and perspectives—shaping your world view, your response to human beings—how are you going to behave in your own life? Who do you respect? People who have lived through really rough things and have survived them and are still laughing—you know, you're able to … just start finding your own compass.

JG: You mentioned earlier that your parents and your grandmother were very influential. Is it safe to say that your family is one of the main influences in your poetry?

NSN: I would say that my family was definitely my first influence, and then a sense of human beings and the human family is definitely my ongoing influence. And I do feel very lucky that my mother read poems to me when I was a child before I could read myself. And by the time I could read, I already knew what an Emily Dickinson poem or a Carl Sandburg poem sounded like; even though I hadn't read it myself, I'd heard it. I'd gotten to bask in that sort of language. I was very attracted to the cadence and composition of poetry, what that language could do that was different from daily conversation and chatter.

JG: You've stated previously that you're a big fan of William Stafford. How would you say Stafford has influenced your writing, if he has influenced your writing?

NSN: His work has meant *everything* to me, since I first read him when I was sixteen. It has given me courage, grounding, clarity, a sense of lyrical movement, vision, wisdom, curiosity, and inquiry—also a way of seeing the world, which is quite elemental. He affected my whole life.

JG: What aspects of Stafford's poetry do you enjoy the most?

NSN: I treasure his honesty and his tip of the head. His "lean into language." His acute perceptions and skills at connection and overlay. His willingness to leap and leap and again. To leave things open-ended. I feel he honored language, human experience, and the ability of a writing process to open our own lives up to us. I love his topics, obviously—his sense of geography—his ways of listening to the world.

JG: You and Stafford are both well known for your personal poems that contain everyday diction and deliver a great deal of insight. Is this a trait that you picked up from Stafford?

NSN: I think I was already leaning that direction quite strongly at the age of sixteen, but he certainly gave me the courage to follow that path, those instincts. We are nourished by the work we love. His continues to nourish me, always, even if I am reading a poem for the hundredth time.

JG: Is there anything else about Stafford that you would like to say that I didn't address?

NSN: We need his commitment to nonviolence more than ever in a country that seems to be sickly obsessed with guns.

JG: In addition to your poetry being very personal and offering a lot of insight, I've also noticed that it tends to move towards compassion and forgiveness. Is this a conscious movement?

NSN: No, I would say it's unconscious. I hope it moves that way. You're very generous to say that it does. But I think as human beings we're always trying to redeem bad situations or apologize or forgive or make something better. I mean, I have a very strong impulse that way, like when I've done something wrong, I really want to rectify it. So I think with poems, you have this sense of looking at the human landscape, the world, and just trying to get below the surface, like why do terrible things keep happening; why is there violence; why are people unhappy? And I think poems often help us put pieces together, even if we can't solve things. This is what I've always thought about poetry: Even if the poems don't solve things, they shine a light on them, and I think that's a big thing. To have a little more light shining even on a mystery is important.

JG: You're often referred to as a "wandering poet." How do you feel about this title?

NSN: I don't know if I said that or someone else said that. Because I've been an itinerant, a freelancer in the world of poetry all these years, I've never had an ongoing, steady job that was longer than one semester. I have taught in different universities for semester-length classes. I'm doing that right now at the Michener Center, at the University of Texas at Austin. But I've jumped around. I've gone from different levels of students, different ages, rural, urban, at-home, overseas, all kinds of places, so that title stuck. There are many wonderful jobs writers can have in a freelance way. You don't have to have one full-time job in order for you to have places you could work. I try to encourage this idea with students interested in writing. Many times people will tell them, "If you like to write, you'll never be able to make a living." Well, that's ridiculous. I've made a living, and I know many people have made livings doing all different kinds of freelance work in the world of writing.

JG: I was wondering. Could you read a few of your poems for us?

NSN: Sure! I would be happy to. I'll read a poem called "Ringing" that was in my most recent book of poems called *Transfer*. This was written after my father's death. By the way, my father was Aziz Shihab, who worked for the *St. Louis Post-Dispatch* for a while. He ran a business in St. Louis for years called World Gifts that was an importing business. He loved the state of Missouri, and we often would drive around with him to different towns. He was also a public speaker, so people might have heard him on different campuses, or even in small-town church congregations.

Ringing

I'm sorry you lost your father, people say,
and I step outside to soak
in stripes of gray cloud.
Hand touches iron rail.
You needed it, I don't.

Blood circulating under skin
and time, that blurred sky shifting.
Air holds everyone visible or not.
Slice lemon you crave by your teacup.
Strange affection for chipped ice.

Maybe the right wind brings
a scent of smoldering twigs,
fresh water over stone.
Maybe tonight your laughter
carpets our rooms.
I keep finding you in ways you didn't know
I noticed, or knew.

Every road, every sea,
every beach by every sea,
keeps lining up with what you loved—
Here's a row of silent palm trees.
It's as if you answered the phone.

You know, I was very, very sad after he died for a long time, and I still am. I'll miss him all my life, but I did feel his presence so … so heartily, so mightily, everywhere around me. That that became a comfort that I could pick up little details that reminded me of him. I'm sure anyone who's lost a very beloved person has had a similar experience. So I say, just, just go with it; cling onto those images and details as much as you can—they help you survive. And I think you also liked the poem, "Arabic."

JG: I did like the poem, "Arabic." I love the poem, "Arabic." I believe it was the first poem I ever read by you, actually.

NSN: That's sweet of you to say. My father was with me on that trip. We were in Jordan, and I was giving presentations around the Middle East in different schools and libraries and working for U.S. libraries and consulates overseas always with the hope of more understanding among people. I was always feeling ashamed that even though I had studied Arabic, Spanish and German, I wasn't fluent in any of them. I could only have the most pedestrian responses to people in any of those three languages, whereas so many people in the Middle East and all around the world are extremely fluent in English. Embarrassing.

Arabic

The man with laughing eyes stopped smiling
to say, "Until you speak Arabic,
you will not understand pain."

Something to do with the back of the head,
an Arab carries sorrow in the back of the head,
that only language cracks, the thrum of stones

weeping, grating hinge on an old metal gate.
"Once you know," he whispered, "you can
enter the room whenever you need to.
Music you heard from a distance,

the slapped drum of a stranger's wedding,
well up inside your skin, inside rain, a thousand
pulsing tongues. You are changed."

Outside, the snow had finally stopped.
In a land where snow rarely falls,
we had felt our days grow white and still.

I thought pain had no tongue. Or every tongue
at once, supreme translator, sieve. I admit my
shame. To live on the brink of Arabic, tugging

its rich threads without understanding
how to weave the rug … I have no gift.
The sound, but not the sense.

I kept looking over his shoulder for someone else
to talk to, recalling my dying friend who only scrawled
I can't write. What good would any grammar have been

to her then? I touched his arm, held it hard,
which sometimes you don't do in the Middle East,
and said, *I'll work on it*, feeling sad

for his good strict heart, but later in the slick street
hailed a taxi by shouting *Pain!* and it stopped
in every language and opened its doors.

[Laughs] It was a true experience, and it made me laugh when I wrote it down. Some people ask about poems—would anyone really do that? Raise your hand and call a taxi by shouting "Pain"? I said, "Well, I did. So—you might." People do all kinds of quirky things, and I love the capacity of poems to contain quirky human experience, too. Odd things we do that give us memories, make us feel really alive —strange little unpredictable things that pop up.

JG: Right. I completely agree. Naomi, thank you so much for speaking with me.

NSN: You are so kind to talk to me and I can't wait to come there. Any time I see Missouri, it's a very touching experience. I look forward to meeting the students and community, so thank you very much for listening to me.

Naomi Shihab Nye

But What Happened to Her?

Her parents were tightly closed German boxes.
You couldn't get anything out of them

if you fiddled with the latch all day. Ask a question?
They looked away. I combed through her old drawers

in Grandma's bedroom. One silver bracelet engraved
with teepees and canoes. A cameo ring that fit no one.

The pale face without features could have been
a million women.

Naomi Shihab Nye

Houses of Depression

The children who live in them hope to fix things.
Causes remain mysterious.

Like a bulldozer in a bedroom, that heavy.
Dump truck pulled up right next to the dining room table.

One person learns to knit.
Another plants heritage tomatoes.

If there is a thread they are reaching for it
but tangles confound them,

knotting, snagging, tricking
attempts to disengage. Doors creak,

someone new might be entering. Let's start over.
Let's solve just this one thing.

A kitchen feels like a cage.

Naomi Shihab Nye

You Have No New Messages

O St. Louis, we drowsed in the cool room
under pines, the muddy swirl in our creek.
My teachers sent only two notes home;
She carries the devil within her, and,
Her mind tends to wander. And I did just fine.
No one was looking for me. I touched a telephone
maybe twice a year. You could hear soft scratchings
of pencils under the hours. Crickets in weeds,
someone hammering a For Sale sign,
the sad river glooming south.
Norma practiced her piano scales for years,
her mother taught me to sew a hem.
Daddy was gone making a deal,
he would be home late.
And my mother wept in a bedroom, wildly,
for whole seasons, it seemed. I monitored her pitch
while rinsing cherries in a sieve.
Stems plucked, pits removed. I was more scared
when she went silent. Called under the crack of her door.

Forty years later old friends gathered,
sat on same ground. So what
was the secret in your house? No one knew
about the tears. You didn't hear them? I said.
The screens were open.
But each house was its own full world.

Naomi Shihab Nye

Coming Home From School

Always one worry;
is she still alive?

Laundry flapping from lines
was a good sign—

why would you wash
if you were planning to die?

Sometimes I pressed my bicycle
recklessly up those hills as if

her thirty years of grief
were pushing the pedals saying

no, no, no, no.

Reviews

Train Shots: Stories **by Vanessa Blakeslee.** Orlando, Florida: Burrow Press, 2014. 150 pages. $15.99, paper.

At first, the short stories included in Vanessa Blakeslee's collection, *Train Shots*, seem disjointed. The reader is taken from the bleak reality of employment at a Mexican restaurant in "Clock In," and the struggling middle-American marriagein "Ask Jesus" to the harsh Central American farm life of "Welcome, Lost Dogs." It soon becomes apparent, however, that beneath the vivid scenery and gritty reality, Blakeslee presents the reader with characters in transition.

In "Uninvited Guest" and "Barbeque Rabbit," newly single mothers try to negotiate a balance between their own desires and their children's needs. "The Sponge Diver" and "Don't Forget the Beignets" feature younger girlfriends coping with disappointment in their respective relationships. The drug-addicted widower of "Hospice of the Au Pair" reconnects with his children, with the help of his domestic assistant, with whom he began an affair during his wife's illness. "The Lung" chronicles the struggle of a cancer survivor to find intimacy with his girlfriend. "The Princess of Pop" contemplates suicide, and the train conductor of "Train Shots" searches for meaning and connection after a young women is killed by his train.

While each story could stand alone, placing them in one collection creates a microcosm of contemporary relationships. Blakeslee's characters choose not between right and wrong, but between their own conflicting desires. Whether it is the investigation of security fraud in "Don't Forget the Beignets" or the lack of communication in "The Sponge Diver," each struggle is of equal importance to the characters experiencing them. Rather than using the common themes of change and loss to teach the reader a lesson, Blakeslee crafts complex relationships and conflicts. Each character comes to a fork in the road and must choose his or her own direction. Each choice is different and each journey unique.

Settings alternate between small-town America and several Central American locations--namely Nicaragua and Costa Rica. No matter the location, Blakeslee draws the reader in with detailed imagery, while avoiding overwhelming blocks of description. Rather than using Central America as simply an exotic backdrop, the geographical displacement of the expatriates and travelers in *Train Shots* intensifies feelings of disconnection, as well as the desire for personal freedom.

The collection is nicely bookended, beginning with "Clock In" and concluding with the titular story, "Train Shots." "Clock In" sets a humorus tone, while touching the surface of the less-than-glamorous lives of the subject's new coworkers. As the subject is introduced to the inner workings of a Mexican restuarant, the reader is given a glimpse into the witty, dark, and sometimes funny web of relationships that Blakeslee weaves into each narrative. In each following story, the reader is reminded that, though life may not go as planned, it always goes on. The final scene of "Train Shots" finds the train conductor, P.T., lying awake at night, imagining himself on a train home, "enjoying the gaps between cities and stations." For the characters in *Train Shots*, it is not the destination that matters, but learning to live in the "space between places."

—*Kelly Baker,* Moon City Review

☾

Byrd by Kim Church. Westland, Michigan: Dzanc Books, 2014. 228 pages. $14.95, paper.

Kim Church's debut novel *Byrd* compels readers to face central questions through each evolution of life transitions. With her reinvention of coming- of-age tropes, the author paints the two distinct personalities of Addie Lockwood and Roland Rhodes through their growth from estranged grade school classmates to disenchanted lovers in their thirties.

Church first introduces their disparate natures through the lens of *Byrd*'s protagonist, Addie Lockwood, a first-grade girl who puts her faith in books and carries on that belief into her adult life, working in a bookstore. In the fourth grade, Roland Rhodes comes in, standing out above the rest of class in his matchless clothes and upper-class parents. Straightaway, the readers get a sense of their forthcoming relationship, one where Addie is overlooked in Roland's limelight, even with the grandeur of his own name: "She thinks his name sounds like a place.

Roland Rhodes. A faraway place. One that would take a long time to get to, and once you did, you would never want to come back."

This foreshadowing transitions into high school, where Addie stands out in their American Counterculture class, where her voice and intellect are finally seen by Roland—something that he is now clearly accustomed to, a magnet to others when he talks about his guitar or music. This initiates a new dynamic in their relationship, one that carries on even when they meet again well after high school. At the same time, there is still that obvious element of isolation present, an element that yields the overall motivation of the book.

Through epistolary transitions to the son, Byrd, put up for adoption, the readers get to know Addie on a much deeper level than they would without them. Here, a raw Addie is found, one that exposes her vulnerability through privacy. Addie is, without a doubt, remarkable and singular without these letters. Church creates her protagonist in a way that gets underneath the reader's skin, and readers come to know her intimately by relatable imperfections and how she suffers through them.

The motifs and characters alone are standout. However, it is Kim Church's simple—yet elevated—use of language that brings the book to life. Each character, although familiar in vague stereotypes, stand out as inventive and personable through their own individual traits and descriptions. Simply put, Church makes the reader notice things in a different light, no matter how simple they are: the way a friend writes fat letters in a word, hair that is shiny and dark like Coca-Cola, or how remembering can sting the brain. Her entrancing rhythm, inimitable descriptions, and inventive characters create a distinctive and captivating world for *Byrd*, forcing its readers into a unique world in its raw humanness.
—*Bailey Gaylin Moore*, MCR

☾

Necessary Myths by **Grant Clauser**. Milton, Delaware: The Broadkill River Press, 2013. 71 pages. $14.95, paper.

Grant Clauser speaks the language of stones in his full-length collection *Necessary Myths*, in which he gives elemental voice to human characters living the lives of fossils in his poems. While the collection moves broadly across themes of survival and a defiance of a fate that looms in the periphery of every page, Clauser suspends the reader between a melancholic past just beyond the fingertips and a future that can only be glimpsed through the storms that repeatedly strike out with lightning,and yet the language reminds its audience of the boldness of stones.

Clauser's poetry delivers the swelling tension of the tired and the restless with the stoicism of a boulder. Clauser introduces tragedies of natural disaster, suicide, futility, and Armageddon as if these things were portended to him in contempt: "The end of the world / was the biggest joke of the day." Though this tension is undoubtedly the subject of ridicule, it nonetheless leaves the reader with tauter muscles, a rigid spine, and perhaps a horrible habit of grinding teeth. Clauser takes the stone he's placed at the most infinitesimal moment between hope and disregard and prods the carbon nerves revealed by a dead grandmother, a fraudulent priest, and a nameless companion with whom he drives across the country in what seems to be an endless pursuit of fulfilment.

Necessary Myths begs the reader to assume that vigil between destiny and history, and asks which path would be more merciful: "It's hard, yes, to love / the stone in your shoe / when your whole life / is spent walking." Clauser holds the essence of what it means to be human as a pebble in the palm of his hand; hands, he notes, bear the evidence of living, the doing of it all, the step he takes toward assuming some purpose for which his characters sigh.

The people presented in these poem are not weak. The days roll on and they meet them all stubbornly in the face of this jinxed atmosphere of loss and longing. These people learn to live with drowning in the face of so much absence, to live without bees and their fruits, an apocalypse they were promised, a destination. Clauser shows them just how deep the water goes, maybe even considers dropping them into its blind depths, then drags their heads above the surface, its physical walls continually present in many poems, showing few signs of corroding from that single moment where Clauser waits on the verge of this great stillness to break.

—*Taylor Supplee*, MCR

((

Sylph by **Abigail Cloud**. Warrensburg, Missouri: Pleiades Press, 2014. 88 pages. $17.95, paper.

Abigail Cloud's first collection of poems, *Sylph*, is marked by its quiet and ethereal tone that captures her awareness of poetry's relationship to both body and mind. Cloud's manuscript was selected as a winner of the Lena-Miles Wever Todd Poetry Book Prize.

The first section of *Sylph* is largely composed of a series of poems about the "demons" that haunt our lives in indirect but distressing ways, such as in "Lost Wedding Ring Demon" and "Choked Peppermint Demon." In this manner, Cloud ascribes the causes of humanity's trials to the personifications of what might otherwise be labeled simply happenstance or bad luck as a way of bringing some semblance of order to a disorganized world, where things happen by chance or no reason at all. In "Lost Wedding Ring Demon," Cloud writes: "Because isn't that what good demons / do? Bottle your faith into one small object, pressed / like the taut skin of a bubble not yet breathed / forward?" In this way she suggests that these demons thus serve as small comforts because their existence explains the seemingly random tragedies we experience.

Cloud's poems also take on a mythic quality, as if she is working from half-forgotten fairytales, leaving the reader with a sense that the mystical imagery she captures is ephemeral in nature. For instance, "From the Compendium of Old Madge" reads as a recipe book of spells or old wives' tales that spin remedies ranging from quieting a man's rage to catching an air spirit known as a "sylph." Cloud writes:

> When the sylph
> comes to you, wrap her in the scarf.
> Her wings will shrivel to be plucked
> away, or drift to the ground
> of their own accord.

This passage suggests that these antiquated instructions, through either science or cynicism, have been lost to us, but perhaps Cloud believes that they are worth rediscovering.

Her poems, however, are not without realism. In "Bonnie Parker, After the Second Heist," Cloud gives voice to a figure so infamous one might say her name carries its own mythic air. Still, Cloud gives the reader insight into Parker's mind through the poem's clever column structure that invites the reader to read both horizontally across columns and vertically down each column, both readings revealing something different from the other and yet part of the same whole. She also employs clichés like "(Bank on it:)" and "(revenge is a dish) / best served cold" to add a refreshingly humorous effect as a playful contrast to her serene and careful craftsmanship.

Sylph is a collection of poems wrought with delicate imagery that will leave its readers suspended in the stillness of Cloud's meditations. Her poems vary in subject matter and form, but her focus remains closely connected with the mythos of the past and present. However, she is equally attuned to the subtle darknesses that permeate our lives.

—*Allys Page,* MCR

☾

Commercial Fiction by Dave Housley. San Francisco: Outpost19, 2013. 98 pages. $12, paper.

Reading a body of work that constantly makes reference to popular culture can become uninteresting and even distracting. Dave Housley, however, has created a collection of stories that observes both the realism and the absurd of contemporary advertisement. *Commercial Fiction* is a layered body of work that utilizes the familiar scenes of commercials as framework for dynamic stories as well as a reference for the reader to better create more concentrated settings.

Although there is the overarching theme of consumerism that is a permanent partner of this subject matter, other themes and ideas are equally represented and prohibit it from becoming overbearing. The body of work contains a varied mix of stories, like "Lexus," that address common problems within normal life, and others like "Coors Light" and "Super Bowl" that present similar scenes in a more abstract way. Because of this variety, the reader can move from one story to the next without the worry of the book becoming monotonous.

One of the most intriguing elements of this work is the subtlety in the use of the settings of the commercials. The choices in companies and the products of the advertisements have no connection to one another other than their commercials being some of the most memorable on TV. It is not difficult to remember which commercial serves as the inspiration behind each story and this adds an extra element visually to Housley's work. These preconceived images give the reader room to suspend disbelief when they read from one story based in reality and another dealing with the absurd.

As well as the variety in setting, there is also a variety in form. The first several stories of the book are presented in traditional forms and then other stories organized into sections or written as interviews and formal reports begin to become interspersed within the book. One of the most successful stories in the collection, "Canada Dry," is a more abstract piece both in form and setting. The story is focused on a group of people who begin to worship the "Canada Dry Ginger Ale Girl" for her ability to keep them healthy and obese by supplying them with a constant supply of ginger ale pulled up from the ground. This cult's story is told through formal reports, interviews, and quotes taken from an unreleased documentary. These sources, most of which are told as first-person accounts, build on the recurring theme of consumerism that is hereditary in this book and well as presenting other ideas of health and happiness.

Commercial Fiction's success as a collection has to do more with the variety of its elements and the frameworks provided by the settings of the commercials rather than the commercials themselves. The familiarity the reader will feel towards the settings of the stories will only add the reading experience.

—*Sierra Sitzes*, MCR

☾

Chapel of Inadvertent Joy by Jeffrey McDaniel. Pittsburgh: University of Pittsburgh Press. 2013, 88 pages. $15.95, paper.

Themes of adultery, middle age, and human duality, as well as questions of the assignment of blame, hang over almost every moment of Jeffrey McDaniel's fifth full-length collection, *Chapel of Inadvertent Joy*. McDaniel preps readers for these subjects in the first poem, "Hello," which asks us to "lean forward a little, friend, / and drag your fragrant strands over my voluptuous grief."

And voluptuous it is. "Eliot Spitzer in Grad School" imagines a young Spitzer with every possible pathway still available. Coins serve as the vehicle for considering the dark-and-light dichotomy we all possess:

> One side of the coin says:
> *you will do great things in your lifetime.*
> The other side reads: *you will rain shame*
> *upon your family.* I flip the coin in the air,
> as if only one of them can be true.

In "Satan Exulting Over Eve," Satan presents himself as set-up by God to be the bad guy, and we are asked to empathize. Satan says, "*Dear Eve,*

I had to do it, / without you, I'm not Satan—just a squandered angel. / Now I'm the inventor of heaven," and we understand the need to makes one's life mean something. We must also question the true source of original sin. Was Satan a "patsy" who, out of loyalty, only did what was asked so that God "could hero in under a balcony of stars"? Or does he need to see himself that way because even Satan must alleviate his own guilt?

The second section, "Reflections of a Cuckold and Other Blasphemies," requires readers to play voyeurs to a wife's adultery, all presented lushly by the speaker. In "I Am Not an Idiot," the cuckold imagines the act of betrayal: "I know / he was scribbling cave paintings / onto your thigh" and "his crushed pearls were drying / on your skin." We watch passively with a speaker who does not overtly assign blame. Our instinct may be to condemn, but the cuckold seems to have expected it to happen, as indicated in "The Birds and the Bees," in which the teenage speaker is advised by his father to "Be preparing now" for the day when his future wife will cheat. Prepare so as not to be destroyed by it.

By the final section of the book, youth's piss-and-vinegar is presented more blatantly alongside the existential crisis of middle age. There are to-do lists in the man cave, and aging is seen as a punishment for previous wrongs. The speaker recognizes that "I'm searching for a metaphor to connect the old and new me." But he also seems more accepting of himself: "I don't want to get away with it / anymore. Getting away with it / is the worst punishment of all."

As heavy as the bulk of the collection may be, it is not bleak, and while the joys in life may be unplanned, they are "yours anyway: the gold-tipped spurs of this moment, / a red bird flinging praise through the sky."
—*Sara Burge*, MCR

☾

***Praying Drunk* by Kyle Minor.** Louisville, Kentucky: Sarabande Books, Inc. 2014, 192 pages. $15.95, paper.

Kyle Minor's second book, *Praying Drunk*, is more than just a simple collection of great short stories. It is a treasure hunt of connectivity told through beautifully crafted prose. In fact, I quote him when I use the term book; he warns us readers at the very start, "These stories are to be read in order. This is a book, not just a collection." This is the first clue to this treasure hunt; what ties these stories together? And what meaning is behind it all?

This entire concept is worthless without strong stories to pull it off and Minor's prose offer us more than just merely strength. His stories pull on the emotions in many directions as he deftly maneuvers between shifting scenes that transition widely from where they start, but then always seems to circle back. For example, the story "The Truth and All Its Ugly" starts with an unexplained medical procedure, shifts to relationship problems, to father and son dealing with said problems in drug abuse, to tragic death, and then comes back to the procedure that started the story in a scene that might leave one crying for the second time.

Each story has this ability. Minor writes with a sock-you-in-the-mouth, break-your-heart one minute, leaving you happy the next, and then go-and-do-it-all-over-again style. His characters make you feel alongside them on their tragic journeys. His ability brings their pain, their happiness, their regret, their love to life on the pages, connecting us to them, turning these stories into experiences. These are not for the faint of heart and will leave you gasping for air by the end.

The variety in the style of the story also speaks to the talent Minor displays. "Glossolalia" is a young love relationship entirely told through two characters' dialogue. There is not even a single "he said she said." Only dialogue. And it's brilliant. Everything required for a great story is delivered —characterization, setting, context, plot, climax, resolution, love, and loss. Or the novella-length "In a Distant Country," told through traditional epistolary form. It narrates the story of missionaries in Haiti through a series of letters by different people, giving multiple perspectives to the events unfolding, portraying the differences in the same story told.

Which leads us back to the original question; what ties all these stories together? Are they different perspectives of the same stories? Are they retellings of the same story, as is hinted at during one of the "Q&A" sections of the book, where we meet the narrator? Speaking of the narrator, in the first story, "The Question of Where We Begin," the narrator calls himself "the god of telling"; perhaps this hints at these being stories of one narrator's life, retold in different ways.

These questions will beg readers to come to the book again, if the quality of the stories themselves doesn't. I know I did.

—*Antony LePage*, MCR

☾

Thought That Nature by **Trey Moody.** Louisville, Kentucky: Sarabande Books, Inc,. 2014. 80 pages. $14.95, paper.

"I dreamt I was Surfer Joe, and what that means I don't know," Paul Westerberg sang on the Replacements' album *Don't Tell a Soul*. Trey Moody, in "Exercise in Patience," talks of a man who waits on the beach, for "I don't know what." The following page, Moody is in his back yard: "I am here. So far / this seems to have been true."

Moody, like Westerberg, is looking for meaning but at the same time not expecting any. There is a hint of fear beneath his calm, an echo of the earlier poem, "Salina, Kansas": "Is this how God terrifies?" one character wonders.

"A Weather" pops up now and again throughout the book—same title, different forces. It becomes expected as we go further into the book, but the results are harder to anticipate. "Tomorrow, crows announce pallid company. Winter, / without smell, leaves." What happens is out of the speaker's hands.

In section two, "Lancaster County Notebook," we get a close examination of thought processes during survival. Moody applies historical words from *The Lewis and Clark Journals* as a stepping-stone from his own untamed Nebraska into a wilderness that nowadays exists only in campfire songs. In "Spring," there is no preparing for the attack. Someone is going to lose.

> When winter
> has gone for good
> we're left with
> more than thought
> yet not ready to feel
> when *the Musquetoes*
> *begin to Suck our blood*
> *this afternoon."*

Section three, untitled like the first, returns to the footprint-like pace of the openers, but finds more ghosts this time around. Sometimes the ghosts are found beneath the trees, like in "The Forest Isn't a Room"; other times the ghosts are found nibbling on apples late at night in the kitchen. In "Both," memories float in limbo:

267

Barn owl
of my childhood
both here
and not here.

Are the memories trustworthy? Moody's search for answers appears again in "This Hemisphere of Leaves":

The moon kept finding
me through the trees, or I found
the moon between objects—
both were probably true.

Maybe the answers are right in front of us, as in "Praise:" "Bless the tree, for without it / to what could we compare ourselves?" In "Backyard," Moody makes a confession, knowing his inquiries might be fruitless:

Sitting in a chair
I'm full of absurdities.
Wind blows—

I can't make sense
of it, even.

There are bits of absurdity imbedded in Moody's work, but we look past it, and accept his words as truth in the end.
—*Anthony Isaac Bradley*, MCR

☾

Pages From the Textbook of Alternate History by **Phong Nguyen.** Plano, Texas: Queen's Ferry Press, 2014. 256 pages. 25.95, cloth.

Pages From the Textbook of Alternate History is a collection of fiction that could be considered a themed collection of stories or even a novel-in-parts, depending on the definition used. It is the second collection from Phong Nguyen, and the premise behind it is intriguing and imaginative, blending speculative and literary fiction with a deft hand. The collection begins with the fantastic frame of a man who, while working in data recovery, is given a decaying hard drive that contains the textbook of alternate history. He tries to get the data from the drive off of it; "I spent the rest of that night tinkering with the drive, abandoning my usual algorithms, relying on trial and error—an approach to which I hadn't needed to make recourse since I was a cub hacker, cracking open my first Commodore." What this framing narrator finds within that drive are the stories of historical figures that are familiar but not. The collection is speculative in the literal sense, imagining the outcomes if one point in history went in a slightly different direction. What if Plato was given a city to administer? What if Joan of Arc became a mother? What if Hitler was accepted to art school? These questions are at the center of Nguyen's collection, and the answers are not always what the reader might expect.

Each historical figure is given a frame to reference what happened around them in the world that is being discussed. This frame is then followed by a firsthand account of another person close to the historical figure, and each chapter ends with reflective questions that might be found in any standard history textbook. The contemplative mood that results from this reflective format is one of the major strengths of Nguyen's collection, because the reader begins to consider other possibilities and what would have happened next in the world that Nguyen has created. Even if you aren't a history buff, the archetypes that are portrayed will be familiar, like the repentant conqueror or the tamed revolutionary.

While the concept of this collection is what stands out, the prose is strong as well. Nguyen's writing style varies based on the narration. When the style needs to be simple, that's exactly what it is. When a more authoritative tone is called for, the style conforms to that need. Not every chapter can be as strong as the chapters on Plato, Benjamin Franklin, and Jesus, but the variability of the prose is enough to carry the reader through any less powerful sections. This collection may not be for everyone, but anyone who enjoys the blending of speculative and literary, or anyone interested in history in general, should definitely give this collection a chance.

—*Matt Kimberlin, MCR*

☾

Between Wrecks by George Singleton. Westland, Michigan: Dzanc Books, 2014. 300 pages. $15.95, paper.

Whether a metaphor for birth and death or the literal wrecks trapping Stet Looper in a diner with the seventeen-year-old son of a neighbor in *Between Wrecks'* titular story, George Singleton creates the sort of thesis Stet Looper is obsessively seeking for in his low-residency master's program in Southern Cultural Studies. A compatriot, at one point exclaims to Looper, "Good God, man, there's a term paper a minute going on around you," summing up Singelton's collection well. Each story is a statement and exploration of Southern culture.

Stet is a member of the Looper clan, who staked out their piece of South Carolina by harvesting river rocks. Raised by an uncle after his parents set out for unknown parts, all of whom hoped he would escape Poke, South Carolina, to "fix the world," his journey is either a tragedy of failed potential or liberation from expectations. Each story, though not in chronological order, introduces the reader to another stage in Stet's journey. Along the way, the reader learns about perceptions of education, work, and culture.

At the diner in the titular story, Looper finds himself washing dishes and asking himself, "Why would anyone choose to wash dishes for a living unless he either had lost hope altogether or never knew that there were self-satisfying vocations out there?" At the heart of the fourteen-piece collection is whether the characters Singleton introduces are trapped by ignorance or abandoned futures, and perhaps, whether the fault lies with them or some external agent.

Singleton's characters are those you would expect to encounter on a journey through economically destitute parts of the rural South. There's your drunks, holier-than-thous, small-time diners, and more than a fair share of gossip and hushed-over history. Far from stereotypes, Singleton's South Carolina is populated by characters whose lives we are invited to consider. His characters beg the reader to see beyond crass expectations of rural life towards the seedy reality of economic hardship faced daily in every aspect of residents' lives.

For those readers who prefer traditional narrative story structures, the collection's final story, "I Would Be Remiss," may strike a nerve. While its untraditional nature may be off-putting, the collection is still solid and can stand without this last addition. This final story is a mix between stream-of-conscious and an acknowledgement section for a fictional book about the lynching of Columbus Choice, titled *No Cover Available: The Story of Columbus Choice, African-American Sushi Chef from Tennessee*. While ostensibly covering and thanking those necessary to produce this opus of Southern Cultural Studies, the acknowledgements serve as a piecemeal biography of Looper's life.

In the end, Stet Looper concludes his opus, "I hope I didn't forget anyone." Through the fourteen stories, it is hard to think whom he might have.

—*Jeff Van Booven*, MCR

☾

The Isle of Youth by Laura van den Berg. New York: FSG Originals, 2013. 256 pages. $14, paper.

Laura van den Berg's second collection is an eye-opening experience that follows the moments of young, female protagonists whose lives are on the brink of failure. Each character is trying to fill a void within them, whether that is accepting their unhappiness in their marriage or losing a sibling in a lab explosion; the protagonists are trying to fill the void that has been created by the loss of a male counterpart.

The Isle of Youth has seven short pieces that develop a central theme of women coming to understand themselves. The author keeps the reader in a constant state of suspense when it comes to each ending, and there is never any sense of closure for the protagonist. Even though the audience is left hanging over the edge, the reader can easily be drawn back in with the author's elegant descriptions of the landscapes that are presented in her text. From the tropical port city of San Antonio Oeste to Paris, the city of romance, the author seamlessly illustrates the picturesque scenery of each location.

The title story follows the journey of a young woman traveling to see her identical twin sister in Miami, Florida. As is the case for many of the female protagonists within this collection, her marriage is crumbling beneath her feet and she is uncertain of the path she must take to regain her happiness. The trip to Miami is unexpected due to her sister's urgent telephone call, but with no specific details provided for the urgency. When the protagonist finally reaches her sister, Sylvia, she explains how she needs her to pose as her for a week so she can go on a trip with the married man she has been having an affair with. After an intense makeover given to her by her sister, she takes Sylvia's place as her sister supposedly travels to the Isle of Youth. What the main character comes to realize is that her sister's life is not what it seems, and pretending to be Sylvia is more than what she has bargained for.

This collection focuses on the secrets that are shared throughout the human race, especially when it comes to the secrets that are kept by women. Each character deals with secrets in different ways, but each secret revolves around central conflicts, such as deception, infidelity, or unhappiness. The secrets of these protagonists are sometimes vocalized or sometimes remain untold, but the author is able to convey the inner conflict that each character is battling against in different destinations around the world; this displays how secrets connect humans to one another.

—*Amanda Conner*, MCR

(

The Old Priest by **Anthony Wallace.** Pittsburgh: University of Pittsburgh Press, 2013. 184 pages. $24.95, cloth.

The stories collected in Anthony Wallace's debut collection, *The Old Priest*, are concerned with storytelling. There are stories about old men telling their stories at blackjack tables in Atlantic City, coworkers telling the stories about past jobs, and grandmothers telling stories on their deathbeds.

This focus on storytelling is strongest in the title story, a bit of metafiction about a novelist, whose book is also called *The Old Priest*. Wallace shows readers the protagonist interacting and listening to stories told by a former teacher. These interactions take course over years and the reader gets the opportunity to hear the Old Priest repeat his stories and hear about the priest from other characters. The story includes this criticism of the protagonist's fictional novel, "… it is also derivative, a retelling of the old priest's stories combined with some mildly ambiguous hints about homosexuality …." It is hard to read this statement as anything but Wallace critiquing his own work, or at least laying bare his process and being unapologetic about how the stories in this collection came to be written.

Putting the title story as the first story in the collection does make the reader wonder about the inspiration for the rest of the stories in the collection, most of which take place in Atlantic City casinos and feature card dealers and pit bosses as protagonists. While this repetitive use of setting could be taxing on the reader, Wallace fills these spaces with unique and vivid characters. Rather than having characters who pity themselves for falling into jobs they see as being beneath them, Wallace's characters are incredibly aware of the roles they play. "And I don't mind it, the familiarity that is, and going along with it all, the cigar smoke and the stories and really acting like I give a shit if he bets for me or not," says the narrator of "Jack Frost," the fourth story in the collection.

It would have been easy for Wallace to let each one of these characters throw out some gambling lingo, but he deftly avoids this trap by giving each character a completely unique voice that reflects where they come from and reflects where the position they hold in the casino system. A young blackjack dealer sounds flippant, A pit boss sounds authoritative, and an executive's nineteen-year-old girlfriend sounds as naive as her choices. Varied as they are, all of these characters are warm and sympathetic. It is easy to care about these characters despite the choices they make, and that is what will drive readers through these stories. These stories cut the bone and get heart of why we tell stories.

—*Andy Myers,* MCR

Contributors' Notes

Albert Abonado is the editor of *The Bakery* and curator of the Deep Fried Reading Series. His poems have appeared or are forthcoming in *Rattle*, *Guernica*, and *Gargoyle*.

C.D. Albin's stories, poems, and reviews have appeared in a number of publications, including *Arkansas Review*, *Cape Rock*, *The Georgia Review*, *Harvard Review*, and *Natural Bridge*. He teaches English at Missouri State University-West Plains, where he edits *Elder Mountain: A Journal of Ozarks Studies*.

Benny Andersen is the foremost contemporary poet and lyricist in Denmark. Author of twenty books of poetry, his work is renowned for its humor, expressionistic wordplay, and colloquial depth. He has won a multitude of literary honors, including the Danish National Arts Award for Lifetime Achievement.

Emily May Anderson earned her Master of Fine Arts at Penn State University. Her poems have appeared in *Sweet, Poetry East*, and *Diverse Voices Quarterly*. She teaches English and reviews books for *NewPages*.

Kelly Baker is working toward her Master of Arts in English at Missouri State University. She is a contributing author of *Edgar Allan Poe: A Guide for Readers Young and Old* and an assistant editor at *Moon City Review*.

Roy Bentley has received fellowships from the National Endowment for the Arts, the Florida Division of Cultural Affairs, and the Ohio Arts Council. His books include *Boy in a Boat* (University of Alabama Press, 1986), *Any One Man* (Bottom Dog Press, 1992), *The Trouble with a Short Horse in Montana* (White Pine Press, 2006), and *Starlight Taxi* (Lynx House, 2013).

Vanessa Blakeslee's debut short story collection, *Train Shots*, is forthcoming on Burrow Press in March. Find her online at VanessaBlakeslee.com.

Melissa Boston is currently in her second year of the Master of Fine Arts program at the University of Arkansas. Her poetry is forthcoming in *PMS*, *Bird's Thumb*, and *The Fourth River*.

Anthony Isaac Bradley's stories and poems have appeared or are forthcoming in *Slipstream*, *The MacGuffin*, *Atticus Review*, and other journals. He was recently nominated for a Pushcart Prize and a *storySouth* 2013 Million Writers Award.

Luci Brown received her degree in creative writing from the University of Tennessee. She lives in Knoxville.

Sara Burge's first book, *Apocalypse Ranch*, won the De Novo Award and was published by C&R Press in 2010. Her poems have appeared in *The Virginia Quarterly Review*, *River Styx*, *Juked*, *Cimarron Review*, *The Los Angeles Review*, and elsewhere.

Doug Paul Case is an MFA candidate at Indiana University, where he is associate poetry editor of *Indiana Review*. His poems have appeared in *Salt Hill*, *Redivider*, *Court Green*, and *Barrow Street*.

Lisa J. Cihlar's chapbook, *The Insomniac's House*, is available from *Dancing Girl Press* (2012), and a second chapbook, *This is How She Fails*, is available from *Crisis Chronicles Press* (2012). She lives in rural southern Wisconsin.

Amanda Conner is a graduate student at Missouri State University, where she serves as an assistant editor of *Moon City Review*.

Christopher Crabtree is studying creative writing at Missouri State University. His work has appeared in *Midwestern Gothic*, *Sundog Lit*, *Elder Mountain*, and other journals.

Tim Craven is originally from Stoke-on-Trent, England, and was a neuroscientist until he began his MFA program at Syracuse University. His poems have appeared or are forthcoming in *Obsessed With Pipework*, *Fourteen*, *Natural Bridge*, and *New Delta Review*.

Pat Daneman lives in Lenexa, Kansas. Recent work appears or is forthcoming in *Bellevue Poetry Review*, *Naugatuck River Review*, *I-70 Review*, and *The Comstock Review*, where she won first prize in their Muriel Craft Bailey Competition. In 2012, she was a runner-up for *Poets & Writers'* Maureen Egan Writers Exchange Award.

Jim Ray Daniels' latest book of poems, *Birth Marks*, was published by BOA Editions in 2013 and was selected as a Michigan Notable Book. His next book of short fiction, *Eight Mile High*, will be published by Michigan State University Press in 2014. A native of Detroit, Daniels teaches at Carnegie Mellon University.

Darren C. Demaree is living in Columbus, Ohio, with his wife and children. He is the author of *As We Refer to Our Bodies* (2013) and *Not For Art Nor Prayer* (2014), both from 8th House Publishing. He is also the author of *Temporary Champions* (2015), due from Main Street Rag.

Laura Dimmit will graduate from the University of Nebraska-Lincoln. Her poetry has previously appeared in *Cape Rock*, *Cave Region Review*, and *Moon City Review*.

Allison Doyle lives in Los Angeles. Her work has appeared in several online and print publications. She can be found at www.allisondoyle.com

Meg Eden has been published in various literary magazines and anthologies. Her chapbooks include *The Girl Who Came Back* (Redbird Chapbooks, 2013), *Rotary Phones and Facebook* (Dancing Girl Press, 2012), and *Your Son* (National Federation of State Poetry Societies, 2012).

Matthew Fogarty was born amd raised in the suburbs of Detroit and currently lives in Columbia, South Carolina, where he is fiction editor of *Yemassee*. He also edits *Cartagena*, a literary journal. His fiction has appeared or is forthcoming in *Passages North*, *Fourteen Hills*, *Midwestern Gothic*, and *PANK*.

Jacek Frączak was born in Warsaw, Poland, and moved to Springfield, Missouri, in 2007. He is a visual artist and designer, as well as an assistant professor in the Art and Design Department at Missouri State University. He has had over thirty solo shows in Poland, Denmark, Germany, and the United States, and his etchings, drawings, and photos can be found in museums around the world.

Timothy Geiger is the author of two full-length poetry collections, most recently *The Curse of Pheromones* (MSR, 2008). He teaches poetry, creative writing, and letterpress printing at The University of Toledo.

Megan Giddings is currently an MFA candidate at Indiana University. She has work recently published or forthcoming in *SmokeLong Quarterly*, *MARY*, *Printers Row*, and *Monkeybicycle*.

Michael Goldman's translations of Benny Andersen's poetry have appeared in journals such as *The Cincinnati Review*, *The Massachusetts Review*, and *Metamorphoses*. He taught himself Danish over twenty-five years ago by translating a Danish copy of *The Catcher in the Rye* word for word.

Julia Greene is currently a senior studying English literature and communications at Missouri State University. She is also a reporter and producer for KSMU News, Ozarks Public Radio.

Khanh Ha is the author of *Flesh* (Black Heron Press, 2012) and the forthcoming *The Demon Who Peddled Longing* (Underground Voices, 2014).

Ken Haas lives in San Francisco, where he works in health care and sponsors a poetry writing program at the UCSF Children's Hospital. His poems have appeared or are forthcoming in *Natural Bridge*, *Spoon River Poetry Review*, *Alabama Literary Review*, and *The Coachella Review*.

Jeff Hardin is the author of *Fall Sanctuary* (Story Line Press, 2004), *Notes for a Praise Book* (Jacar Press, 2013), and *Restoring the Narrative* (Story Line Press), which recently received the Donald Justice Poetry Prize and will appear in 2015.

Kirsten Hemmy is a Fulbright Fellow living in Senegal. Her book *The Atrocity of Water* was published in 2010 by Press 53.

Cynthia Marie Hoffman is the author of two poetry collections: *Sightseer* (Persea Books, 2011), winner of the Lexi Rudnitsky First Book Prize in Poetry, and the forthcoming *Paper Doll Fetus* (Persea Books), slated for late 2014. A chapbook, *Her Human Costume* (Gold Line Press), is also forthcoming this spring.

Amorak Huey teaches writing at Grand Valley State University in Michigan. His chapbook *The Insomniac Circus* is forthcoming in 2014 from Hyacinth Girl Press. His poems appear in *The Best American Poetry 2012*, *The Southern Review*, *The Cincinnati Review*, and many other journals.

Zeke Jarvis is an associate professor at Eureka College. His work has appeared in *2 Bridges*, *Bitter Oleander*, and *Knock*, among other places.

Amaris Feland Ketcham's work has appeared in *Glassworks*, *The Los Angeles Review*, *The Rio Grande Review*, and *The Utne Reader*.

Matt Kimberlin received his MA in English from Missouri State University. He is an assistant editor for *Moon City Review* and a contributor for *Unstuck*'s blog. His fiction has appeared in *Paddle Shots: A River Pretty Anthology*.

Dan Lambert is an MFA candidate at Bowling Green State University.

Gary Leising is the author of *The Alp at the End of My Street* (Brick Road Poetry Press, 2012) and *Temple of Bone* (Finishing Line Press, 2013). He teaches at Utica College and lives in upstate New York.

Antony LePage recently graduated from Missouri State University, where he served as an assistant editor for *Moon City Review*.

Keegan Lester is the poetry editor and co-founder of the journal *Souvenir*. His work is published or forthcoming in *The Barn Owl Review*, *CutBank*, and *The Adroit Journal*, among others. He works at West Virginia University's Division of Diversity, Equity, and Inclusion.

Alexis Levitin's thirty-four books of translation include Clarice Lispector's *Soulstorm* and Eugenio de Andrade's *Forbidden Words*, both from New Directions. Recent books include Salgado Maranhão's *Blood of the Sun* (Milkweed Editions, 2012), Eugenio de Andrade's *The Art of Patience* (Red Dragonfly Press, 2013), and Ana Minga's *Tobacco Dogs* (The Bitter Oleander Press, 2013).

Christopher Locke is nonfiction editor for *Slice*. His first full-length collection of poems, *End of American Magic*, was released by Salmon Poetry in 2010. *Waiting for Grace & Other Poems* (Turning Point Books) and the memoir *Can I Say* (Kattywompus Press) were both released in 2013.

George Looney's books include *Monks Beginning to Waltz* (Truman State University Press, 2012), *A Short Bestiary of Love and Madness* (Stephen F. Austin University Press, 2011), *Open Between Us* (Turning Point, 2010), *The Precarious Rhetoric of Angels* (2005 White Pine Poetry Press Poetry Prize), *Attendant Ghosts* (Cleveland State University Press, 2000), *Animals Housed in the Pleasures of Flesh* (1995 Bluestem Award), and the 2008 novella *Hymn of Ash* (Elixir Press).

Angie Macri's recent work appears in *The Cincinnati Review* and *Alaska Quarterly Review*. An Arkansas Arts Council fellow, she lives in Hot Springs and teaches in Little Rock.

Conor Robin Madigan's work will be serialized in *The Fortnightly Review* in 2014.

Salgado Maranhão's *The Color of the Word* won Brazil's highest poetry award in 2011. An earlier collection, *Mural of Winds*, won the prestigious Prêmio Jabuti in 1999. His work has appeared in numerous magazines in the United States, including *Cream City Review*, *Florida Review*, *Massachusetts Review*, and *Spoon River Poetry Review*.

Amanda Marbais' fiction has appeared in *The Collagist*, *Hobart (web)*, *Monkeybicycle*, *McSweeney's Internet Tendency*, and elsewhere. She's the co-founder and managing editor of *Requited Journal* and lives in Chicago.

Alex Mattingly is a writer living and working in Indianapolis.

Jon Chaiim McConnell is a graduate of the Emerson College MFA program and the associate editor of *Whole Beast Rag*. His work has appeared or is forthcoming in *SmokeLong Quarterly* and *The Knicknackery*.

Bryan Merck has published in *American Amethyst Arsenic*, *Eunoia Review*, *Literary Juice*, and others. He is a past winner of the Southern Literary

Poetry Prize and the Barksdale-Maynard Fiction and Poetry Prizes. He lives in south Georgia.

Nancy Carol Moody lives in Eugene, Oregon, and is the author of *Photograph With Girls* (Taprock Books, 2009).

Bailey Gaylin Moore is a graduate student at Missouri State University, where she teaches English and serves as an assistant editor of *Moon City Review*.

Andy Myers is currently working on an MA in English at Missouri State University, where he also works as an assistant editor of *Moon City Review*. His work is forthcoming in *SmokeLong Quarterly*.

Richard Newman is the author of the poetry collections *Domestic Fugues* (Steel Toe Books, 2009) and *Borrowed Towns* (Word Press, 2005). He lives in St. Louis, where he serves as editor of *River Styx* and co-director of the *River Styx* Reading Series.

Phong Nguyen is an associate professor at the University of Central Missouri and the editor of *Pleiades* and Pleiades Press. He is the author of *Memory Sickness and Other Stories* (Elixir Press, 2011) and *Pages From the Textbook of Alternate History* (Queen's Ferry Press, 2014).

Samuel Nichols lives with his wife and two children in Springfield, Missouri, where he is a senior creative writing student at Missouri State University. This is his first publication.

Naomi Shihab Nye lives with her husband, photographer Michael Nye, in old downtown San Antonio. She won the NSK Neustadt Prize in Children's Literature for 2013.

Allys Page is a graduate student at Missouri State University, where she teaches creative writing and is an assistant editor for *Moon City Review*.

Alan Michael Parker is the author of seven collections of poems, including *Long Division* (Tupelo Press, 2012), and three novels, including *The Committee on Town Happiness* (Dzanc Books, 2014). The Douglas C.

Houchens Professor of English at Davidson College, he also teaches in the University of Tampa low-residency MFA program.

Ricardo Pau-Llosa's seventh book of poems, *Man,* is forthcoming from Carnegie Mellon University Press (2014), which also published his previous four titles.

Jody Reale lives in Hawaii and maintains the blog *Kill Your Lunch Hour.*

Phoebe Reeves earned her MFA at Sarah Lawrence College and now teaches English at tahe University of Cincinnati Clermont College. Her chapbook, *The Lobes and Petals of the Inanimate*, was published by Pecan Grove Press in 2009.

Katy Resch's work has appeared in *Blackbird, West Branch, Painted Bride Quarterly,* and other journals.

Jenna Rindo's poems have been published in *Shenandoah, American Journal of Nursing, Crab Orchard Review,* and other journals.

J.T. Robertson earned his creative writing degree at Missouri State University and works in nonprofit development. His work previously appeared in *Moon City Review, The MacGuffin, TheNewerYork,* and *Paddle Shots: A River Pretty Anthology.* He lives in Creve Coeur, Missouri.

Bobby Ross' work has been exhibited widely throughout the United States, and it has been featured in many galleries and reviewed in many periodicals.

Brandon Rushton is an MFA candidate in poetry at the University of South Carolina, where he serves as the poetry editor of *Yemassee.*

Brittney Scott received her MFA from Hollins University. She is the 2012 recipient of the Joy Harjo Prize for Poetry, as well as the Dorothy Sargent Rosenberg Poetry Prize. Her poems have appeared or are forthcoming in such journals as *Prairie Schooner, Alaska Quarterly Review, Crab Orchard Review,* and *Copper Nickel.*

Brian Simoneau's manuscript won the De Novo Prize and will be published by C&R Press in 2014. His poems appeared or are forthcoming in *Crab Orchard Review*, *Georgia Review*, *Mid-American Review*, and other journals.

Sierra Sitzes is a student at Missouri State University and an assistant editor for *Moon City Review*.

Noel Sloboda is the author of the poetry collections *Shell Games* (Sunnysideout, 2008) and *Our Rarer Monsters* (Sunnysideout, 2013), as well as several chapbooks. He teaches at Penn State York.

Hali Fuailelagi Sofala is a Samoan-American poet and teacher originally from Eatonton, Georgia. She earned an MFA in poetry from the University of Wisconsin-Madison and is currently a doctoral student in English at the University of Nebraska-Lincoln. Her work appears in *Arcadia*, *Calyx*, *New Madrid*, and *Juked*.

Amber Sparks is the author of the story collection *May We Shed These Human Bodies* (Curbside Splendor, 2013) and co-author of the hybrid text novel *The Desert Places*, along with Robert Kloss and illustrator Matt Kish. You can find her at www.ambernoellesparks.com.

Eve Strillacci is a recent product of the Hollins University MFA program. Her work has appeared in *JMWW*, *Sixth Finch*, *The Paris-American*, and elsewhere. In 2013, she received the Gertrude Claytor Poetry Prize.

Taylor Supplee is currently an undergraduate at Missouri State University, where he serves as an assistant editor for *Moon City Review*. His poetry has appeared in *Midwestern Gothic* and *Paddle Shots: A River Pretty Anthology* and is forthcoming in *Rattle*, *SLAB*, *Revolver*, and *Shadow Road Quarterly*.

Danilo Thomas received his MFA in fiction at the University of Alabama, where he was the fiction editor for *Black Warrior Review*. He has taught in Alabama's maximum security prison systems through a fellowship from the Alabama Prison Arts + Education Project. His chapbook, *Murk*, was published by AB Gorham Press in 2012.

Jeff Van Booven holds an MA from Missouri State University. Since graduating, he's taken up making and editing videos.

Santiago Vizcaíno's first book of poetry, *Destruction in the Afternoon*, won the Premio Proyectos Literarios Nacionales award from the Ecuadorian Ministry of Culture in 2008. His second book, *In the Twilight*, won second prize in the Pichincha Poetry Prize competition in 2010. His work has appeared in *Bitter Oleander*, *Connotation Press*, *Lake Effect*, *Saranac Review*, and *Words Without Borders*.

Matthew Vollmer is the author of two story collections—*Future Missionaries of America* (MP Publishing Limited, 2010) and the forthcoming *Gateway to Paradise* (Persea Books)—as well as a collection of essays, *Inscriptions For Headstones* (Outpost19, 2012). He is co-editor of *Fakes: An Anthology Of Pseudo-Interviews, Faux-Lectures, Quasi-Letters, "Found" Texts, And Other Fraudulent Artifacts* (W. W. Norton & Company, 2012).

Kellie Wardman is a poet and writer living in southern New Hampshire. She serves as an adjunct faculty in writing and communications at Southern New Hampshire University and is a non-profit consultant. She received her MFA from Emerson College.

Geoff Watkinson founded *Green Briar Review* in June 2012. He is an MFA candidate in creative nonfiction at Old Dominion University, where he is the managing editor of *Barely South Review*. He has contributed to *The Good Men Project*, *Bluestem*, *Prick of the Spindle*, and *The Flagler Review*.

Gabriel Welsch is the author of *The Four Horsepersons of a Disappointing Apocalypse* (Steel Toe Books, 2013), *The Death of Flying Things* (WordTech Communications, 2012), *Dirt and All Its Dense Labor* (WordTech Communications, 2006), and the chapbook, *An Eye Fluent in Gray* (Seven Kitchens Press, 2010).

Gary Wilkens, an assistant professor of English at Norfolk State University, was the winner of the 2006 Texas Review Breakthrough Poetry Prize for his first book, *The Red Light Was My Mind* (Texas Review Press, 2007).

KV Wilt is a writer of poems, stories, and plays and teaches writing, mythology, and Native American literature at Saint Leo University.

faultline
JOURNAL OF ARTS AND LETTERS

A Pushcart Prize-winning Literary Journal

Volume 23 available
June 2014

Featuring stories by
Joe Wenderoth, Andrew Tonkovich,
Ryan Ridge and Mel Bosworth

Current issue: $10
Archive issues available

Find out more at
faultline.sites.uci.edu

RECENT CONTRIBUTORS INCLUDE

Fiction: Kim Chinquee
Brian Evenson
Tao Greenfield
Lee Ann Roripaugh
Luke B. Goebel
Lou Beach

Poetry: Tony Hoagland
Julianna Baggott
Olena Kalytiak Davis
Major Jackson
Matthew Lippman
Joshua Marie Wilkinson

Hadar Bar-Nadav
Emilia Phillips
Elizabeth Bradfield
Cynthia Huntington
Melissa Broder

poetry
ART
interviews
prose

Submit
&
Subscribe

www.
jubilat
.org

Department of
English

482 Bartlett Hall
University of Massachusetts
Amherst, MA
01003

The editors of *Mid-American Review* are pleased to announce

the **2014**

Fineline Competition
for prose poems, short shorts, and anything
in between

$1000 First Prize
Deadline: June 1, 2014

2014 Final Judge: Lindsay Hunter, author of *Don't Kiss Me* (FSG, 2013) and *Daddy's* (Featherproof, 2010)

submit: marsubmissions.bgsu.edu

or

Mid-American Review
Department of English
Bowling Green State University
Bowling Green OH 43403

500-word limit for each poem or short. $10 entry fee (payable online or by check/money order) for each set of three works. Contest is for previously unpublished work only—if the work has appeared in print or online, in any form or part, or under any title, or has been contracted for such, it is ineligible and will be disqualified. Entry fees are non-refundable. All participants will receive *Mid-American Review* v. XXXV, no. 1, where the winner will be published. Submissions will not be returned. Manuscripts need not be left anonymous. Contest is open to all writers, except those associated with the judge or *Mid-American Review*, past or present. Judge's decision is final.

PUERTO DEL SOL

a journal of new literature

Enter the 2014 Puerto del Sol Poetry and Fiction Contests, judged by Sarah Vap and Lydia Millet, for a chance at a cash prize and publication in a journal that has featured great literary voices such as David Foster Wallace, Lee K. Abbott, and Jenny Boully.

The entry fee of $15 includes a yearlong subscription to Puerto del Sol. All entries will be considered for publication.

Deadline: March 15, 2014.

The 2014
Moon City
Poetry Award

- The Moon City Poetry Award is for an original collection of poetry written in English by a single author.
- Individual pieces in the collection may be published in periodicals or chapbooks, but not yet collected and published in full-length manuscript form.
- Open to all writers not associated with Moon City Press or its judges, past or present. Students, alumni, and employees of Missouri State University are ineligible.
- Manuscripts should be at least 48 pages long.
- Manuscripts should be paginated. Please include a Table of Contents and an Acknowledgements page.
- Manuscripts should be submitted via Submittable, https://mooncitypress.submittable.com
- A $25 entry fee is due via Submittable at the time of submission; entry fees are nonrefundable.
- Simultaneous submissions are permitted, though manuscripts should be withdrawn immediately if accepted elsewhere.
- Deadline: May 1, 2014. Winners will be notified in late 2014 and the winner will be published in 2015.
- First prize: $1000, publication by Moon City Press (including international distribution through the University of Arkansas Press), and a standard royalty contract. Three additional finalists will be named and considered for publication.
- For questions, please visit http://mooncitypress.com/ or contact Moon City Editor Sara Burge at saraburge@missouristate.edu.

Moon City Review
2015

Call for Submissions
Fiction
Poetry
Nonfiction
Translations
Reviews
https://mooncitypress.submittable.com